FAITH IN GOD AND GENERALS

AN ANTHOLOGY OF FAITH, HOPE, AND LOVE IN THE AMERICAN CIVIL WAR

★ ★ ★ ★ ★ ★ ★ ★ ★ ★ ★ ★ ★ ★ ★ ★ ★ ★ ★ ★

FAITH IN GOD AND GENERALS

AN ANTHOLOGY OF FAITH, HOPE, AND LOVE IN THE AMERICAN CIVIL WAR

★★★★★★★★★★★★★★★★★★★★

COMPILED BY TED BAEHR AND SUSAN WALES

FOREWORD BY RON MAXWELL

BROADMAN
& HOLMAN
PUBLISHERS

NASHVILLE, TN

© 2003 by Ted Baehr and Susan Wales
All rights reserved
Printed in the United States of America

0-8054-2728-7

Published by Broadman & Holman Publishers,
Nashville, Tennessee

Dewey Decimal Classification: 241
Subject Heading: FAITH
UNITED STATES—HISTORY—1861–65, CIVIL WAR—PERSONAL NARRATIVES
WAR—RELIGIOUS ASPECTS

All color still photographs from the film *Gods and Generals*
copyright © 2003, Ted Turner Film Properties, LLC; all rights reserved.
All still photographs from the film *Gods and Generals* were photographed by Van Redin, copyright © 2003
(pages 1,11,29,41,61,79,103,123,143,169, endsheets, front and back cover)

The Generals of the American Civil War (www.generalsandbrevets.com): 63,69,117,119,125,147,159,172,177.
Library of Congress: x,3,5,8,9,10,12,16,20,23,31,32,34,35,37,40,44,45,46,38,55,56,57,60,68,69,72,76,
77,78,82,85,87,102,105,107,108,122,130,131,141,149b,151,152,154,156,158,160,165,166.
U.S. National Archives & Records Administration: vi,2,7,15,18,26,28,30,33,39,
42,59,65,80,101,114,121,126,133,139,150a,153,157,158,161,168.
Virginia Military Institute Archives: 66,67,89,92,94,128,134,178.
Moorland-Spingarn Research Center, Howard University: 149.
U.S. Army Signal Corps: 167. Ohio Historical Society: 24.
Eyewire, Inc.: 62,99,104,144. Comstock Images: 124.

1 2 3 4 5 6 7 8 9 10 07 06 05 04 03

CONTENTS

★★★★★★★★★★★★★★★★★★★

CONTENTS *continued*

★ ★ ★ ★ ★ ★ ★ ★

Three Confederate prisoners from the Battle of Gettysburg, July 1863.

FOREWORD

BY RON MAXWELL

★ ★ ★ ★ ★ ★ ★ ★ ★ ★ ★ ★ ★ ★ ★ ★ ★ ★ ★ ★

Those who cannot remember the past are con-
demned to repeat it.

—*George Santayana*

Literally millions of people in our own country and
around the world have come to know Joshua Lawrence
Chamberlain since the premier of our 1993 Civil War
film, *Gettysburg*. Few people ten years ago, outside of a
circle of scholars and Civil War enthusiasts, knew about
this extraordinary man until seeing the movie. Now our
countrymen, women, and people around the world will
come to know Thomas Jonathan "Stonewall" Jackson in
a very intimate way when they view the next film, the prequel: *Gods and Generals*.

Thomas Jonathan Jackson—what an extraordinary
man—walked among us 130 years ago! The more you
come to know him, and the more you come to know that
generation—the men who wore the blue and the men who
wore the gray—the more difficult it is to endure the politically correct cant that is espoused by many in the chat-
tering classes on an almost daily basis. I find solace in the
fact that when they see this film those who have been so
irresponsible to that generation perhaps will be shamed
into some silence.

Faith in God and Generals was penned and collected
by my friends Ted Baehr and Susan Wales. As the pages of
this anthology unfold, you will also become acquainted
more intimately with many of the characters in the film.
(Even in a three-plus-hour film, there is much more to be
told about the historical characters.) The author/editors
have provided us with a closer look at these brave men
and women as a companion piece to the movie. While the
contributors of this inspiring book have expanded brilliantly on some of the characters appearing in the film,
others in *Faith in God and Generals* are faces without
names, and now, they, too, will come alive on the pages of
this book. Some of these gripping tales depict the
strength, the angst, and the faith of the women left behind
who loved these brave men.

The Civil War was a brutal episode in our history.
More than a half million soldiers were killed or wounded.
Tens of thousands were made refugees. The suffering was
beyond our reckoning. *Faith in God and Generals* is a
must-read for anyone who sees the film or plans to see the
film to further their study and increase their understanding of these important historical characters who helped
shape the future of the generations who followed.
Individual heroism and courage, duty and honor only
make sense in the context of these trials and tribulations.

The last thing the world needs is a mindless, glossy
entertainment on the Civil War. None of us wants that,
so it is important to accept the seriousness of this challenge: to keep our eyes wide open, to be relentlessly honest, to refrain from perpetuating myth and folklore—

to get to the truth of the matter. Nothing will be more dramatic, and nothing will be more worthwhile.

As a writer, I spend a lot of time alone in the research and the writing of screenplays. I've come to recognize that I'm not really alone because I'm with the characters that I am researching. I feel as though I come to know them intimately, as friends, and at some point they are speaking through me onto a page. Eventually, they are embodied in a cinematic sense and resurrected for the world to see. For me, it is a spiritual process.

In the private world of my writing and research, which is a great contrast to the time of making the movie—when you're surrounded by hundreds of people in the crew and hundreds of people in the cast—I have come to rely on some friends who've lived over the generations. The characters in the story are what move me. The movies I've made, and the movies I've wanted to make, center around the characters. We have everything to learn from those who lived in the past. I try to give them back their authentic voice. Telling the truth about the individuals and the moral climate in which they lived creates understanding of the past and touches our hearts.

I am passionate about representing history accurately, and I pay attention to detail, to portray individuals as they were. We are all very susceptible to the power of the media. The media, particularly films, have a powerful influence on our lives. Movies have the ability to tell stories with such authority that the stories they tell can pass as truth, whether or not they are truth. I have a moral obligation to exercise responsibility in my telling of history. The telling of history is the life and death of a people. An inaccurate portrayal can be the death of a culture over the years.

The same thing is true in the research I've done for the last two years, which I understand is only a blink of an eye compared to historians who spend their entire lives researching this. Among the many issues that are involved in the American Civil War—and there are many, as we all know (and they conflict and they overlap and they support one another, and the motivations of the war changed as the war went on)—no one in 1860 or 1861 could have imagined the conflagration, the immense destruction and death that would ensue, and the years the war would endure. But certainly, one of the motivating factors you see at work in both the Northern and Southern troops is patriotism—a positive love of country, love of place, love of people, love of community—which one needs to defend.

Of course, in the 1860s, it was a different world. The allegiance to state was often more powerful than allegiance to country. When you study the Confederate characters—when you study Robert E. Lee, Thomas Jonathan Jackson, the other Confederate generals—you see an agonizing time between two loyalties: a loyalty to the flag of the United States (the flag they all fought under in the Mexican War) and a loyalty to home, place, and heritage.

Society is an open-ended partnership between generations. The dead and the unborn are as much members of society as the living. To dishonor the dead is to reject the relation on which society is built—a relation of obligation between generations. Those who have lost respect for the dead have ceased to be trustees of their inheritance. Inevitably, therefore, they lose the sense of obligation to future generations. The web of obligations shrinks to the present tense.

—Edmund Burke
speaking in the 1780s in England

Certainly we are living in a time—maybe all times were thus—when we are obsessed with the present tense and obsessed with our own wisdom, our own knowledge, and our own expertise. The act of writing and compiling a book, making a movie, or making a historical film is doing in a sense exactly what Edmund Burke is saying. It is reaching back to that generation—in the case of *Gods and Generals* and *Gettysburg,* to the generation of the 1860s in the United States, in giving them a voice. It is not about imposing our voice on them. It is not about sitting in judgment from our high and mighty place at the beginning of the twenty-first century in moral indignation and moral superiority over that generation. But, unfortunately, that is where the attitude of the Hollywood entertainment industry too often comes from—in this smug air of superiority that persists, the received wisdom that we are better than any generation that ever lived before and, worse, that we can sit in judgment of them. The only point of making a historical film is to give them a voice, to try to find out what they have to say—the lives they lived. And maybe, by this process, that generation can illuminate our own.

Of course, I don't mean to say for one second that those generations were a host of saints or that they should necessarily be emulated. That would be nonsensical. We do, however, need to look back with a sense of humility and with a sensitive ear to what these people have to tell us.

The 1860s were not that long ago. Everything that generation was concerned about, every single issue, is alive today and burning in our contemporary society. Think of it, every one of those issues. The Confederacy was kept by force in the United States, slavery was abolished, the nation saved as "one nation under God." But the underlying issues—states rights, individual liberty, sectionalism, industrialism, arbitrary taxations, Federal usurpations, racial justice, cultural identity, the uses and misuses of the military force, loyalty, and patriotism—all are alive and contentious in the great national debate.

There is another part of Edmund Burke's admonition, not only in looking to the past, but also in looking to the future. In a movie or any other work of art, you are holding hands between generations, with those who once lived and with generations yet unborn. You are at that connecting point.

The film *Gettysburg* with all its flaws (and I'd be the first to admit it has them) will be a connecting point for generations to come. Generations from now will get the DVD, or whatever the technology is, and they will say, "This is what this generation did in 1993. This generation is connecting us with an earlier one. Were they truthful?" Because they will be able to get to the truth the same way we can. They will be able to get to the letters, the diaries, the regimental records, and the newspapers of the day. Were they telling the truth? Does the truth matter?

Just the other night, I saw an episode of "Murder She Wrote." It happened to catch my attention because I heard a character in it say First Manassas. So, I sat down and watched it. Again, it was filled with caricature, filled with falsehood, and filled with the received wisdom you're supposed to have if you want to get ahead in Hollywood. Which means, anybody who ever lived south of the Mason-Dixon line is either a bumbling fool, a racist monger, or . . . you know the list. Filmmakers have to get beyond these clichés and caricatures to a deeper place.

The philosopher Vico was writing in the fourteenth century in Italy, at the beginning of the Renaissance. His words, what I am going to include here, are paraphrased by Isaiah Berlin. He kind of put his finger on the process that I and other filmmakers have to do, which is striving to the truth through this alchemical process. Vico wrote about "fantasia," without which the past cannot, in his view, be resurrected. The crucial role he assigns to the imagination must not blind us, and did not blind him, to the necessity for verification. He allows that critical methods of examining evidence are indispensable.

Yet without fantasia, the past remains dead. To bring it to life, we need, at least ideally, to hear men's voices . . . to conjecture, on the basis of such evidence as we can gather, what may have been their experience, their forms of expression, their values, outlook, themes, ways of living. Without this, we cannot grasp whence we came, how we came to be as we are now. Not merely physically or biologically, and, in a narrow sense, politically and institutionally, but socially, psychologically, morally. Without this, there can be no genuine self-understanding. We call great historians not those who only are in full control of the factual evidence obtained by the use of the best critical methods available to them, but also possess the depths of imaginative insight that characterizes gifted novelists, and that is what we call the muse.

"The patriot volunteer, fighting for country and his rights, makes the most reliable soldier on earth."
—Stonewall Jackson

PREFACE

BY TED BAEHR

★ ★ ★ ★ ★ ★ ★ ★ ★ ★ ★ ★ ★ ★ ★ ★ ★ ★ ★

JACKSON: *My esposita! Come, before I leave, we must sit, read together . . . a verse.*

Jackson finds his Bible on a shelf.

JACKSON: *Yes, yes, here. Corinthians, Second Corinthians, chapter 5. I have been thinking about this verse.*

Anna puts her hand on his, and they read it together.

"For we know that if our earthly house of this tabernacle were dissolved, we have a building of God, a house not made with hands, eternal in the heavens."

They kneel together. His arm is around her.

—*from the script of* Gods and Generals, *written by Ron Maxwell*

Depending on your point of view, there may never have been an historic event in the life of the United States of America that influenced the nation and its people as much as the Civil War a.k.a. the War Between the States a.k.a. the War of Northern Aggression. This tragic and yet heroic event pitted brother against brother on an immense scale. Although countless war movies have been made, it is rare that a big budget Hollywood movie comes along that accurately and faithfully reflects history *and* the Christian faith of the protagonists in an historic event.

Gods and Generals, based on the best-selling book by Jeff Shaara, is such a movie. It accurately portrays the human characters and honors the faith of the key players. Ron Maxwell—the renowned director of the critically acclaimed epic movie *Gettysburg*—wrote, directed, and coproduced *Gods and Generals.* The film is also produced by Ted Turner Pictures.

Because the book is so vast, the movie covers the years 1861 through 1863 and focuses on General Stonewall Jackson—up through his death—with General Joshua Lawrence Chamberlain and General Robert E. Lee featured as dictated by history and the arc of the movie's storyline.

Gods and Generals is the prequel to *Gettysburg,* a film based on the novel *The Killer Angels* written by Jeff's father, Michael Shaara. *Gods and Generals* was filmed in and around Sharpsburg, Maryland, the site of the Antietam Battlefield, and on actual historic locations in Virginia and West Virginia. Many of the actors from the movie *Gettysburg* will reprise their roles in the new film, and additional historical figures are Stonewall Jackson, Mary Anna Morrison Jackson, Myra Hancock, Mary Custis Lee, and Fanny Chamberlain.

From the Battle of Fredericksburg to the Battle of Chancellorsville, when Jackson is mortally wounded by his own men, *Gods and Generals* paints a brilliant portrait of the lives of these great leaders during the tumultuous decade leading up to the Battle of Gettysburg.

Prof. James I. Robertson, Alumni Distinguished Professor and Executive Director of the Virginia Center for Civil War Studies at Virginia Tech and award-winning author of *Stonewall Jackson: The Man, The Soldier, The Legend,* had this to say about the *Gods and Generals* screenplay:

> I very much appreciate the opportunity to read the script for Gods and Generals. Quite frankly, I have never been more enthusiastic about a movie project. As a lifelong student of Gen. "Stonewall" Jackson, as well as one who spent seven years producing the most recent biography of the man, I have the strongest desire to see him depicted on film in the most accurate light. Anything less would be insulting to Jackson's memory and more fodder for the long-standing criticism that movie makers have neither the desire nor the ability to be truthful in historical productions. The Turner movie of Gods and Generals would go farther than any other modern film in dispelling those charges. Indeed, I see an even more positive contribution. The present script would reveal for the first time the real essence of one of history's most famous individuals. Most important of all, you have the opportunity to present a film that will inspire as well as inform.

The *Washington Post* reporter who visited the set of the movie commented that he had never seen such a powerful love scene as Jackson praying with his wife.

The religious fervor of Jackson and Lee in the movie is a commentary on the war fervor of the South in general. How could one fight to dissolve the Union without God on one's side?

If you have seen *Gettysburg*, then you must see *Gods and Generals*. If you have not seen *Gettysburg*, then see *Gods and Generals* first, then immediately watch *Gettysburg*.

The book you are about to read, *Faith in God and Generals,* is filled with stories that will help you understand the true story of the faith and values of the historic participants in this epic feature film.

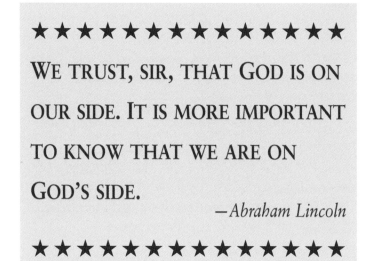

★ ★ ★ ★ ★ ★ ★ ★ ★ ★ ★ ★ ★ ★ ★

WE TRUST, SIR, THAT GOD IS ON OUR SIDE. IT IS MORE IMPORTANT TO KNOW THAT WE ARE ON GOD'S SIDE.

—*Abraham Lincoln*

★ ★ ★ ★ ★ ★ ★ ★ ★ ★ ★ ★ ★ ★ ★

PREFACE

By Susan Wales

★ ★

Neither party expected for the war, the magnitude, or the duration, which it has already attained. Neither anticipated that the cause of the conflict might cease with, or even before, the conflict itself should cease. Each looked for an easier triumph, and a result less fundamental and astounding. Both read the same Bible, and pray to the same God; and each invokes His aid against the other. It may seem strange that any men should dare to ask a just God's assistance in wringing their bread from the sweat of other men's faces; but let us judge not, that we be not judged. The prayers of both could not be answered; that of neither has been answered fully. The Almighty has His own purposes."
—*President Abraham Lincoln,*
Second Inaugural Address, March 4, 1865

Having descended from a Southern Baptist family steeped in tradition with a rich history and faith deeply rooted in the War Between the States (my Southern ancestors fought for both the North and the South), I was profoundly affected by filmmaker Ron Maxwell's epic masterpiece, *Gods and Generals*. The movie, like its predecessor, *Gettysburg*, enhanced my own understanding of the conflicted choices that our forefathers were forced to make as Ron Maxwell brilliantly brings these godly characters alive on the screen.

Because slavery was condoned in biblical times and Jesus Christ never addressed the issue, as well as the Apostle Paul telling slaves to obey their masters, Southerners felt justified in defending their cause; yet, the Northerners were confident that they were fighting on God's side to set the captives free. When a *Yankee* prisoner reported the earnestness of the *Rebels'* faith-filled prayers, coupled with the fact that the Union army was experiencing heavy casualties and losses at the onset of the battles, the Northerners grew concerned. The question was asked: Can we be praying to the same God? Lincoln addressed this issue: "The will of God prevails. In great contests each party claims to act in accordance with the will of God. Both may be, and one must be, wrong. God cannot be for and against the same thing at the same time."[1]

Out of this conflict and the words from Lincoln's quote, the title of Jeff Sharra's book and subsequently Ron Maxwell's movie, *Gods and Generals*, was born.

Jeff Daniels is one of several actors in the movie *Gettysburg* who reprises his role in *Gods and Generals*, playing the part of Colonel Joshua Chamberlain, one of the finest military leaders of the Union army.

Another actor who also appeared in *Gettysburg* is Stephen Lang, who magnificently portrays the character of Stonewall Jackson, a brilliant soldier and a deeply religious man whose faith and courage are legendary. "Playing a historical figure to me bears a certain responsibility. You've got the ghosts looking over your shoulder," said Stephen Lang.

Oscar winner Robert Duvall plays the role of Confederate General Robert E. Lee, a distinguished twenty-five-year veteran of the United States army and native Virginian. With unwavering faith, Lee is forced to choose between his country and his home state.

Jeremy London excels in the role of Stonewall's trusted aide, Sandie Pendleton, also a devout Christian. "I'm just honored to be a part of this movie," says London. "It's just absolutely incredible exploring the human nature of how people used to be willing to die for something they believed in."

Another Oscar winner, Mira Sorvino, makes a charming appearance as Fanny Chamberlain, wife of Joshua Lawrence Chamberlain; and, newcomer Kali Rocha is superb as General Stonewall Jackson's wife, Mary Anna Morrison Jackson. Five current United States congressmen have roles in the film, including noted historians Senator Phil Gramm of Texas and Senator Robert Byrd of West Virginia.

The original orchestral score for this major motion picture was composed by John Frizzell and Randy Edelman in London and features a solo virtuosity by renowned country fiddler Mark O'Connor and Chieftain's own Uilene Pipe player, Paddy Moloney. The original end-title song, "Cross the Green Mountain," written and performed by legend Bob Dylan, was recorded in Los Angeles.

According to Maxwell, Bob Dylan's new song, released by SONY Records and featured over the closing titles of *Gods and Generals,* is "a haunting, moving ballad, reminiscent of his earliest works with the added insights of a lifetime." Upon hearing the song, performed by Dylan and his band, Maxwell noted, "Dylan has in a sense returned to his roots—the same roots that nourished the mountain men of western Virginia, the home of Thomas Jonathan Jackson and countless others who fought for both the Blue and the Gray."

Praised by film critics, historians, and theologians, *Gods and Generals* is one of the most spiritually influential films of our times. Coauthor of this book and chairman of the Christian Film & Television Commission ministry and MOVIEGUIDE®, Ted Baehr said, "*Gods and Generals* breaks the mold of most Hollywood feature films because it also contains a strong faithful Christian perspective that was true to the characters at that turbulent time in America's history."

The film's screenplay writer, director, and producer, Ronald F. Maxwell, was educated at New York University, first in the College of Arts and Sciences and later in the Graduate School of the Arts' Institute of Film. He has since compiled a lengthy filmography by writing, producing, and directing movies for television and theatrical release. In addition to *Gettysburg,* he has directed such movies as *Little Darlings, The Night the Lights Went Out in Georgia, Kidco,* and *Parent Trap II.*

Maxwell is currently in preproduction on yet another Civil War story, *Last Full Measure. Gods and Generals* is a prequel to his landmark film, *Gettysburg,* and *Last Full Measure* will be a sequel. Altogether, they will comprise Ron Maxwell's epic Civil War Trilogy. As this trilogy unfolds, the viewer will understand the magnitude of the gift that Ron Maxwell has given us as we gain a deeper understanding through his films of the historical characters, their issues, and the freedom our ancestors fought to obtain for future generations.

ACKNOWLEDGMENTS

★ ★ ★ ★ ★ ★ ★ ★ ★ ★ ★ ★ ★ ★ ★ ★ ★ ★

We want to extend heartfelt gratitude and appreciation to the remarkable and talented individuals at Broadman and Holman: Ken Stephens, David Shepherd, Len Goss, Lisa Parnell, and Diana Lawrence for taking on this challenging project. With your great faith and attitude that nothing is impossible with God, you have truly accomplished miraculous things!

We are also grateful to Matt Jacobson of Loyal and Ken Curtis of *Christian History* magazine for their help and especially our distinguished contributors, without whose dedication the book could not have been published. Read their great books to become better acquainted with this period of history!

Thanks to Mick Mayhew at Warner Brothers who allowed us to spend hours going through the photographs from the movie, and to Robert Wussler, Suzanne Arden, and Tina Knight at Ted Turner Pictures for their dedication, time, and assistance.

Susan Wales and Ted Baehr

FROM SUSAN WALES

A special thanks to my longtime friends, Ted Baehr and his wife Lili, who invited my participation, and to Ron Maxwell, one of the most passionate and godly filmmakers in the business, who offered us this incredible opportunity.

Love to my husband Ken and my daughter Megan and granddaughter Hailey who exhibit love and the patience of Job while I am meeting impossible deadlines.

Seeing the film *Gods and Generals* and researching this book, *Faith in God and Generals*, affirms my appreciation for our ancestors' sacrifices—some with their lives—so we enjoy freedom in America today, and especially for our Lord Jesus Christ who lives in our hearts and guides our paths on our journey.

Susan Wales

FROM TED BAEHR

This book is joyfully dedicated to:

Jesus, our Lord and Savior;

Lili, my beautiful wife; Peirce, James, Robert, and Evelyn, my wonderful children; and Ted "Bob 'Tex' Allen" Baehr, my loving father and a truly great actor who now resides with his beloved Savior!

Also, to my good friend and valiant believer in the truth, Ron Maxwell, who accepted my heartfelt suggestion to write this book as a complement to his great movie, *Gods and Generals;* and to the children and generations who will follow us who need to know about their godly heritage and the Truth that will set them free from the confusion of every age. May God protect them and help them to remember so that they may be more than conquerors in Jesus Christ.

Finally, I want to thank the directors, advisers and friends of MOVIEGUIDE®, the Christian Film & Television Commission ministry, and Good News Communications, Inc.

In His Name, Ted Baehr

★ ★

History, in general, is often a story of civil strife. It's so important for our people to know the stories of earlier Americans, of the character of the people that came before us. I seek to bring understanding, compassion, and illumination of the trials of the 1860s. There were enormous challenges, terrible choices to be made. It was never an easy issue of allegiances. Yet, our country made it through. Understanding the complex issues of our history can strengthen us and give us wisdom in our approach to issues today.

—Ron Maxwell

★ ★

1
THE PARTING SEA
REVOLUTIONARY FAITH IN NORTH AND SOUTH

★★★★★★★★★★★★★★★★★★★★★★★

In the movie *Gods and Generals,* actors (l-r) Stephen Lang, Robert Duvall, Bo Brinkman, and Bruce Boxleitner are General Thomas Stonewall Jackson, General Robert E. Lee, Major Walter Taylor, and General James Longstreet.

What is often spoon-fed to our generation is an oversimplified, one-dimensional view of the conflict. The issues of the Civil War include slavery—my film recognizes that people were tarnished and impaired in their judgment by slavery—but the war was much more complex and paradoxical than is being taught to society.

—Ron Maxwell, director of the movie
Gods and Generals

"ONE OF THE KNIGHTLIEST SOLDIERS"

★ ★ ★ ★ ★ ★ ★ ★ ★

How could we help falling on our knees, all of us together, and praying God to pity and forgive us all!"
—Joshua Chamberlain after the war

Joshua Lawrence Chamberlain looked out upon the masses of men streaming by, clad in tattered gray, and ordered that his men salute the vanquished. Years of monumental struggle, bloodshed, and suffering had ended here, in this quiet knoll called Appomattox, where the armies passed silently. Chamberlain ordered a "carry arms" salute that spread down the Union line as they faced the forces of Major General John B. Gordon.

Surprised, Gordon reared on his steed and saluted back. The dignity of that act led Gordon to later call Chamberlain "one of the knightliest soldiers" of the war. In the person of this knight of the North coexisted the twin strands of a warrior and a scholar, a deeply thoughtful and religious man who bore the burden of his country's call to take up arms against treachery, aristocracy, and slavery.

His faith, honesty, and persistence in overcoming obstacles marked Chamberlain's formative years. His tenacity is best understood by a story from Lawrence's youth. As the firstborn son of a Maine farming family, Lawrence was well accustomed to brutal work, dawn to dusk. One day, he was driving an ox cart and collecting hay with his father when one of the front wheels caught between two stumps. His father, a stern man, demanded that he "clear the cart." Lawrence, thinking his father couldn't see how firmly the cart was lodged, asked of his father, "How do I do it?" His father responded forcefully, "Do it—that's how!" Thus, Chamberlain, with all of the force he could muster, did it. In his memoirs Chamberlain said, "'Do it—that's how!' was a maxim whose order far exceeded the occasion. It was an order for life that was worth infinitely more than years of book learning and dilatory resolution."

While his father wished the boy would go into the military, his mother believed he should go into the ministry. Ultimately, he decided to become a missionary, but he was too far behind in his studies to enter Bowdoin College. In nine months' time, Lawrence built a solitary study in his attic and learned Greek and Latin with the aid of tutors, passing the entrance requirements to Bowdoin. While there, Chamberlain was forced to confront another shortfall: a nagging stammer. He learned to overcome this by speaking in a sing-song manner, not unlike how he would sing as a member of chorus in church, and went on to become a gifted orator and linguist. By his graduation from Bowdoin and Bangor Theological Seminary, Chamberlain was fluent in nine other languages. He accepted a job offer as a professor of rhetoric at Bowdoin before war called him to markedly different services.

The path to war for Chamberlain must have been a difficult one. He had benefited greatly from times of peace: he had a beautiful family (his wife, Fanny Adams, was animated and charming and the daughter of the local pastor), was a beloved professor, and knew little about the art of war. Nonetheless, he could not be restrained after the Rebel victory at Bull Run led President Lincoln to call for more recruits. Though the college tried to keep him from entering service, he was committed to the cause. He said of his willingness to participate, "I have always been interested in military matters, and what I do not know in that line, I know how to learn. But, I fear, this war, so costly of blood and treasure, will not cease until the men of the North are willing to leave good positions, and sacrifice the deepest personal interests, to rescue our Country from desolation, and defend the national existence against treachery at home and jealousy abroad. This war must be ended, with a swift and strong hand; and every man ought to come forward, and ask to be placed at his proper post."

Chamberlain considered the Confederate attack on Federal forces an assault on the sacred Union, and the democracy it represented, a nation which had been paid for by the blood of his Puritan ancestors, three of whom fought in the Revolution. The "jealousy abroad" he spoke of was also no small matter: English papers at the time praised the

Joshua Chamberlain

South for ending the "horrible nightmare" that was the American experiment of democracy and individual merit. They believed the break-up of the Union would prove that aristocracy and monarchy are the proper forms of government, and that men of humble origins such as Abraham Lincoln, or Lawrence Chamberlain, had no business as leaders. In taking up arms, Chamberlain recognized the risks and accepted the great sacrifices that his involvement entailed.

Chamberlain requested a commission from the governor of Maine and received the position of lieutenant colonel under Colonel Adelbert Ames: the 20th Maine Regiment had been born. Under Ames, Chamberlain learned how to lead men and how to fight. Later, Ames would be given charge of a division, and Chamberlain would lead the 20th.

His body bore the proof of his dedication: in twenty-four engagements—including Antietam, Fredericksburg, Chancellorsville, Gettysburg, Spotsylvania, and Cold Harbor—Chamberlain was wounded six times. At Fredericksburg in December 1862, where Chamberlain led his men "up slopes slippery with blood," a Confederate ball grazed by his ear and neck. At Gettysburg on Little Round Top, Chamberlain held the end of the Union line against wave after wave of Alabaman Confederates. Had he lost the position, the entire Union flank would have been exposed, and the Confederates would have swept over the ridge and probably won the battle, and the war. Chamberlain vividly described the battlefield: "everywhere men torn and broken, staggering, creeping, quivering on the earth, . . . Things which cannot be told—nor dreamed."

During the Petersburg campaign Chamberlain was struck by a minié ball that ripped through his body, hip to hip, shattering bones and cutting the bladder and urethra. The injuries were so severe that the Union army sent out his obituary prematurely, and the division surgeons predicted that he had no chance of survival. Chamberlain, however, hung on to life as he was transferred from field hospital to hospital and quickly scrawled his wife a message attesting both to his faith and love for her: "My darling wife I am lying mortally wounded the doctors think, but my mind & heart are at peace Jesus Christ is my all-sufficient savior. I go to him. God bless & keep & comfort you, precious one, you have been a precious wife to me. To know & love you makes death & life beautiful . . . Oh how happy to feel yourself forgiven. God bless you evermore precious precious one. Ever yours Lawrence."

Chamberlain survived the encounter and after a period

★ ★ ★ ★ ★ ★ ★

In great deeds,
something abides.

—Joshua Chamberlain

★ ★ ★ ★ ★ ★ ★

of recovery in Maine returned to the field to again shed blood for the cause of freedom. He justified his return to war, in part, by remarking that "there is no promise of life in peace, & no decree of death in war. And, I am so confident of the sincerity of my motives that I can trust my own life & the welfare of my family in the hands of Providence." He went on to be wounded again at Quaker Roads and continued to rally his troops after being shot across the arm. His fearlessness and bravery were such that, amazingly, both his troops and the Confederates who faced him cheered him on in that engagement. Again, after that occurrence, the New York papers mistakenly published his obituary.

"In great deeds, something abides," said Chamberlain in memory of the actions that occurred in the battle of Gettysburg, including his defense of Little Round Top. Indeed, he was awarded the Congressional Medal of Honor for the bloody task of holding the line against consistent rebel onslaughts. In 1889, Chamberlain would return to Gettysburg to pay tribute to the great loss in words perhaps as stirring as Lincoln's:

> In great deeds something abides. On great fields something stays. Forms change and pass; bodies disappear; but spirits linger, to consecrate ground for the vision-place of souls. And reverent men and women from afar, and generations that know us not and that we know not of, heart-drawn to see where and by whom great things were suffered and done for them, shall come to this deathless field, to ponder and dream; and lo! the shadow of a mighty presence shall wrap them in its bosom, and the power of the vision pass into their souls. This is the great reward of service. To live, far out and on, in the life of others; this is the mystery of the Christ—to give life's best for such high sake that it shall be found again unto life eternal.

In years after the war, Chamberlain did indeed "live, far out and on" as he became the president of Bowdoin College, became Governor of Maine, and then went into business in the last years of his life. For a man so visibly scarred by the war, Chamberlain was the last man to die of war-related injuries. In 1914, as he succumbed to his wounds, another war another world away was beginning, but Chamberlain can be credited with standing his ground and ensuring that this nation would remain united under God.

★ *James S. C. Baehr*

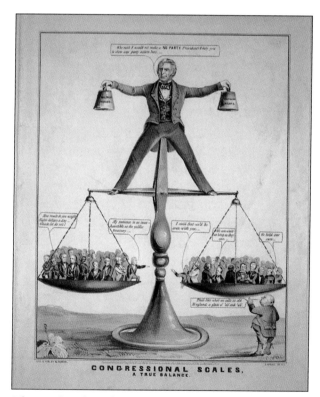

The North and South disagreed about slavery for years prior to the Civil War. This satirical print by Currier & Ives illustrates attempts to balance southern and northern interests on the question of slavery in 1850.

OFFICIAL PROCLAMATIONS

★ ★ ★ ★ ★ ★ ★ ★ ★

Both parties deprecated war; but one of them would make war rather than let the nation survive; and the other would accept war rather than let it perish. And the war came.
—*Lincoln's Second Inaugural Address, March 4, 1865*

In his second inaugural address, President Abraham Lincoln recognized that people on both sides of the Civil War were Christian people who looked to God for assistance in the struggle. Both North and South "read the same Bible, and pray to the same God; and each invokes His aid against the other." Both Northern and Southern leaders believed that the morality and religion of the soldiers were just as important to victory as was their fighting strength.

Leaders of both sides issued orders and proclamations encouraging Christian prayers and observances among the soldiers and the citizenry. At the beginning of the war, on November 15, 1862, President Lincoln wrote a letter to his army commanders encouraging Sabbath observance among the troops as well as the avoidance of vice and immorality:

The President, Commander-in-chief of the Army and Navy, desires and enjoins the orderly observance of the Sabbath by the officers and men in the military and naval service. The importance, for man and beast, of the prescribed weekly rest, the sacred rights of the Christian soldiers and sailors, a becoming deference to the best sentiment of a Christian people, and a due regard for the Divine will demand that Sunday labor in the army and navy be reduced to the measure of strict necessity.

The discipline and character of the national forces should not suffer, nor the cause they defend be imperiled by the profanation of the day or name of the Most High.

At this time of public distress, adopting the words of Washington in 1776, "Men may find enough to do in the service of God and their country, without abandoning themselves to vice and immorality." The first general order issued, by the Father of his Country after the Declaration of Independence, indicates the spirit in which our institutions were founded, and should ever be defended: "The general hopes and trusts that every officer and man will endeavor to live and act as becomes a Christian soldier, defending the dearest rights and liberties of his country."[1]

In July 1862, General Robert E. Lee issued a general order to the army similarly stating that all duties except inspection were to be suspended on Sunday so that the soldiers could rest and attend religious services. When some officers began to use Sunday as a gala day for inspections and military reviews, General Lee issued a general order reinforcing Sabbath observance in the army as a moral and religious duty, as well as contributing to the health of the troops. Only the most necessary duties would be required on the Sabbath. Inspections would be performed at a time that would not interfere with the men attending divine service.[2]

Both North and South continued the practice and tradition—dating back to the earliest days of colonial America—of proclaiming fast days and days of prayer for the respective nations.

★ ★ ★ ★ ★ ★ ★ ★ ★

It has seemed to me fit and proper that God should be solemnly, reverently, and gratefully acknowledged, as with one heart and one voice, by the whole American people.

—Abraham Lincoln

★ ★ ★ ★ ★ ★ ★ ★

The most famous of these proclamations is undoubtedly Lincoln's Thanksgiving Proclamation of 1863, which established an annual Thanksgiving as a national holiday:

It is the duty of nations as well as of men to own their dependence upon the overruling power of God; to confess their sins and transgressions in humble sorrow, yet with assured hope that genuine repentance will lead to mercy and pardon; and to recognize the sublime truth, announced in the Holy Scriptures and proven by all history, that those nations are blessed whose God is the Lord.

We know that by his divine law, nations, like individuals, are subjected to punishments and chastisements in this world. May we not justly fear that the awful calamity of civil war which now desolates the land may be punishment inflicted upon us for our presumptuous sins, to the needful end of our national reformation as a whole people?

We have been the recipients of the choicest bounties of heaven; we have been preserved these many years in peace and prosperity; we have grown in numbers, wealth and power as no other nation has ever grown.

But we have forgotten God. We have forgotten the gracious hand which preserved us in peace and multiplied and enriched and strengthened us, and we have vainly imagined, in the deceitfulness of our hearts, that all these blessings were produced by some superior wisdom and virtue of our own. Intoxicated with unbroken success, we have become too self-sufficient to feel the necessity of redeeming and preserving grace, too proud to pray to the God that made us.

It has seemed to me fit and proper that God should be solemnly, reverently, and gratefully acknowledged, as with one heart and one voice, by the whole American people.

I do therefore invite my fellow citizens in every part of the United States, and also those who are at sea and those who are sojourning in foreign lands, to set apart and observe the last Thursday of November as a day of Thanksgiving and praise to our beneficent Father who dwelleth in the heavens.

The Confederate government similarly recognized the need for the people to pray to the Lord with reverent thanksgiving and humility about the affairs of the nation. After the Army of the Potomac was repulsed and the capital city of Richmond was spared from the invading armies, the Confederate Congress called for a day of prayer. The leaders felt that just as the American colonies had been helped by God in their fight for independence from Great Britain, so the Confederate States needed to seek God to achieve independence from the United States. President Jefferson Davis issued the proclamation for a day of prayer to the citizens of the Confederate States:

The Senate and House of Representatives of the Confederate States of America have signified their desire that a day may be set apart and observed as a day of humiliation, fasting, and prayer, in the following language, to wit: "Reverently recognizing the Providence of God in the affairs of man, and gratefully remembering the guidance, support and deliverance granted to our patriot fathers in the memorable war which resulted in the independence of the American colonies, and now reposing in Him our supreme confidence and hope in the present struggle for civil and religious freedom, and for the right to live under a government of our own choice, and deeply impressed with the conviction that without Him nothing is strong, nothing is wise and nothing enduring; in order that the people of this Confederacy may have the opportunity, at the same time, of offering their adoration to the great Sovereign of the Universe, of penitently confessing their sins and strengthening their vows and purposes of amendment in humble

reliance upon His gracious and almighty power: The Congress of the Confederate States of America do resolve, That Friday, the 8th day of April next, be set apart and observed as a day of humiliation, fasting, and prayer, that Almighty God would so preside over our public counsels and authorities; that He would inspire our armies and their leaders with wisdom, courage and perseverance; and so manifest Himself in the greatness of His goodness and majesty of His power, that we may be safely and successfully led, through the chastening to which we are being subjected, to the attainment of an honorable peace; so that while we enjoy the blessings of a free and happy government we may ascribe to Him the honor and the glory of our independence and prosperity." A recommendation so congenial to the feelings of the people will receive their hearty concurrence; and it is a grateful duty to the Executive to unite with their representatives in inviting them to meet in the courts of the Most High.[3]

*Jefferson
Davis*

After the major Confederate defeats at Vicksburg and Gettysburg in July 1863, President Davis again called upon the Confederate people to seek the Lord in prayer for the nation:

★ ★ ★ ★ ★ ★ ★ ★ ★ ★ ★ ★ ★ ★ ★ ★

Again do I call the people of the Confederacy —a people who believe that the Lord reigneth, and that His overruling Providence ordereth all things—to unite in prayer and humble submission under His chastening hand, and to beseech His favor on our suffering country.

—Jefferson Davis

★ ★ ★ ★ ★ ★ ★ ★ ★ ★ ★ ★ ★ ★ ★ ★

Again do I call the people of the Confederacy—a people who believe that the Lord reigneth, and that His overruling Providence ordereth all things—to unite in prayer and humble submission under His chastening hand, and to beseech His favor on our suffering country. It is meet [or fitting] that when trials and reverses befall us, we should seek to take home to our hearts and consciences the lessons which they teach, and profit by the self-examination for which they prepare us. Had not our successes on land and sea made us self-confident and forgetful of our reliance on Him? Had not the love of lucre eaten like a gangrene into the very heart of the land, converting too many among us into worshippers of gain and rendering them unmindful of their duty to their country, to their fellow men, and to their God? Who, then, will presume to complain that we have been chastened or to despair of our just cause and the pro-

tection of our Heavenly Father? Let us rather receive in humble thankfulness the lesson which He has taught in our recent reverses, devoutly acknowledging that to Him, and not to our feeble arms, are due the honor and the glory of victory; that from Him, in His paternal providence, comes the anguish of defeat, and that, whether in victory or defeat, our humble supplications are due at His footstool. Now, therefore, I, Jefferson Davis, President of these Confederate States, do issue this, my proclamation, setting apart Friday, the 21st day of August ensuing, as a day of fasting, humiliation, and prayer; and I do hereby invite the people of the Confederate States to repair on that day to their respective places of public worship, and to unite in supplication for the favor and protection of that God who has hitherto conducted us safely through all the dangers that environed [surrounded] us.[4]

In accordance with President Davis's call for prayer, General Robert E. Lee issued the following order to his army:

Robert E. Lee

Headquarters,
Army Northern Virginia,
August 13, 1863.

The President of the Confederate States has, in the name of the people, appointed August 21st as a day of fasting, humiliation, and prayer. A strict observance of the day is enjoined upon the officers and soldiers of this army. All military duties, except such as are absolutely necessary, will be suspended. The commanding officers of brigades and regiments are requested to cause divine services, suitable to the occasion, to be performed in their respective commands. Soldiers! We have sinned against Almighty God. We have forgotten His signal mercies, and have cultivated a revengeful, haughty, and boastful spirit. We have not remembered that the defenders of a just cause should be pure in His eyes; that "our times are in His hands," and we have relied too much on our own arms for the achievement of our independence. God is our only refuge and strength. Let us humble ourselves before Him. Let us confess our many sins, and beseech Him to give us a higher courage, a purer patriotism, and a more determined will; that He will convert the hearts of our enemies; that He will hasten the time when war, with its sorrows and sufferings, shall cease, and that He will give us a name and place among the nations of the earth.[5]

The pathos of the American Civil War was that it was indeed a war in which brother was fighting brother. Christian fought against Christian, and both sides prayed to God for guidance, direction, and victory.

Diana L. Severance

Soldiers from the North and South often spent long periods of time together after being captured in battle. In Fair Oaks, Va., Lt. James B. Washington, a Confederate prisoner, with Capt. George A. Custer of the 5th Cavalry, U.S.A.

GOD IS ON OUR SIDE
SELECTIONS FROM SERMONS DURING THE CIVIL WAR ERA

THE NORTH

The following words were part of a sermon delivered by Henry Ward Beecher on Thanksgiving Day 1860.

THE SOUTHERN STATES have organized society around a rotten core—slavery: the North has organized society about a vital heart—liberty . . . . They stand in proper contrast. God holds them up to ages and to nations, that men may see the difference. Now that there is a conflict, I ask which is to yield?

The truth that men cannot hush, and that God will not have covered up, is the irreconcilable difference between liberty and slavery! Which will you advocate and defend? . . .

The secret intentions of those men who are the chief fomenters of troubles in the South cannot in anywise be met by compromise. What do those men that are really at the bottom of this conspiracy mean? Nothing more or less than this: Southern empire for slavery, and the reopening of the slave-trade as a means by which it shall be fed. Their secret purpose is to sweep westward like night, and involve in the cloud of their darkness all Central America, and then make Africa empty into Central America, thus changing the moral geography of the globe. And do you suppose any compromise will settle that design, or turn it aside, when they have made you go down on your knees, and they stand laughing while you cry with fear because you have been cozened and juggled into a blind helping of their monstrous wickedness?

They mean slavery. They mean an Empire of Slavery.

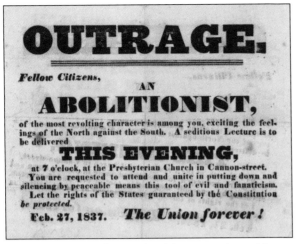

Slavery supporters obstructed antislavery meetings with handbills like this in 1837.

They don't any longer talk of the evil of slavery. It is a virtue, a religion! You cannot compromise with them except by giving up your own belief, your own principles, and your own honor. Moral apostasy is the only basis on which you can build a compromise that will satisfy the South!

THE SOUTH

These words were delivered by L. W. Tucker, a Presbyterian minister in Fayetteville, North Carolina, in May 1862.

WE SHOULD PRAY TO GOD to give success to our cause, and triumph to our arms. God will defend the right. . . .

Our cause is sacred. It should ever be so in the eyes of all true men in the South. How can we doubt it, when we know it has been consecrated by a holy baptism of fire and blood? It has been rendered glorious by the martyr-like devotion of Johnson, McCulloch, Garnett, Barlow, Fisher, McKinney, and hundreds of others who have offered their lives as a sacrifice on the altar of their country's freedom.

Soldiers of the South, be firm, be courageous, be brave; be faithful to your God, your country and yourselves, and you shall be invincible. Never forget that the patriot, like the Christian, is immortal till his work is finished.

You are fighting for everything that is near and dear, and sacred to you as men, as Christians and as patriots; for country, for home, for property, for the honor of mothers, daughters, wives, sisters, and loved ones. Your cause is the cause of God, of Christ, of humanity. It is a conflict of truth with error—of the Bible with Northern infidelity—of a pure Christianity with Northern fanaticism—of liberty with despotism—of right with might.

In such a cause victory is not with the greatest number, nor the heaviest artillery, but with the good, the pure, the true, the noble, the brave. We are proud of you, and grateful to you for the victories of the past. We look to your valor and prowess, under the blessing of God, for the triumphs of the future.[6]

★ *David B. Chesebrough*

★ ★ ★ ★ ★ ★ ★ ★ ★ ★ ★ ★ ★ ★ ★

By 1860, there were nearly 4 million slaves in the United States. One of every seven Americans belonged to another. (Yet, most Confederate soldiers didn't own any slaves.)

★ ★ ★ ★ ★ ★ ★ ★ ★ ★ ★ ★ ★ ★ ★

2
GOD-FEARING ARMIES
FIGHTING FOR THE "RIGHT"

Stephen Lang, actor who portrays General Stonewall Jackson in the movie *Gods and Generals*

I think that [Jackson's] relationship with the Bible and with God played a tremendous role in this film.... He looked for sustenance on a daily basis from both testaments.... Many times Jackson was looked upon as kind of a silent and forbidding figure. Yet, if you look at many of the discussions he had with all the preachers — you know, the Southern army was just ripe with preachers—because there was a great Christian revival going on in 1861–62. The dialogues that he had with these men are extremely animated and vital.... They are terrific to read about. I thought it was really interesting last year that the Presbyterian Church in Lexington, where Jackson prayed, burned to the ground from the interior. Of course, the whole town of Lexington stood and wept as it was going. The only thing from the interior that did not burn completely was Jackson's pew.... Jackson's stuff, his uniform, hat, the horse—these things in the Valley, they are considered relics in a religious sense, I think.... Can you imagine the emotional and spiritual value of this pew that is left—the only thing left.

—actor Stephen Lang (Stonewall Jackson *in* Gods and Generals)

"MUST ETERNITY BE LOST?"
ORGANIZING THE CHAPLAINCY

★ ★ ★ ★ ★ ★ ★ ★ ★

At their great victory at First Manassas, many in the South believed the war was virtually over. They expected England and France to soon recognize the Confederacy, clearly establishing Southern independence. During this period, profanity, gambling, drunkenness, and other vices were rampant throughout the Army of Northern Virginia. There were few chaplains to minister to the spiritual needs of the soldiers. On October 26, 1862, hospital steward John Samuel wrote in his diary: "I have not heard a sermon for a long time. Preaching is so seldom and irregular in camp that I greatly fear all of us will lose all the taste we ever had for serious solemn discourse. The truth is very obvious that we are all becoming depraved. The character of our fallen nature is such that the life we are leading meets no rebuffs as we go down, down in the mire of sin and folly. And there is scarcely a soldier in our ranks who will not admit [that] of all classes of men a soldier in this struggle should strive harder to gain the aid and approbation of Divine control."[1]

The Confederate defeats at Roanoke Island and Forts Henry and Donelson began to work a change in the Southern people. They became more humble and began to increasingly realize their need to depend upon God for their success. In the summer and fall of 1872, the Army of Northern Virginia faced intense fighting around Richmond, at Second Manassas, and at Sharpsburg.

Seeing the dead bodies of their comrades on the field deeply affected many of the soldiers, and they began to more seriously consider the uncertainty of their own lives. As the army went into its winter camp, there was more time for reflection, and many of the soldiers underwent a spiritual awakening.

General Jackson was most concerned about the spiritual condition of the men in his Second Corps, and he made plans to organize the chaplains in the army. Jackson believed the chaplains should be as systematically organized as any of the other departments of the army. He wrote his pastor, Rev. White of Lexington, some of his thoughts on the matter:

Each denomination of the Christian Churches throughout the South should send into the army some of its most prominent ministers who are distinguished for their piety, talents, and zeal; and such ministers should labor to produce concert of action among chaplains and Christians in the army. These ministers should give special attention to preaching to regiments which are without chaplains . . . . Denominational distinctions should be kept out of view and not touched on; and as a general rule, I do not think that a chaplain, who would preach denominational sermons, should be in the army. His congregation is his regiment, and it is composed of persons of various denominations. I would like to see no question asked in the army as to what denomination a chaplain belongs, but let the question be, Does he preach the Gospel?[2]

Jackson believed a lack of spirituality and morality was hampering the success of the Confederate army and nation. If he could lead a Christian, converted army, then victory seemed much more assured for the struggling Confederate nation. An organized chaplaincy would be an important step to that end. Jackson asked Beverly Tucker Lacy, pastor of the Presbyterian church in Fredericksburg,

Virginia, if he would join the Second Corps and organize the chaplains in the army. Jackson personally offered to pay two hundred dollars toward Lacy's salary, as well as three hundred dollars for tracts for the soldiers.

★ ★ ★ ★ ★ ★ ★ ★ ★ ★ ★ ★ ★ ★ ★

Originally, the government required chaplains to be ordained ministers of a Christian denomination, but after protests by Jewish leaders, the statute was changed on July 17, 1862, to read "any religious denomination."

★ ★ ★ ★ ★ ★ ★ ★ ★ ★ ★ ★ ★ ★ ★

Rev. Lacy was a graduate of Princeton Theological Seminary and had pastored churches in Virginia and Kentucky before coming to Fredericksburg in May 1861. Within a year after coming to Fredericksburg, Rev. Lacy found his town and church in the middle of the fighting between North and South. The Union soldiers occupied Fredericksburg in May 1862, and many of the citizens fled the town in fear. During part of the fighting, Rev. Lacy took refuge in the basement of a house, leading others there in praying Psalm 27: "Though a host should encamp against me, my heart shall not fear." Preaching from Scripture, "Lo, I am with you always," Lacy reassured the people that God had not forsaken them during this time.

Rev. Lacy's family home of Chatham was on the Rappahannock River and was occupied by Union soldiers in the fall of 1862. Clara Barton even stayed there for a time, ministering to the wounded Union troops. She later went into Fredericksburg itself and ministered to the wounded in the Episcopal and Presbyterian churches. The horrible memories of the suffering in Fredericksburg remained with her until her death. It was during such suffering that the spiritual awakening in the Southern army began.

Rev. Lacy joined Jackson's Second Corps at Moss Neck, near Fredericksburg, in March 1863, and shared a room with Jackson. Lacy immediately started regular family prayers and devotions at breakfast for Jackson's staff. On March 16 he called all the chaplains together at Round Oak Baptist Church near Moss Neck to establish a "Chaplain's Association of Jackson's Second Corps." Weekly, for eight weeks, the chaplains met together for prayer and Bible study, with Rev. Lacy keeping Jackson informed of all the meetings. Lacy developed for the chaplains a description of their duties and defined what relationship they should have with their men. He discussed with them the types of messages the men needed. Comparing the duties of a chaplain to those of commissary officers, he said:

> If the commissariat neglected its duties because of some derangement in its usual routine, the army would starve, although victorious. Yet even with its deranged system, the army must have its bread, if not the full supply, yet how valuable is the dry crust or hard biscuit! Brethren, we are appointed to carry the spiritual bread of life to the men. We

★★★★★★★★★★

"WE BELIEVE THAT GOD IS WITH US, NOT ONLY TO OWN AND BLESS HIS WORD TO THE SALVATION OF MEN, BUT THAT HIS BLESSING RESTS UPON OUR CAUSE AND ATTENDS OUR ARMIES."

—Rev. Beverly Tucker Lacy

★★★★★★★★★★

draw from a never-failing supply . . . . In the fighting many of these men must fall. One sermon more, brethren, for the love of souls, for the glory of God. Let us devise means to get this bread to them. . . . Don't desert the men because they are in the trenches. Go speak a word to them if only to say, "I know you were ready to die for your country; but were you ready to meet your God?" The Gospel hurts no men at any time under any circumstances. Ernest prayer by the camp fire makes men rest better, and march better.[3]

At its first meeting, the Chaplain's Association issued a paper written by Rev. Lacy as an address to the churches of the Confederacy on the needs of the army. In it, Lacy challenged the churches to send more ministers to serve as chaplains among the soldiers:

> We believe that God is with us, not only to own and bless His word to the salvation of men, but that His blessing rests upon our cause and attends our armies . . . . We are thankful to God for the large number of Christian officers who command our armies and aid us in our work. The presence of so many pious men in the ranks gives us a Church in almost every regiment to begin with. The intercourse and Christian communion of Christian brethren in the army is as intimate and precious as anywhere upon earth. It is an interesting fact, that by this work ministers of the different denominations are brought into closer and more harmonious co-operation, thus promoting the unity and charity of the whole Church, and greatly encouraging each other . . . . The near approach of death excites to serious thought. Religious reading is sought and appreciated.

Many opportunities for personal kindness to the sick and the wounded, on the battlefield and in the camp, bind grateful hearts to faithful chaplains. In preaching the word, conducting prayer-meetings and Bible classes, by circulating the Scriptures and other religious reading, and by frequent conversations in private, we have ample opportunity for doing our master's work and laboring for immortal souls. . . .

At this very time a most interesting and extensive work of grace is in progress amongst the troops stationed in and around the desolated city of Fredericksburg. The evidences of God's love and mercy are thus brought into immediate and striking contrast with the marks of the cruelty and barbarity of men.

Brethren, do not these movements of the Holy Ghost

Chapels often were built in soldiers' quarters. In 1864, the Army of Northern Virginia alone boasted fifteen chapels. One chapel built by the Army at the Tennessee seated more than one thousand people.

Chaplain conducting Mass for the 69th New York State Militia encamped at Fort Corcoran, D.C.

indicate where God's ministers should follow, and in what work they should engage? . . . Eternity alone can disclose the extent of the blessed work which faithful chaplains have accomplished in our armies. . . .

Brethren, send us more chaplains. The harvest truly is great, the laborers are few. We send abroad to the Churches the Macedonian cry, Come and help us. . . . The cause will not brook delay. A series of battles, which may speedily follow the opening of the campaign, will sweep away thousands of our brave comrades and friends—thousands of your own sons and brothers. Then come while it is called today. Come up to the help of the Lord, to the help of the Lord against the mighty. . . .[4]

The appeal for more chaplains in the army went beyond the immediate situation, looking forward to the future of the new country the Southerners were attempting to establish. After the war was over, the leaders of the new Confederacy would be the survivors of the army. It was important that these men be

Petersburg, Va. Chaplains of the 9th Corps, 1864.

established Christians. If they were godless men, then the new government would be immoral and godless. The entire fight for constitutional liberty would then be in vain.

In late March, Jackson moved his headquarters from Moss Neck to Thomas Yerby's, near Hamilton Crossing. An outdoor chapel was prepared nearby, and services were held in the open air. Trees were felled and used for benches. There Tucker Lacy led the Sunday morning and evening services and Wednesday prayer meetings. Hymn sings were also held there on Sunday afternoons. Often General Lee and other officers would worship there with men of Jackson's Second Corps. One April Sunday there were at least one thousand present. Rev. Lacy had never addressed such an imposing and respectful audience: "It was a noble sight to see there those, who led our armies to victory and upon whom the eyes of the nation are turned with admiration and gratitude, melted in tears at the story of the cross and the exhibition of the love of God to the repenting and return sinner."[5]

Sandie Pendleton, one of General Jackson's aides, wrote his mother that Rev. Lacy was very effective in energizing the chaplains. He was an eloquent preacher as well as a charming companion at the staff mess. He was a great teller of stories and was full of witticism that always enlivened conversation.

In April, Jackson's wife Anna and baby Julia were able to come and spend some time with General Jackson at the Yerby's house. Jackson had not yet seen his little daughter and was the most doting of fathers when she came. On April 23, Rev. Lacy baptized little five-month-old Julia. The following Sunday, the open air chapel was crowded with soldiers. An hour before the service was to begin, all the seats were occupied, and the soldiers were reading religious material and Bibles that had been distributed to them. General Jackson and Anna later arrived, as did Generals Lee, Early, and Kernshaw. In a strong voice, Rev. Lacy preached to the large congregation a powerful sermon on the rich man and Lazarus, contrasting this world and the next. It was the last sermon General Jackson ever heard, for he was wounded six days later.

On the night of May 2, 1863, General Jackson was seriously wounded; his left arm was amputated in the early morning of the following day. When Rev. Lacy came to the tent where Jackson's arm had been amputated, he exclaimed, "Oh, General, what a calamity." Jackson thanked him and said, "You see me severely wounded, but not depressed, not unhappy. I believe that it has been done according to God's holy will, and I will acquiesce entirely in it. You may think it strange; but you never saw me more perfectly contented than I am today."

With his firm trust in God's providence, Jackson knew his wound was God's will, and he would wait until God revealed His reasons. Jackson told Lacy that when he was lying wounded on the field and when he was being carried in the ambulance, "I gave myself up into the hands of the Heavenly Father without a fear . . . . It has been a precious experience to me, that I was brought face to face with death, and found all was well."[6] In the following days, at Jackson's request, Lacy had daily devotions at Jackson's bedside at ten o'clock.

The following Sunday, between twenty-five hundred and three thousand assembled for worship at Jackson's headquarters. Before the services, General Lee met Lacy and asked him about General Jackson's condition. When told he was growing weaker by the moment, Lee emotionally replied, "Surely, God will not take him from us, now that we need him so much. Surely he will be spared to us in answer to the many prayers which are offered for him." For the text of his sermon, Tucker Lacy used Jackson's favorite Scripture: "And we know that all things work together for good to them that love God, to them who are the called according to his purpose" (Rom. 8:28). All the men were thoughtful and serious as they thought

of all that depended on Jackson's recovery. At the end of the sermon, Rev. Lacy said it might be God's will to spare Jackson's life in answer to their prayers, and he called on all to petition the throne of grace for Jackson. At the conclusion of the time of prayer, Lacy said whatever God would do in the event would be for the best. When Jackson died that day, there was a calm and peace among the soldiers. They accepted Jackson's death as part of divine providence, even if they did not understand it.

During those difficult days in May, Tucker Lacy ministered not only to Jackson and the soldiers, but to Jackson's wife Anna. Often Lacy prayed with Anna that God would spare Jackson's life, if it were His will. When Jackson died Sunday, May 10, Lacy gave spiritual comfort to Anna. She later wrote: "Never shall I forget Mr. Lacy's ministrations of consolation to my bleeding heart on that holiest of Sabbath afternoons. Seated by my bedside, he talked so of Heaven, giving such glowing description of its blessedness, and following in imagination the ransomed, glorified spirit, through the gates into the [heavenly] city that at last peace, the 'peace of God,' came into my soul, and I felt that it was selfish to wish to bring back to this sorrowful earth, for my happiness, one who had made such a blissful exchange."[7]

After Jackson's death, Rev. Lacy continued with the Second Corps under Generals Ewell and Early, preaching fervently, ministering to the wounded, and building up the Chaplains' Association. John Apperson, a hospital steward of the Second Corps, often summarized Lacy's sermons in his diary. In February 1864, before the Wilderness Campaign, Lacy preached on the crucifixion of Christ, which he described as "the most important event in the history of time and the annals of eternity." All history—past, present, and future—centered upon the cross. Then Lacy shared how the witnesses of the crucifixion represented the human race in all its variety, good and bad, virtuous and depraved. According to Apperson's diary, Lacy "drew analogies between many of the beholders of that event and many now in existence. There lives now the Roman official, the priest and pontiff, the centurion and soldier, the thief of both conditions, the militia following public opinion or popularity, the sorrowing disciples, the weeping and prayerful mother. There were the prophets of false religions, the enemies of true religion—just as now."[8]

The same evening Lacy preached from Job 42:5–6: "I have heard of thee by the hearing of the ear: but now mine eye seeth thee. Wherefore I abhor myself, and repent in dust and ashes." Lacy developed the text by showing that the highest knowledge was to know God and the next highest was for man to know himself. Once a man knows God in all His righteousness and holiness, he then knows himself to be a depraved sinner in God's sight, in need of redemption that only comes in Christ. John Apperson wrote, "I have never looked at the history of Job with as much interest as I shall hereafter."

In addition to his sermons, Lacy prepared a popular lecture on "The Life and Christian Character of General T. J. Jackson." The chaplain described the glories of Jackson's military struggles as well as his exemplary Christian life. Lacy's eloquence held his audience spellbound for hours, and his account of Jackson's last days challenged listeners to make their peace with God. He shared the fact that a few days before his death, Jackson had discussed "repentance" with Rev. Lacy and told him, "That, unless he had previously made his peace with God, he did not think it would be possible to collect his thoughts to contemplate such a subject then."[9] Lacy used Jackson's statement as a warning to the unconverted soldiers to not delay their commitment to Jesus Christ.

As always, Tucker Lacy and the chaplains were most concerned with "the salvation of our sons and brothers, the salvation of our dear soldiers. We plead for those who are ready to lay down the life that now is. Shall they lose also the life which is to come? If the sacrifice of the body is demanded, shall that of the soul be made? If time is forfeited, must eternity be lost? The great object for which the Church of God was instituted upon earth is the same as that for which the Son of God died upon the Cross: THE GLORY OF GOD IN THE SALVATION OF MEN."[10]

★ *Diana L. Severance*

Chaplains were also enlisted to serve soldiers aboard ships. Religious services were held on the deck of the U.S. monitor Passaic.

SONGS IN THE CAMPS
FAITH IN THE MIDST OF WAR

★ ★ ★ ★ ★ ★ ★ ★ ★

Modern movies, television programs, historical documentaries, and historians have often overlooked one of the most significant aspects of the war: the Christian faith of those involved. Its effect was profound. The widespread revivals that broke out among the soldiers on both sides were unprecedented in American history, bringing hundreds of thousands of men to Jesus Christ and into the church. The abolitionists, almost all of whom were deeply committed to their Christian faith, made abolishing slavery a defining issue. Three of the country's largest denominations—Presbyterian, Methodist, and Baptist—split into Northern and Southern bodies over issues related to slavery, which caused Senator John C. Calhoun to note that because these denominations had "formed a strong cord to hold the whole Union together," when they broke apart, he predicted that "nothing will be left to hold the States together except force."[11] Finally, the nation's 3 to 4 million slaves endured their years of bondage and triumphed because of their widely held faith in Jesus Christ.

In commenting on the general historical ignorance about the faith of those involved on both sides, historian Gardiner H. Shattuck Jr., the author of *A Shield and a*

★ ★ ★ ★ ★ ★ ★ ★ ★ ★ ★ ★ ★

Three of the nation's leading Protestant denominations—the Presbyterians, Methodists, and Baptists—all divided over slavery or related issues. These church divisions fractured political parties and ultimately helped to divide the nation.

★ ★ ★ ★ ★ ★ ★ ★ ★ ★ ★ ★ ★

Hiding Place: The Religious Life of the Civil War Armies, notes: "The single aspect of the war that the [National] Park Service has failed to highlight is the impact of religion on the soldiers. Orientation films and shows at visitor centers never note how important religion was. Civil War soldiers gathered in great numbers around campfires to participate in revivals, not just to see minstrel shows."[12]

In contrast, the movie Gods and Generals illustrates the faith in Jesus Christ of many of those involved in the war.

IN THE BEGINNING

After the Southern forces fired on Fort Sumter in April 1861, the majority of Northern denominations, except for the historic "peace" churches, supported the war to reunite the country. The Protestant churches emphasized that the Union had to be preserved because of the special place the United States of America occupied in God's history. Because it was founded on Christian principles, they believed the United States stood in the vanguard of civilizing the world.

Preachers and ministers even portrayed the war in millennial terms, quoting the twentieth chapter of Revelation and other Bible passages that described the close of history. Even though most clergy believed in a postmillennial theology, they expected that the war would lead to God's reign being more thoroughly established. One Philadelphia Baptist minister claimed in 1863 that the defeat of the South would inaugurate what the Founding

Fathers "pictured and dreamed about, and prayed for. It will come with blessings, and be greeted with Hallelujahs, it will be the Millennium of political glory, the Sabbath of liberty, the Jubilee of humanity."

Believing that God was at work in the crisis changed the way in which Christian leaders dealt with slavery. In the beginning, the Northern churches were deeply divided about slavery. A few con-demned slavery as a sin, while others argued that the Bible per-mitted slavery. Most Christian leaders held more moderate beliefs. They believed that slavery would be abolished, but they abhorred the abolitionists' attack on slave owners as sinners.

As the war persisted, however, more and more church leaders began to interpret the war as a punishment sent by God. The ini-tial defeats of Union armies appeared to be punishment, and the belief developed that God would chastise the North until it took steps to end slavery. Many became convinced that God was using the conflict to establish His kingdom on earth. Therefore, what had started out as a call to preserve the Union turned into a cry for liberation.

That cry for repentance demanded more than the abo-lition of slavery; it also required citizens to turn from their sins and accept Jesus Christ. The Reverend Horace Bushnell, a Congregationalist minister in Hartford, Connecticut, preached just after the Union army had been routed at Bull Run in the summer of 1861: "There must

One Confederate soldier contended that if the South was lost, the epitaph should be "Died of whiskey."

be reverses and losses, and times of deep concern. There must be tears in the houses, as well as blood in the fields; the fathers and mothers, the wives and the dear children coming into the woe, to fight in hard bewailings." As the war progressed, more and more clergy told their people that "far more blood not only would be shed, it needed to be shed if the war were to attain its God-appointed purpose."

At the beginning of the hostili-ties, religious faith was the excep-tion, not the rule, among the troops. Army chaplains com-plained about the seductive influ-ences among the soldiers. The daily routine of army life was so tedious that men often succumbed to sin, and the camps were full of profanity, gambling, drunkenness, sexual licentiousness, card play-ing, and petty thievery. Those who wanted to practice their faith com-plained that the Sabbath was not observed, and General Robert McAllister complained that a "tide of irreligion" had rolled over his army "like a mighty wave." One Confederate soldier con-tended that if the South was lost, the epitaph should be: "died of whiskey."

Early in 1862, Chaplain James Marks bought a tent and began holding services for the soldiers of the 63rd Pennsylvania Regiment, who were bitter after their defeat at Bull Run. Thus began a revival that lasted until the spring and saw hundreds of men "born again."

Civilize the Army

As the war became more serious and prolonged, the troops began to turn in earnest toward God. President Lincoln believed that Christianity would civilize the Union army, so he provided for organized Christian guidance to soldiers. On May 4, 1861, he ordered regimental commanders to appoint chaplains for their units. These chaplains had to be ordained ministers in Christian denominations and were paid an officer's salary, which at first was $1,700 per year, but later was lowered to $1,200. Lincoln also supported the United States Christian Commission, an interdenominational organization dedicated primarily to the spreading of the gospel of Jesus Christ in the Union armies.

President Lincoln also proclaimed public fast days; on at least three occasions he urged Americans to go to their houses of worship, confess their sins humbly to the Almighty, and ask God's blessing. Moreover, President Lincoln's attitude toward the war was transformed as the country's attitude changed. In 1861, he said his sole purpose was to preserve the Union. By the fall of 1862, however, he decided to free slaves in those areas still in rebellion against the government on the first day of 1863. In 1864, Lincoln stood for reelection by calling for a constitutional amendment abolishing slavery everywhere within the United States. Without the transformation of the clergy's opinions, it is unlikely that the president would have proceeded as he did.

Northern ministers continued to proclaim that the war was a baptism of blood that would cleanse the nation of its sin and prepare it for moral rebirth. Many thought that the blood baptism took place on Good Friday, April 14, 1865, when President Abraham Lincoln died at the hand of John Wilkes Booth, merely five days after Lee's surrender to Grant. Like the death of Jesus, intoned the clergy, Lincoln's blood—and, in fact, all the blood shed over four years—purchased new life for the nation. One minister noted: "He [Lincoln] has been appointed . . . to be laid as the costliest sacrifice of all upon the altar of the Republic and to cement with his blood the free institutions of this land."

In the Southern states, Confederate president Jefferson Davis was less concerned with establishing army chaplains and evangelistic activities within the army. Those chaplains who were appointed received a salary of $1,020 per year, which was soon lowered to $600, but then increased to $960.

Other Christian Confederate leaders made earnest efforts to provide their soldiers with Bibles or New Testaments, and religious tracts. Chaplains sent out a constant stream of letters from the field to churches petitioning them to "send our best men—holy men to assist in evangelizing and ministering to the troops." Although the rural South had limited capacity to print its own Bibles, Southern Christians procured Bibles and tracts for the Confederate men from British, and even some Northern, Bible societies.

Christian Leaders

As noted in the movie *Gods and Generals*, Confederate generals Robert E. Lee and Thomas J. Jackson, as well as many others, encouraged the spread of the gospel in the Army of Northern Virginia (which had 10 percent of its soldiers convert to born-again Christianity). Jackson encouraged the troops to keep the Sabbath holy and attend worship services by trying to avoid battle on the Sabbath, if possible. As the movie shows, his men often witnessed him in prayer before and during battle. Furthermore, Jackson always acknowledged God as the author of his military victories.

William W. Bennett, a minister who ran the Methodist Soldiers Tract Association and wrote *A Narrative of the*

Great Revival Which Prevailed in the Southern Armies, believed the Southern army had truly been "a school of Christ," where pious generals like Stonewall Jackson and Robert E. Lee led their men both in battles and in prayer meetings. He observed that the "moral miracles" that had taken place among Confederate soldiers were the most magnificent of all time. According to Bennett,

> In the army of General Lee, while it lay on the upper Rappahannock, the revival flame swept through every corps, division, brigade, and regiment. [One chaplain explained]: "The whole army is a vast field, ready and ripe to the harvest. The susceptibility of the soldiery to the gospel is wonderful, and, doubtful as the remark may appear, the military camp is most favorable to the work of revival. The soldiers, with the simplicity of little children, listen to and embrace the truth. Already over two thousand have professed conversion, and two thousand more are penitent. Oh, it is affecting to see the soldiers crowd and press about the preacher for what of tracts, etc., he has to distribute, and it is sad to see hundreds retiring without being supplied!"

> [Another minister wrote]: "The cold, mud, and rain, have produced great suffering and sickness among the troops; for we have been entirely without shelter in very exposed positions. In our field hospital we have over 350 sick.

> "I never saw men who were better prepared to receive religious instruction and advice. . . . The dying begged for our prayers and our songs. Every evening we would gather around the wounded and sing and pray with them. Many wounded, who had hitherto led wicked lives, became entirely changed. One young Tennessean, James Scott, of the 32d Tennessee, continually begged us to sing for him and to pray with him. He earnestly desired to see his mother before he died, which was not permitted, as she was in the enemy's lines, and he died rejoicing in the grace of God."

Another chaplain to the Army of Northern Virginia, J.

William Jones, noted in *Christ in the Camp*: "On the bloody campaign from the Rapidan to Cold Harbor in 1864 . . . , Bryan's Georgia Brigade had a season of comparative repose, while held in reserve, when they had from three to five [religious] meetings a day, which resulted in about fifty professions of conversion, most of whom . . . [were] baptized in a pond which was exposed to the enemy's fire, and where several men were wounded while the ordinance was being administered."

In the Northern armies, Union general George B. McClellan decreed that the North's holy cause demanded services every Sunday morning, if possible. Union general Oliver O. Howard, nicknamed "the Christian General," actually preached to the troops when a regular chaplain or minister was not available. The devout Catholic Union general William Rosecrans refused to fight on Sundays. Even during the Battle of Stone's River, after fighting desperately all Saturday, he rested his army on Sunday before reengaging the enemy on Monday. Perhaps, Rosecrans's devotion granted him divine favor, for the Confederate army retreated from his advances.

THE FAITH OF THE DOWNTRODDEN

Christianity also was prevalent in the slave community. Even though not all slaves were Christian, the doctrines, symbols, and vision of life preached by Christianity were familiar to most. Regular Sunday worship in a local church often was augmented by unlawful or informal prayer meetings in the slave cabins, the fields, or the woods. Often those slaves who were forbidden by masters to attend church risked beatings to attend secret meetings to worship God.

Wash Wilson, a former slave, recalled: "When de niggers go 'round singin' 'Steal Away to Jesus,' dat mean dere gwine be a 'ligious meetin' dat night. De masters didn't like dem

Fugitive slaves cross the Rappahannock River in Virginia on their way North in 1862.

'ligious meetin's so us natcherly slips off at night, down in de bottoms or somewhere. Sometimes us sing and pray all night."

The slaves frequently held their own meetings because the white folks' preacher would strip the gospel of its meaning. One slave noted: "The preacher came and he'd just say, 'Serve your masters. Don't steal your master's turkey. Don't steal your master's chickens. Don't steal your master's hawgs. Don't steal your master's meat. Do whatsomever your master teds you to do.' Same old thing all the time . . . . Sometimes they would . . . want a real meetin' with some real preachin'. They used to sing theft songs in a whisper and pray in a whisper."

Since slaves faced severe punishment if caught attending secret prayer meetings, they devised several techniques to avoid detection of their meetings, such as meeting in secluded woods, gullies, ravines, and thickets. Peter Randolph, a former slave from Prince George County, Virginia, described a secret prayer meeting as follows: "The slave forgets all his sufferings, except to remind others of the trials during the past week, exclaiming: 'Thank God, I shall not live here always!' Then they pass from one to another, shaking hands, and bidding each other farewell. . . . As they separate, they sing a parting hymn of praise."[13]

Many slaveholders permitted their slaves to attend church, and some openly encouraged Christian meetings among the slaves by hiring licensed preachers. Annual revival meetings were held for blacks as well as for whites.

The slave preacher held a special position in the African American community and presided over slave baptisms, funerals, and weddings. One correspondent from Georgia wrote to the editor of the American Missionary and exclaimed, "What wonderful preachers these blacks are! I listened to a remarkable sermon or talk a few evenings since. The preacher spoke of the need of atonement for sin. 'Bullocks c'dn't do it, heifers c'dn't do it, de blood of doves c'dn't do it—but up in heaven, for thousan' and thousan' of years, the Son was saying to the Father, "Put up a soul, put up a soul. Prepare me a body, an' I will go an' meet Justice on Calvary's brow!"' He was so dramatic. In describing the crucifixion he said: 'I see the sun when she turned herself black. I see the stars a fallin' from the sky, and them old Herods comin' out of their graves and goin' about the city, an they knew 'twas the Lord of Glory.'"

The testimonies of the slaves indicated that they understood the restrictions under which the slave preacher labored. They respected his authority because it came from God. He preached the Word of God with power and authority, which sometimes humbled white folk and frequently uplifted slaves.

Josiah Henson, at the age of eighteen, was transformed by the words of a slave preacher: "Jesus Christ, the Son of God, tasted death for every man; for the high, for the low, for the rich, for the poor, the bond, the free, the negro in his chains, the man in gold and diamonds." Henson recalled, "I stood and heard it. It touched my heart and I cried out: 'I wonder if Jesus Christ died for me.'"[14]

"Spirituals" also were a vital part of the slave community's worship. Unable to read the Bible, and skeptical of the white interpretation of it, most slaves learned the message of the gospel from songs that expressed their own experience. Drawing from the Bible, hymns, sermons, and African singing and dancing, these spirituals made the characters, themes, and lessons of the Bible become dramatically real and take on special meaning for the slaves.

Ted Baehr

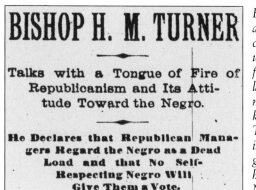

BISHOP H. M. TURNER

Talks with a Tongue of Fire of Republicanism and Its Attitude Toward the Negro.

He Declares that Republican Managers Regard the Negro as a Dead Load and that No Self-Respecting Negro Will Give Them a Vote.

Blacks were not allowed to serve as chaplains (or soldiers) until 1863. Altogether, fourteen black chaplains served U.S. regiments. One of the best known was H. M. Turner, whose preaching had drawn congressmen to hear him; he was known as "the Negro Spurgeon."

THE GREAT REVIVAL

★ ★ ★ ★ ★ ★ ★ ★ ★ ★

As noted previously, revivals broke out throughout the Civil War in the Northern and Southern armies alike. As seen in the movie *Gods and Generals*, chaplains were often attached to regiments of both armies, and preachers frequently visited the troops. There were a few revivals in 1861–62, but the "Great Revival" occurred in the winter and spring of 1863. Even though it occurred in both Northern and Southern armies in the various Virginia and Tennessee battlefields, the best documentation for the Great Revival is for Lee's Army of Northern Virginia. The Confederate chaplain Reverend J. William Jones—who wrote *Christ in the Camp*, one of the best accounts—estimates that no less than 150,000 soldiers came to know Jesus Christ as Lord and Savior that year. The religious revival also affected the leaders of the Confederacy, including Jefferson Davis; Generals Bragg, Ewell, Hood, Hardee, and Joseph E. Johnston; as well as the rank and file.

Almost every night, troops came together for prayer, worship, and to listen to preachers proclaim the good news of Jesus Christ. Almost every meeting ended with soldiers coming forward to accept Christ or receive prayer. If the meeting was near a body of water, then the soldiers frequently stepped forward for baptism, with no concern for the temperature.

Rev. Jones also reported that Confederate soldiers formed Bible reading clubs, wherein they would pass around a well-worn Bible, sharing the gospel. Since the soldiers were always desperate for scarce Testaments and religious tracts, when Chaplain Jones approached, the soldiers would cry out, "Yonder comes the Bible and Tract Man!" and hurry to him to beg for Bibles. The good Chaplain Jones would soon give away his small supply of reading material and then have to turn down most of the soldiers. Jones reported, "I have never seen more diligent Bible-readers than we had in the Army of Northern Virginia."

Here is an account by Private Benjamin W. Jones, who served in the 3rd Virginia Infantry Regiment:

Camp Roper, Va., Feby 20, 1863

My dear Friend:

I hear that a great religious spirit and revival is spreading throughout Lee's army, and some of the other armies of the South, and there are some evidences of it here, and in other camps about Richmond. Old professors that had become lukewarm in their zeal, are arousing to a sense of their duty, and many of the openly sinful are growing more temperate and reverent in their conversation and regard for religious things. There is less of cursing and profligacy, and much less of card playing in our Company now than formerly. The voice of prayer is often heard in camp among the men, and . . . commands now have regular, or at least, occasional, preaching. Many ministers have gone out as evangelists to the armies, and some have gone into the ranks as private soldiers, or have become regular chaplains. . . . Their example and teaching are exerting a wide-spread and salutary influence. Rev. J. W. Ward, of Isle of Wight, has preached to our Company once recently, and other ministers hold meetings near us occasionally.

Almost nightly now, before the tattoo is sounded, we hear the voice of song in our camp, religious and revival songs and hymns. There are several men here who sing well, and these assemble together and pass an hour or two together at night very pleasantly. Sergeant N. B. Pond's tent is headquarters for these exercises, and doubtless, to some extent, this method of praise and prayer is doing good here and toning down some of the rougher vices of the men. May it lead finally to a great outpouring of the Holy Spirit upon all the armies, and all the people of all the South. A soldier may fight and be a religious and God-fearing man, too.

But let me tell you of a little incident that has really taken place in our camp lately—one of the little comedies, not altogether innocent, but wholly harmless, that are occasionally happening and which serve as safety-valves to let off the superfluous steam engendered by the life of confinement and idleness in camp.

★ ★ ★ ★ ★ ★ ★ ★ ★ ★ ★

Major revivals broke out in the Civil War armies. In the Union army, between 100,000 and 200,000 soldiers were converted; among Confederate forces, approximately 150,000 men converted to Christ. Perhaps 10 percent of all soldiers experienced conversions during the conflict.

★ ★ ★ ★ ★ ★ ★ ★ ★ ★ ★

One of the songs that were being sung quite frequently, almost nightly in fact, by our religious choir was that somewhat eccentric refrain: *Scotland's burning! Scotland's burning! Cast on water! Cast on water!*

And so some of the prankish set among our boys conceived the idea of turning a little joke on the men in Sergeant Pond's tent. As a few of the tents had been fixed up with rude dirt chimneys for fireplaces, and Sergeant Pond's was one of these, it gave the boys a fine chance to play their game. And, one night, one of the smallest among the men, with a bucket of water in hand, was lifted up by a big, strong fellow to the top of the little stick chimney. And just as the choir rang out the alarm, "Scotland's burning! Cast on water!" the little fellow on the chimney cast his bucket of water down upon the fire inside, which deluged the whole fireplace, put out the fire, and scattered the embers in every direction.

Of course, too, it put a sudden stop to the song, and sent the men quickly out of the tent after the offenders. But not in time to discover who they were. Before they were fairly out of the tent, the boys had gained their own bunks, and were enjoying the fun at a distance.

The choir soon saw the joke, and, as they could do no more, submitted quietly. But it is presumed that nothing more will be heard of "'Scotland's burning" for some time.

With a prayer for your continued safety and welfare at home, I remain,
Your friend, B.

John Dooley, who enlisted in the famous 1st Virginia Infantry, reported:

Perhaps this is the night for prayer meeting, for the parsons, taking advantage of this period of calm, are indefatigable in their efforts to draw the soldiers together to sing psalms and assist at prayer. Hundreds and thousands respond to their call and the woods resound for miles around with the unscientific but earnest music of the rough veterans of Lee's army. In doleful contrast to the more enlivening notes of the initiated, the chorus of the Mourners may often be recognized; for conversions among the non-religious members of the army of Lee are of daily occurrence, and when they establish themselves upon the Mourners Bench, it is evident to all how deep and loud is their repentance. There is something very solemn in these immense choruses of earnest voices, and there are, I am sure, hundreds of these honest soldiers truly sincere in believing that they are offering their most acceptable service to God.

Some of the parsons or chaplains are very zealous and persevering in assembling the soldiers to prayer; especially the chaplain of the eleventh Va and the seventh. The latter is held in high esteem by all, whether members of religion or not; for, they say, in times of action, he is as bold as the bravest and is to be seen in the first and fiercest battles, consoling and assisting the wounded. Florence McCarthy of Richmond, chaplain of the 7th inf., is also distinguished for his preaching and zeal among the soldiers. They say he told his congregation the other day that when they heard the doors and windows of the church slamming while the minister of God was preaching, they might be sure that the devil was at work trying to hinder the faithful from listening to the divine word. Some might very naturally presume from this that his Satanic Majesty was most at large during the blustering month of March than at any other time in the year.

The records from the U.S. Christian Commission report similar events in the North's Army of the Potomac

Members of the Christian Commission at their field headquarters near Germantown, Md.

at the same time. The brigade chapels of the Army of the Potomac were so full that many men were frequently turned away. One Union general recorded that he had "never seen a better state of feeling in religious matters in the Army of Potomac."

From the fall to the winter of 1863, a strong Confederate force, entrenched in the mountains around the city, besieged the Union army in Chattanooga, Tennessee. Trans-formed by the revival, many of the Union soldiers attributed their surprising victory over the Confederates as a visible interposition of God. The Union troops pursued their enemy as the Confederates retreated toward Atlanta. In Ringgold, Georgia, hundreds of Union troops were baptized in Chickamauga Creek.

While retreating toward Atlanta, the Confederate's Army of the Tennessee also was swept up by the fires of the Great Revival. As they retreated from Dalton, Georgia, the Reverend C. W. Miller says that a Confederate brigade determined to worship in a field. They read the Bible out loud, sang a song of praise, and prayed. As one soldier was praying out loud with his comrades kneeling in silence, they heard the Northern artillery and were soon greeted with the burst of a thirty-two-pound cannon shell overhead. As shells shrieked toward them and shrapnel fell nearby, the men continued to pray as if there was no danger. Finally, the chaplain said the benediction, and the soldiers sought cover.

The revivals continued amongst Sherman's troops as they marched across Georgia and through the Carolinas. When the soldiers stopped for the night, they frequently assembled in local churches and worshiped.

TRANSFORMED

More than 150,000 Confederate and between 100,000 and 200,000 Union troops are estimated to have accepted Jesus Christ during the hostilities, which is about 10 percent of the men engaged in the War Between the States. Not only did these men come to know Jesus Christ as Lord and Savior, but also there were numerous reports of the change that took place in the men, during the war and afterward, as a result of the outpouring of the Holy Spirit.

For example, when Major P. B. Bird was mortally wounded in the trenches of Richmond near the end of the war, he intoned, "But for leaving my wife and children, I should not feel sad at the prospect of dying. There is no cloud between God and me now."

During one prayer meeting, a young soldier reportedly exclaimed, "O that my mother were here!" When asked why he wanted to see his mother, he replied, "Because she has so long been praying for me, and now I have found the Savior." Another wounded Christian soldier asked a friend to "tell my mother that I read my Testament and put all my trust in the Lord. . . . I am not afraid to die."

Although the revivals initiated an intensely spiritual experience, they had a social impact by encouraging the soldiers to abandon sinful behavior, such as card playing or swearing, and to develop a rich prayer life and Bible reading. A disciplined life was beneficial for a soldier, and the assurance of eternal salvation removed the fear of death so that believing soldiers were more heroic than their unconverted comrades. As an anonymous black soldier of the 1st South Carolina (U.S.) Regiment noted, "Let me lib wid de musket in one hand an' de Bible in de oder—dat I may know I hab de bressed Jesus in my hand, an' hab no fear." William Russell of the 26th Virginia Regiment recorded this prayer in his diary: "Oh Lord, if we should go into battle, be thou our shield & hiding place. If it is consistent with thy will, that any of us should be killed, may we have a happy admittance into thy Kingdom above."[15]

A POWERFUL IMPACT

The revivals may have made a more lasting effect on Christianity in the South than in the North. Although the North's overall victory encouraged them to convert immigrants entering their cities, alleviate oppressive social conditions, and bring the gospel to "benighted heathen" overseas, even so, traditional doctrines began to come under attack. Liberal theologians undermined Christian orthodoxy and rejected the idea of a changeless faith. Flush with materialism and secularism, many in the North drifted away from the faith in Jesus Christ that had sustained them in the war.

For many in the South, on the other hand, all that was left after Appomattox was faith, and Southern Christians spoke of the spiritual benefits they had gained through adversity. They noted that prosperity made men and women arrogant and seduced them into believing they did not need God. The hardship of their loss taught the Southerners forbearance and Christian humility.

William Faulkner, in his novel *The Unvanquished*, wrote: "Victory without God is mockery and delusion, but defeat with God is not defeat" at all.

While traveling through the South after the war, Rev. J. William Jones saw a crippled veteran working in a field, guiding a plow with his one good arm. Recognizing him from the war, Jones stopped to provide some encouragement. The veteran had left college and a promising career when the war broke out, had been wounded in battle, and had been baptized by Jones during the war. Jones reflected, "To see him thus, then, his hopes blighted, his fortune wrecked, and his body maimed for life, deeply touched my heart. . . . I shall never forget how the noble fellow, straightening himself up, replied, with a proud smile: 'Oh, Brother Jones, that is all right. I thank God that I have one arm left and an opportunity to use it for the support of those I love.'"

The Great Revival truly transformed soldiers' lives both during and after the war. President Lincoln wrote that "the will of God prevails. . . . Both [sides] may be wrong. . . . In the present civil war it is quite possible God's purpose is something quite different from the purpose of either party." In the midst of the crucible of war, God did, in fact, bring men by grace into an eternal relationship with the Lord Jesus Christ.

Ted Baehr

A refugee family leaving a war area with belongings loaded on a cart

3
"HE DESCENDED INTO HELL"

HOLDING FAST TO HOPE

★ ★ ★ ★ ★ ★ ★ ★ ★ ★ ★ ★ ★ ★ ★ ★ ★ ★ ★

Wounded soldiers being tended in the field after the Battle of Chancellorsville

July 3, 1863, about 2 o'clock (p.m.), we were ordered to charge one of the most impregnable batteries that ever human beings tried to take by cold steel; we made a very successful failure in the attempt. Our losses were heavy in killed, wounded prisoners. I was wounded in the right leg about 200 yards from the Yankee batteries."

Left for dead, without food, water, or medical aid until July fifth, Captain Hill "was found by a Negro farmer who brought him buttermilk and rendered him other assistance."
—Captain Andrew Adams Hill, wounded at Gettysburg excerpt from a family history by his son, Vernon James Hill, in 1900

ADELBERT AMES: CARPETBAGGER OR SAINT?

★ ★ ★ ★ ★ ★ ★ ★ ★

Born on October 31, 1835, in Rockland, Maine, Adelbert Ames was the son of a sea captain, Jesse Ames, and his wife, Martha Bradbury Tolman. Adelbert, like many young men who grew up on the rugged coast, spent his youth attending school and sailing on clipper ships. In 1856 he entered the Military Academy at West Point. He graduated fifth in the celebrated class of 1861, which included the legendary General George Armstrong Custer.

Assigned to the front lines as a lieutenant in the Union army during the Civil War, Ames commanded a section of the 5th U.S. Artillery at the first battle of Bull Run (First Manassas) on July 21, 1861. Wounded in the thigh and bleeding profusely, the lieutenant refused evacuation from the battlefield and continued to give orders until he was too weak to sit upon the caisson where his men had placed him.

In August of 1862, Ames was promoted to colonel of Volunteers of the 20th of Maine Infantry and reported for duty at Camp Mason in Portland. A strict disciplinarian, Ames was unimpressed by the menagerie of slovenly fishermen, shopkeepers, teachers, builders, and sailors who had enlisted. Even his second in command, Joshua Lawrence Chamberlain, a bookish college professor, had no military experience. "This is a hell of a regiment,"[1] Ames complained.

Faced with the dauntless challenge of transforming this group of stubborn inexperienced Mainers into soldiers over a short span of time, Ames began successfully imparting the contents of the Regulation Drill Manual to an impressive Chamberlain and relentlessly drilling the not-so-impressive recruits until the would-be soldiers began secretly devising a plot to shoot their harsh leader once they engaged in a battle.

On September 2, 1862, the 20th of Maine left Camp Mason and caught a steamer in Boston. After a four-day voyage they arrived at Alexandria, Virginia, and camped overnight in Washington. The next morning, witnessing the regiment's sloppy marching performance as they joined the Third Brigade, Ames lost his temper and bellowed, "If you can't do any better than you have tonight, you better all desert and go home!"[2]

None of the men went home, and as they reaped the benefits of his rigorous training, they abandoned their plans to shoot Ames and grew to respect him. The 20th of Maine became one of the most able and famous regiments in the Northern army, fighting at Antietam, Fredericksburg, and Chancellorsville. Ames's protégé, Chamberlain, emerged as one of the greatest heroes of the war.

Following the Chancellorsville battle, the 20th of Maine was quarantined as a result of a bad batch of smallpox vaccines and placed under the command of Chamberlain, who was promoted to lieutenant colonel. Ames, promoted to brigadier general, U.S. Volunteers, was sent to command a brigade in the Army of the Potomac, which he later led at the Battle of Gettysburg.

During the Siege of Petersburg in 1864, Ames attained the brevet rank of major general, U.S. Volunteers, and in later years won the Medal of Honor. By the war's end, he

had an outstanding record and reputation at the age of twenty-nine years old.

On July 15, 1868, the highly decorated war hero was appointed the provisional governor of Mississippi, under acts of Congress providing for such temporary government, and on March 17, 1869, his challenging command extended to include the Fourth military district. Ames left Mississippi in 1870 when he was elected a U.S. senator. "In some counties it was impossible to advocate Republican principles, those attempting it being hunted like wild beasts; in others, the speakers had to be armed and supported by not a few friends."[3] The senator explained to Congress the difficulties he faced in Mississippi to carry out the law of Reconstruction in the Southern state.

Adelbert Ames

While serving in the Senate, Ames met and fell in love with the beautiful daughter of his Civil War crony, the colorful General Benjamin Butler, with whom he had served in the Fort Fisher expedition. Blanche Butler had arrived in Washington while Congress was in session to manage the house her father had bought there, and she became quite popular among the young Washington crowd. Blanche married Ames on July 21, 1870, at St. Anne's in Lowell, Massachusetts, the same church where, in 1844, her father had married her mother, former Shakespearean stage actress Sarah Hildreth.

In 1873 Ames was elected governor of Mississippi by popular vote, but upon his return, the white Southerners were clearly regaining control of the state, and the freed slaves were being intimidated out of voting. Ames requested that President Grant send in Federal troops to

In 1850, Congress passed the Fugitive Slave Law, which allowed slave-hunters to seize alleged fugitive slaves without due process of law and prohibited anyone from aiding escaped fugitives or obstructing their recovery. The law threatened the safety of all blacks, slave and free, and forced many Northerners to become more defiant in their support of fugitives.

protect the blacks, and Ben Butler added his urging, but the troops were never sent. Tragically in 1874 three hundred blacks were killed by white vigilante groups in Vicksburg. A devastated Governor Ames asked, "Why should I fight a hopeless battle . . . when no possible good to the Negro or anybody else would result?"

Ames was impeached by the white-Democrat-controlled legislature for his efforts to maintain civil rights for the former slaves. He was put on trial for misappropriation of funds and a variety of other false accusations. To defend his son-in-law, Butler hired attorneys Thomas J. Durant and Roger A. Pryor, who struck a deal with the legislative leaders to have the impeachment charges withdrawn if Ames resigned as governor. On March 29, 1876, Ames resigned, his impeccable military reputation unjustly

tarnished by dirty Southern politics. Even in 1876 when the deadly Northfield Bank robbery took place in Minnesota, Cole Younger was able to evoke sympathy for the James-Younger gangs simply because of the South's hatred for Ames and his father-in-law, Benjamin Butler, who had money deposited in the bank where both Ames's father and brother served on the board.

Leaving politics for business, Ames moved his family to New York and then to Lowell, Massachusetts, where he and Blanche sought a more sedate life to raise their children near her family. Ames enjoyed success in the flour business with his father and brother operating mills in Minnesota. After serving his country as brigadier general of the American troops in Cuba during the Spanish-American War, Ames retired to his home in Lowell. He died in their summer home in Ormand Beach, Florida, at age ninety-seven, the last surviving full rank general officer of either side in the Civil War.

Years after her father's death, daughter Blanche Ames challenged then Senator John F. Kennedy for his writings in *Profiles in Courage.* She accused Kennedy of incorporating the standard white supremacist view that Radical Republicans had persecuted the South during Reconstruction, which defamed the Mississippi Reconstructionist governor Adelbert Ames. "You have been influenced to form your opinion of a former fellow member of the Senate by the gossip and writings of his enemies,"[4] Blanche Ames complained, but Kennedy never retracted his accusations.

Despite his unpopularity in Mississippi and the South for his attempts to carry out the laws of freedom for the freed slave, history has finally proven that Adelbert Ames was not only a war hero but also a revered champion of civil rights.

★ *Susan Huey Wales*

Private Battles

★ ★ ★ ★ ★ ★ ★ ★ ★

In both armies—North and South—soldiers clung to their faith in God and love for those back home to give them the courage to keep pressing on.

A devoutly religious Baptist family in North Carolina who owned no slaves, the Huntleys were gravely concerned when their son George Job Huntley went off to fight in the Civil War without being saved. The family prayed that George might be spared long enough to come home and make his profession of faith. They made a "bargain with God" that if this could happen they would accept the death of another family member who was already saved or that of a young child presumed to heaven at death.

Huntley came home with a leg wound, which he received at Second Manassas. While recuperating at home, George made his profession of faith, and his younger sister Martha Catherine Huntley, age seven, died on December 9, 1862.

George Job Huntley's conversion is beautifully evident by these words excerpted from a letter written to his family on April 24, 1863.

The future is misty and hard to fathom. Time and nothing else will develop all things. The weather is rather bad, yet though, much better than it has been. We have had some very lovely days here and in viewing the budding nature around me my mind is involuntary carried back to other

Soldiers in the trenches before battle.

days and other scenes when I was not trampled down by the fetters of a soldier's life, when on a lovely day like this I could view, while my heart throbbed with emotions of gratitude to the Giver of all things, the disentombing of all nature from her wintry grave, the budding forth of all vegetable creation and the soft and inviting appearance that everything wears when nature smiles and the works of nature praise their Maker.[5]

Huntley died on July 2, 1863, after being wounded on July 1, the first day of the battle of Gettysburg.

⭐ *Tom Huntley*

Field hospital after the battle at Savage Station, Va.

Oftentimes the reality of war caused the soldiers to see beyond this world, expressing their hope in the Kingdom above. Sullivan Ballou wrote to his wife Sarah only one week before he and twenty-seven of his close comrades—and four thousand Americans in all—died in the battle at First Manassas. This is one of the most beloved love letters written during the war.

July the 14th, 1861
Camp Clark, Washington D.C.

My very dear Sarah:

The indications are very strong that we shall move in a few days—perhaps tomorrow. Lest I shall not be able to write you again, I feel impelled to write a few lines that may fall under your eye when I shall be no more.

Our movement may be one of a few days' duration and full of pleasure—and it may be one of severe conflict and death to me. "Not my will, but thine O God, be done." If it is necessary that I should fall on the battlefield for my Country, I am ready. I have no misgivings about, or lack of confidence in, the cause in which I am engaged, and my courage does not halt or falter.

I know how strongly American Civilization now leans upon the triumph of the Government, and how great a debt we owe to those who went before us through the blood and suffering of the Revolution, and I am willing—perfectly willing—to lay down all my joys in this life, to help maintain this Government and to pay that debt, but, my dear wife, when I know that with my own joys I lay down nearly all of yours, and replace them in this life with cares and sorrows—when, after having eaten for long years the bitter fruit of orphanage myself, I must offer it as their only sustenance to my dear little children—is it weak or dishonorable that while the banner of my purpose floats calmly and proudly in the breeze underneath my unbounded love for you, my darling wife and children, I shall struggle in fierce, though useless, contest with my love of country?

I cannot describe to you my feelings on this calm summer Sabbath night, when two thousand men are sleeping around me, many of them enjoying the last, perhaps, before that of death—and I am suspicious that Death is creeping behind me with his fatal dart, while I am communing with God, my Country, and thee.

I have sought most closely and diligently, and often in my breast for a wrong motive in thus hazarding the happiness of those I loved and I could not find one. A pure love of my country and of the principles I have often advocated before the people and "the name of honor that I love more than I fear death" have called upon me, and I have obeyed.

Sarah, my love for you is deathless, it seems to bind me to you with mighty cables that nothing but Omnipotence could break; and yet my love of Country comes over me like a strong wind and bears me irresistibly on with all these chains to the battlefield.

The memories of all the blissful moments I have spent with you come creeping over me, and I feel most gratified to God and to you that I have enjoyed them so long, and how hard it is for me to give them up and burn to ashes the hopes of future years when God willing, we might still have lived and loved together and seen our sons grow up to honorable manhood around us. I have, I know, but few and small claims upon Divine Providence, but something whispers to me—perhaps it is the wafted prayer of my little Edgar—that I shall return to my loved ones unharmed. If I do not, my dear Sarah, never forget how much I love you, and when my last breath escapes me on the battlefield, it will whisper your name.

Forgive my many faults, and the many pains I have caused you. How thoughtless, how foolish, I have oftentimes been! How gladly would I wash out with my tears every little spot upon your happiness, and struggle with all the misfortune of this world, to shield you and my dear children from harm, but I cannot. I must watch you from the spirit land and hover near you, while you buffet the storms with your precious little freight and wait with sad patience till we meet to part no more.

But, O Sarah! If the dead can come back to this earth and flit unseen around those they love, I shall always be near you; in the gladdest day and in the darkest night—

amidst your happiest scenes and gloomiest hours—always, always; and if there be a soft breeze upon your cheek, it shall be my breath; or the cool air fans your throbbing temple, it shall be my spirit passing by.

Sarah, do not mourn me dead; think I am gone and wait for thee, for we shall meet again.

Children watch as soldiers approach near Bull Run, Va.

As for my little boys, they will grow as I have done, and never know a father's love and care. Little Willie is too young to remember me long, and my blue-eyed Edgar will keep my frolics with him among the dimmest memories of his childhood. Sarah, I have unbounded confidence in your maternal care and your development of their characters and feel that God will bless you in your holy work. Tell my two mothers I call God's blessing upon them. O Sarah, I wait for you there! Come to me, and lead thither my children.

Sullivan

★ *Susan Huey Wales*

COMFORT YE MY PEOPLE

★ ★ ★ ★ ★ ★ ★ ★ ★

As the war wore on and people in the South saw their homes ravaged, property destroyed, churches in ashes, and loved ones dead, Christian pastors were challenged to bring comfort to the people. One woman in deep distress came up to Rev. William White, pastor of the Presbyterian church in Lexington, Virginia, and said, "It seems to me I have no faith at all. I certainly have not enough to determine whether the Lord is on our side in this war or on that of the enemy." Rev. White kindly told the lady that faith could not settle such issues: "The Bible says, 'Faith comes by hearing, and hearing by the Word of God.' Since the Word of God has nothing to say on the war itself, this is not a question of faith. The Scriptures, however, do have much to say that will increase faith during such a time. Faith can take its stand and be comforted by such Scriptures as, 'The Lord omnipotent reigned'; 'The very hairs of your head are numbered'; 'A sparrow shall not fall to the ground without your Father'; and 'All things work together for good to them that love God.'"[6] This simple encouragement to faith based on Scripture greatly quieted the dear lady's mind.

William White could comfort others with the Scriptures because they had comforted him in difficult times, including at the death of his son Hugh. Hugh was killed at the battle of Second Manassas, August 30, 1862. He had been an outstanding Christian and a loving son, and his loss was severely felt by his father. In his last letter home, Hugh had written, "I feel more and more deeply that I must live altogether for God and in God." With Hugh's death, Rev. White found God a present help in time of trouble: "I have had a very sweet experience of God's great goodness in giving him to us, in making him what he was, and in taking him to himself just *when* and *as* he did I firmly believe that he had filled the allotted measure of his days, that he had accomplished his mission, and answered the end of his being. He ardently desired to preach the gospel, but his will was to do and suffer the will of God."[7]

Rev. White's most famous church member, Stonewall Jackson, had that implicit faith in God that could take him through all trials. Rev. White thought Jackson was the happiest man he ever knew: "His faith and trust were so implicit that his own will was in perfect subjection to that of his Heavenly Father, and no suffering or trial could make him wish it had been otherwise."[8]

In victory or in defeat, in life or in death, Rev. White counseled his people to faith in God's sovereign purposes and ways. God's purposes might be hidden and not fully understood, but the Christian could have confidence and faith that His will would be done and all things would indeed work together for good and for His glory.

★ *Diana L. Severance*

Since the Word of God has nothing to say on the war itself, this is not a question of faith. The Scriptures, however, do have much to say that will increase faith during such a time.

—Rev. William White

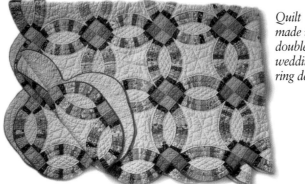

Quilt made with double wedding ring design

GRANDMOTHER'S QUILT

★ ★ ★ ★ ★ ★ ★ ★ ★ ★

The following story, originally printed sometime prior to 1881,[9] beautifully illustrates God's faithfulness and sovereignty.

As a young girl growing up in Cleveland, Ohio, I was especially enchanted by Grandmother Barkin's most cherished possession, a quilt she had made with swatches from the wedding gowns of generations of brides in our family.

When Grandmother would preside over tea, she would spread out the quilt, enthralling her guests, and especially me, with her tales of each delicate piece of fabric and the bride who wore it. The well-to-do brides in our family left behind swatches of silk, satin, brocade, and velvet, while the pioneer brides of lesser means contributed their soft muslin and calico. A swatch of lace from Grandmother's own wedding gown was proudly displayed in the center of the quilt where she had embroidered "Love One Another" atop the exquisite fading blue satin.

To my delight, when her guests departed, and Grandmother would fold up the priceless heirloom she

would often smile sweetly and say, "This wedding quilt will be yours one day, dear Mary." Since grandmother had only sons and no daughter, and I was the eldest granddaughter, the quilt would be passed down to me if I married first.

Although I was approaching twenty-five, I was more concerned with the kind of man I wanted to marry than getting married just for the sake of getting married. For this reason I feared that the quilt might never be mine, but go to one of my younger cousins. That fear quickly dissolved when my childhood playmate Leonard Wynn and I began to take the same path to work each day.

As Leonard and I wound our way through the narrow street leading to town, he would amuse me with his stories. However, one day in 1861, my hopes of owning the wedding quilt were suddenly dashed when Leonard informed me that he had enlisted in the Union Army. When the day came to see him off at the train station, I felt as though my heart would break.

As the Civil War unfolded, so did the enthusiasm and patriotic spirit of the women of Cleveland. Grandmother Barkin and I were no exception. Freely and abundantly Grandmother sent supplies from her stores. But her crowning sacrifice was yet to be made.

Early one bright winter morning a carriage rolled up to Grandmother's door, and out of it stepped two eager young ladies who took Grandmother aside and spoke in whispered tones.

"So you see, Mrs. Barkin, we are desperate for quilts for our soldiers."

Slowly rising from her chair, the elderly lady stood and then proceeded to her wardrobe. Out came her treasured quilt, wrapped in white and fragrant with lavender. Calling to me, she said, "Mary, they need quilts at the hospital. I have no other ready-made ones. Are you willing to give this one up?"

I hesitated for only a brief moment, realizing every gift added one more chance of comfort for my Leonard.

So Grandmother's quilt adorned one of the cots in the hospital and gave warmth and pleasure to many a poor sufferer, serving a purpose far greater than its maker had originally intended.

Grandmother and I joined the tireless group of women from Cleveland and both volunteered at the hospital. One Christmas as I was passing from cot to cot distributing grapes and oranges, I watched the eager looks of the poor fellows. Having emptied my basket, I went to assist in feeding those who were unable to help themselves.

Nurses and officers of the U.S. Sanitary Commission in Fredericksburg, Va.

Taking a plate of jelly in my hand, I stepped to the side of one of the cots, noticing as I did that Grandmother's quilt lay upon the bed! The sight of it brought a rush of tender memories, filling my eyes with tears so that for a moment I didn't see the face upon the pillow. The soldier who lay beneath its folds was missing his arm.

Then, with a sudden start, I recognized the face. I saw Leonard Wynn, my beloved Leonard! As I dried my eyes, I got a closer look at the pale face with sunken eyes, revealing the depth of his pain. "No, it can't be. I'm mistaken," I assured myself.

But the familiar voice erased all doubt. "Ah, Mary, I've been watching and waiting for you!"

Overjoyed, I asked, "Why didn't you send for me?"

"I knew you would come sometime. The sight of this," he said, touching the quilt, "made me sure of it."

During the next few weeks, Leonard and I rediscovered the joys of our companionship. That happiness was quickly extinguished, however, when I arrived at the hospital one morning to find Leonard's bed occupied by another wounded soldier. A nurse informed me that the officers had deemed Leonard healthy enough to return to his regiment. Along with Leonard, Grandmother's quilt had also vanished.

And so, the Christmas of 1862 came and went, bringing with it joyous surprise only to snatch it and Grandmother's quilt away.

Another long year passed. I was as busy as ever, assisting the cause by trying to impart the Christmas spirit to the weary, sick, and wounded soldiers in the hospital. One evening at the close of the day's proceedings, I wearily laid my head down on a table. It was growing dark, and I closed my eyes to snatch, if possible, a brief interval of much needed rest.

Suddenly I was startled awake from my sleep. How long had I been asleep and what was lying under my head? One glance revealed that it was Grandmother's quilt. How did it get there?

I squealed with delight as I heard a familiar voice—Leonard's. "I have come for my Christmas gift, sweet Mary," he said as he drew the quilt to his chest and pointed to the inscription Grandmother had embroidered over the faded blue satin: "Love One Another."

"I wanted to ask you a year ago but decided that I would not ask you to take a maimed, sick soldier. I kept the quilt in memory of you. See, I fixed it so it would come back to you if anything happened to me." He showed me the label fastened securely to the quilt: "To be sent to Miss Mary Barkin, Cleveland, Ohio."

Then he told me how on one cold winter's day the quilt had saved his life. While sitting close to the fire to warm himself and to cook some potatoes, a stray ball from the enemy's batteries came whistling through the air, taking a straight course toward him. Luckily, he was wrapped in the quilt. The ball struck him but, because of the thickness of the quilt, got no further than his coat.

That night Grandmother's quilt went back to its original owner, and my right to it as a wedding gift was firmly established by Leonard's proposal.

★ *Retold by Susan Huey Wales*

Medical ward in the Carver General Hospital, Washington, D.C.

★ TRAGEDIES OF WAR

Executive Mansion
Washington, November 4, 1864

Burial of soldiers in Fredericksburg, Va.

Mrs. Bixby
Boston, Massachusetts

Dear Madam:
I have been shown in the files of the War Department a statement of the Adjutant-General of Massachusetts that you are the mother of five sons who have died gloriously on the field of battle. I feel how weak and fruitless must be any words of mine which should attempt to beguile you from the grief of a loss so overwhelming. But I cannot refrain from tendering to you the consolation that may be found in the thanks of the Republic they died to save. I pray that our Heavenly Father may assuage the anguish of your bereavement, and leave you only the cherished memory of the loved and lost, and the solemn pride that must be yours to have laid so costly a sacrifice upon the altar of freedom.

Yours very sincerely and respectfully,
Abraham Lincoln

4
"JUDGE NOT THAT WE BE NOT JUDGED"

ABRAHAM LINCOLN

Before rushing to the bedside of her wounded husband, General Stonewall Jackson, a relieved Anna Jackson, escorted by Captain James Power Smith, left, and Dr. Hunter McGuire, pays her respects to an unknown soldier she had first believed to be her husband. From left are actors Stephen Spacek, Kali Rocha, and Sean Pratt.

ABRAHAM LINCOLN: SAVIOR OF A NATION

★ ★ ★ ★ ★ ★ ★ ★ ★

Never before in the nation's history had there been so *unusual a time!* A man had been elected president though not even appearing on the ballot in ten states! Even before arriving in Washington, every mail delivery brought more death threats and ominous warnings. Close friends advised that he resign before taking the oath of office! A plot to assassinate the president-elect had been uncovered, forcing the last leg of his trip to Washington to be in the dead of night, without family, under heavy guard, and incognito!

Never before had a president-elect faced so *unusual a task!* Six states had already seceded from the Union before the inauguration! A secessionist government had been established, large quantities of munitions were on their way to Confederate forts, a siege on the City of Washington had been plotted! Disunity reigned . . . hatred and distrust abounded . . . the North against the South, friend against friend, and brother against brother!

But, never before had so *unusual a man* been elected president of the United States!

THE UGLIEST MAN IN THE WORLD

A tall, gaunt, strange-looking man stood looking in a mirror. With arms and legs totally out of proportion to his torso, a face that resembled a rutabaga, shriveled skin, hair that was absolutely rebellious and ears that seemed to "flap in the wind," he at last exclaimed aloud to himself, "It's true, Abe Lincoln, you are the ugliest man in the world. If I ever see a man uglier than you, I'm going to shoot him on the spot!"

Who was this grotesque individual destined to become the sixteenth president of the United States? After a span of 125 years since his death, and in the wake of more than ten thousand books describing his life and times, many Americans still ask that very question and still seek to fathom the complexities that comprised this "man who belongs to the ages."

Nominated only narrowly on the fourth ballot by a seriously divided Republican Party and elected with less than a 40 percent popular vote by his countrymen, in 1861 he became the president of a nation torn by bitter disunity.

LOG-CABIN CHILDHOOD

A personal trek to greatness from the depths of insignificance and the overcoming of tremendous obstacles along the way to success is a familiar tale in America. But one would be hard-pressed to discover a rise to greatness

Abraham Lincoln

from a more wretched origin than is chronicled in the life of Abe Lincoln. Recent research has shown that his father, Thomas Lincoln, was not the improvident, irresponsible and indolent parent to young Abe that early biographers have suggested. Nevertheless, the dirt floor, one-room cabin long associated with Lincoln is not apocryphal and well depicts the stark poverty, dearth of cultural refinement, and sheer difficulty of life that surrounded Lincoln as a young boy.

And yet, little Abe Lincoln was well blessed and enriched by a religious heritage that would shape his life and prepare him for one of the most monumental tasks of all history. Nancy Lincoln created a religious atmosphere in that cabin home and spent Sunday afternoons often with Abe upon her knee, reading to him from the family Bible and especially impressing upon him the Ten Commandments. Her last words to him when he was but nine years of age were, "Abe, I'm going to leave you now and I shall not return. I want you to be kind to your father and live as I have taught you. Love your heavenly Father and keep His commandments." Sarah Bush, who was to become Abe's stepmother, only served to reinforce the religious impact of his mother. She took Abe and his sister, Sarah, to the Pigeon Creek Hard Shell Baptist Church every Sunday. Sunday after Sunday young Abraham sat motionless and listened intently to the long, fiery orations of simple but devout prairie preachers as they expounded on predestination, the fear of the Lord, and the new birth.

It appears Tom Lincoln would have been content for Abe to have gained a "real 'eddication of readin', writin', and cipherin'," but the young man had an insatiable appetite for something far greater. Having learned to read and write in a one-room "blab" school, a nine-mile walk from home, he began eagerly to devour every printed page that fell into his hand. He read and reread *Aesop's Fables, Robinson Crusoe, Pilgrim's Progress,* a short history of the United States, Weema's *Life of George Washington,* and, of course, the King James Version of the Bible.

"I'll Hit It Hard"

In part it was the thirst for knowledge that led Lincoln away from the prairie homestead, now moved to Illinois, and caused him as a flatbed hand to set sail for New Orleans. There Lincoln witnessed a scene that was to shape his heart and mind for a lifetime. In May 1831, for the first time, he encountered the horrors of a slave auction. He stood in silence while his heart bled and his resolve became forever fixed. William Herndon, his life-long law partner, said, "Slavery ran the iron into him then and there, and bidding his companions follow him Lincoln said, 'By God, boys, let's get away from this. If I ever get a chance to hit that thing, I'll hit it hard.'"

Defeated in his first endeavor to seek a seat in the Illinois State Legislature in 1832, he won with an overwhelming plurality in 1834 the first of what would result in four successive terms. Persistence in his self-styled law study resulted in his being formally admitted to the Illinois Bar on March 1, 1837. Soon after he moved to the new capital of Illinois, Springfield, on an invitation to become a law partner there. A few months later, he and several other lawyers attended a camp meeting on the outskirts of Springfield. A Bible preacher by the name of Rev. Dr. Peter Akers preached a sermon that night on the subject, "The Dominion of Jesus Christ."

The point of the sermon was that the dominion of Christ could not come in America until slavery would eventually be destroyed by civil war. "I am not a prophet, nor the son of a prophet," the preacher declared, "but I am a student of the prophets. As I read prophecy,

American slavery will come to an end in some near decade. I think in the sixties." After a graphic description of the war that was to come, he brought his sermon to a climactic end by exclaiming, "Who can tell but that the man who shall lead us through the strife may be standing in this presence!" Only a few feet away from him stood Lincoln, absorbed in every word. "Those words were from beyond the speaker . . . ." Abe Lincoln quietly remarked. "The doctor has persuaded me that slavery will go down with the crash of a civil war." The next morning he said, "I am utterly unable to shake from myself the conviction that I shall be involved in that tragedy." Many were the epic moments in the shaping of Lincoln's life: this was certainly one of them.

SUCCESSFUL LAWYER

Along with the growth of his reputation and influence as a politician, his law practice now escalated. His sense of truth and justice contributed a great deal to his effectiveness. His very appearance in a court of law came to cause judges and juries to presume that right was on his side!

In 1846 he was elected to the United States Congress after a hard-fought campaign against Peter Cartright, the famed Methodist circuit rider. While the campaign was under way, Cartright's supporters proclaimed Lincoln to be an infidel. Lincoln waited until he had won the election before replying to the charge. In a handbill (which was undiscovered until 1942) Lincoln responded, "That I am not a member of any Christian church is true; but I have never denied the truth of the Scriptures; and I have never spoken with intentional disrespect of religion in general...."

Lincoln visits soldiers in the field

Returning to Springfield a retired member of Congress after just one term, Lincoln's law practice now reached new heights of success. The Illinois Central Railroad retained him on a permanent basis, and Erasmus Corning of Albany, New York, president of the New York Central Railroad, also sought his services on a permanent basis. Corning introduced their first meeting with the statement: "I understand that in Illinois, you never lose a case." For all practical purposes, it appeared that Lincoln had withdrawn permanently from the political scene.

Fortunately for the nation, his time was but drawing near. In 1854 the slavery issue began to polarize the nation as nothing had ever done before, and God's purposes in Lincoln's life were about to unfold dramatically.

CATAPULTED TO FAME

The Republican Party rather suddenly emerged, and Abe Lincoln found himself catapulted to national reputation as the most logical combatant to the famed proslavery senator, Stephen Arnold Douglas from Illinois. The Whigs strongly considered Lincoln for a Senate seat in 1854, and the first Republican national convention gave him respectable but unsuccessful support for the vice presidential nomination in 1856. But now, with Douglas's senatorial seat expiring in 1858, Lincoln seemed the natural opponent and was given the Republican Party nomination. In his acceptance speech he set the tone for what was to follow with the memorable and famous words: "A house divided against itself cannot stand. I believe the government cannot endure half slave and half free. I do not expect the Union to be dissolved . . . but I do expect it will cease to be divided."

The eyes of the nation were now turned upon the series of even Lincoln-Douglas debates. On the surface, Lincoln was thought to have been no match for the distinguished Douglas, and in the early debates the press generally confirmed the presupposition. Yet, even the press changed its stance as the public was more and more impressed with Lincoln's integrity, logic, and eloquence. One easterner inquired, "Who is this man who is replying to Douglas from your State? Do you realize that no greater speeches have been made in the history of our country? . . . That his knowledge is profound, his logic unanswerable, his style inimitable?" Although Mr. Lincoln amassed a majority of votes on election day, under the apportionment law then in effect, it was Douglas who was declared the winner.

Lincoln experienced one of his bitterest moments. "It hurts too bad to laugh," he admitted, "and I am too big to cry." Recovering from his disappointment, Lincoln wrote to Dr. A. G. Henry, "I am glad I made the last race. It gave me a hearing on the great and durable question of the age which I would have had in no other way; and though I now sink out of view and shall be forgotten, I believe I have made some marks which shall tell for the cause of civil liberty long after I am gone."

"Mary, We've Won!"

But by no means was he to "sink out of view." On the contrary, letters of congratulation and encouragement poured in from all over the nation, as well as invitations to speak! In only twelve months he addressed twenty-three major audiences and traveled four thousand miles. Party leaders instantly spoke of him as a potential presidential candidate, and indeed when the heat died down from the 1860 Republican National Convention, Abraham Lincoln emerged as the winner of the party's presidential nomination!

"Mary, we've won!" had been the jubilant shout of Abe Lincoln to his wife on election night, November 6, 1860. But in the weeks that preceded his inauguration he was to discover that no man had ever assumed the Presidency of the United States surrounded by issues of the seriousness and gravity that confronted him!

In the 1860 presidential campaign, brightly colored banners, outrageous political cartoons, sentimental sheet music covers, and patriotic portraits were printed to win the vote. The colorful banner and the bold campaign poster support the candidacy of Abraham Lincoln during his first (and victorious) presidential campaign in 1860.

Within six weeks following the election, there was dancing and fireworks in the streets of Charleston, South Carolina. South Carolina had seceded and declared a new "Declaration of Independence." Six other states would quickly follow, and two days before Lincoln left for Washington, Jefferson Davis was elected president of a newly formed nation!

For three months Lincoln was forced to sit idly by while the outgoing Buchanan administration, torn by disloyalty, did nothing to arrest the dissolving of the Union. Amid scores of threats on his life, countless sleepless, distressed nights, the loss of forty pounds, and with the conviction that he would not return alive, the president-elect bade a tearful farewell to Springfield. On only two occasions did his voice become choked and tears fill his eyes as he spoke publicly; and this was one of them! "I now leave not knowing when or whether I may return, with a task before me greater than that which rested upon Washington. Without the assistance of the Divine Being who ever attended him, I cannot succeed. With that assistance, I cannot fail." For a most unusual task God had prepared a most unusual man. John Hay expressed the sentiments of many when he said, "I believe the hand of God placed him where he is."

The same John Hay, Lincoln's personal secretary, perhaps unwittingly expressed the distinctive qualities of leadership God had cultivated in Lincoln when he said of him, "There is no man in the country so wise, so gentle, and so firm." Lincoln was indeed firm: "You may burn my body to ashes and scatter them to the winds of heaven. You may drag my soul down to the regions of darkness and despair. But you will never get me to support a measure which I believe is wrong."

SAVE THE UNION!

Such firmness was revealed in less than forty-eight hours in the presidential chair! Lincoln traced America's democratic birthright right back to the Declaration of Independence and the founding fathers. He saw the Declaration the cord that bound the states in an indissoluble union. Secession was simply not an option to him, even in the face of contrary views, such as those held by influential Northerners: Horace Greeley, in a two-column article, bitterly attacked the president for his procrastination on the slavery issue. Lincoln responded firmly. "My paramount object in this struggle is to save the Union, and is not either to save nor to destroy slavery."

"Malice toward none" was very much more to Lincoln than a poetic phrase incorporated in an address. It demonstrated the very sensitivity required to lead a broken, bleeding nation . . . a compassion born of a life of personal sorrow.

MORE TEARS

At the age of nine he had known the emptiness that comes to a sobbing child when his mother lies cold in death. He never forgot her, and often referred to her as his "angel mother." At sixteen he had been shattered by the insanity of a close boyhood friend, and his world had been devastated three years later by the death of his beloved sister, Sarah. In 1835, the death of his fiancée, Anne Rutledge, had been almost too much for him to bear. In his despair he said, "There is nothing to live for now," and for years visiting her grave seven miles outside New Salem, Illinois, was a Lincoln ritual.

The sadness that lifelong marked the features of Lincoln and the melancholia that was characteristic of his personality were thus only reinforced by the domestic sorrow that struck the Lincoln home at the height of his professional success, in 1850. Abraham and Mary's second son, Eddie, died after an illness of fifty-two days. They were inconsolable in their grief.

Mary Todd Lincoln

Beneath the firm, determined exterior was to be found now a tender, sensitive, gentle spirit, which was touched by the heartache of a nation in grave emotional crisis. He openly wept over the loss of both Union and Rebel lives, which, by the end of the War, were to number more than six hundred thousand. He frequently paced the floors by night and was discovered one morning having spent the night with head in hands, grieving and praying for the nation he loved. Reading aloud Oliver Wendell Holmes's poem, "Lexington," to his friend Noah Brooks, he came to the lines: "'Green be the grass where her martyrs are lying! Shroudless and tombless they sunk to their rest.'" His voice quavered, he choked, and handing the volume back to Brooks he whispered, "You read it; I can't."

Lincoln's profound wisdom, shown on an almost daily basis, was evidenced in the stand he had taken regarding slavery. "If slavery is not wrong, nothing is wrong," he repeated on several occasions. Regardless of this, his presidential oath demanded that his first responsibility be to preserve the Union.

★ ★ ★ ★ ★ ★ ★

Without the assistance of the Divine Being who ever attended him, I cannot succeed. With that assistance, I cannot fail.

—Abraham Lincoln

★ ★ ★ ★ ★ ★ ★

Freedom

He felt that in preserving the nation, slavery would be contained and would ultimately die a natural death. He reasoned that an ill-timed proclamation would alienate the border states, change the focus of the war, cause additional unrest in the North, and ultimately jeopardize the Union. But when the right time arrived, Lincoln solemnly announced to his Cabinet, "I made a solemn vow before God, that if General Lee was driven back from Pennsylvania, I would crown the result by the declaration of freedom to the slaves." This action caused deep bitterness in the South and much criticism in the North, yet it seemed to rally the Union, brought new hope to the Negro, and deterred European governments from aligning themselves with the Confederacy!

A crude cultural heritage and a meager formal education give no explanation for the wisdom evidenced in this one man. Within the context of his spiritual life was to be found the real secret of his wisdom, for "the fear of the Lord is the beginning of wisdom." Even a cursory study of the life of Abraham Lincoln demonstrates that, even though he was not a conventional church member, he was a devout, God-fearing man. His biographies provide numerous accounts of his respect for deity, knowledge of and reverence for Scripture, and of his devotion to prayer. When the Civil War reached its darkest hour, he called for a "national day of fasting and prayer," and, after Gettysburg, it was he who proclaimed "a day of thanksgiving" that became an annual national event.

Most Honest Lawyer

That his childhood religious training, with its emphasis on the Ten Commandments, had a profound effect upon the life and character of the president is indisputable. He bore the title, "most honest lawyer east of China." On many occasions as a young lawyer he would remind an opponent of the points of his own argument. When in 1860 he took the oath of office, upholding the oath became for him a matter of personal integrity. When asked about his honesty, on a number of occasions he reminisced to his mother's voice, "Thou shalt not steal. . . . Thou shalt not bear false witness," and to her last words, "Love your heavenly Father, and keep His commandments."

But deep in Lincoln's heart, try as he might to keep God's Law, was his awareness of the reality that he fell far short of the glory of God. He knew it even as a boy, as can be seen by the scribbling in his arithmetic book: "Abe Lincoln, his hand and pen, he will be good, but God knows when!" This little verse is witness to the guilt and self-condemnation that surrounded him the greater part of his life and especially during the war years. It is evidenced in his statement to a group of Baltimore clergymen: "I wish I were more pious."

For this one who was called the "most religious of all our presidents," for Abe Lincoln who had tried so valiantly to keep God's law, there was something his closest associates viewed as lacking. His personal bodyguard expressed it well when he said, "The misery that dripped from Lincoln as he walked was caused by his lack of personal faith." For all of his knowledge of Scripture and his association with the great ministers of his day, he failed, for the better part of his life, to comprehend that the salvation of the Lord is "not by works which we have done," and that it is "by grace ye are saved through faith, and that not of yourselves," effort and piousness notwithstanding.

★ ★ ★ ★ ★ ★ ★ ★ ★ ★

Abraham Lincoln, though he knew the Bible thoroughly and spoke often of an Almighty God, was never baptized and was the only United States president never to join a church.

★ ★ ★ ★ ★ ★ ★ ★ ★ ★

CONSECRATED TO CHRIST

It appears that the grace of God was to be understood by Lincoln and a personal relationship with the Savior established only after yet another private tragedy would compound his public sorrow. Tragedy was to make its presence known in the White House with the sudden death of little Willie, the Lincolns' youngest child and the apple of the president's eye. In the hour of his inconsolable grief, Willie's nurse shared with the president her very personal relationship with Jesus Christ and encouraged him to know the Savior. Lincoln, by his own testimony, did not immediately respond, but some time later he related to a friend his newfound peace. He said, "When I left Springfield, I asked the people to pray for me; I was not a Christian. When I buried my son—the severest trial of my life—I was not a Christian. But when I went to Gettysburg, and saw the graves of thousands of our soldiers, I then and there consecrated myself to Christ." With deep emotion he told his friends that he had at last found the peace for which he longed.

In the days that followed, Abe Lincoln worshiped regularly at New York Avenue Presbyterian Church, not only on Sunday, but at the Wednesday evening prayer service as well! Dr. Phineas Gurley, the godly pastor of the church, became the president's personal confidant, and relates the fact that Lincoln had discussed with him his desire to make public his confession of faith and to unite in membership. Some months later, his second inaugural address was like the Gettysburg Address, a classic that reads like a sermon, with two complete verses of Scripture and fourteen references to God! But, within weeks the nation would mourn its tragic loss, and Abe Lincoln would dwell in the presence of the Christ whom he had now come to love and know so personally!

Palm Sunday 1865 was marked by rejoicing in the city streets of the North. General Robert E. Lee had surrendered at Appomattox, and to all intents and purposes the Civil War was over. The president gave thanks to God, and without a triumphal word, directed the attention of the nation to the task of reconstructing the South and to the healing of our Southern "brothers and sisters."

Five days later, on, Good Friday, church bells began to peal in Washington, then in Philadelphia, then in New York City and across the nation—the president was dead! Even before he was buried, the president's name would be linked with Washington's. "Washington the father of the nation . . . Lincoln the savior of the nation!"

Humble, self-effacing Abe Lincoln would have been very uncomfortable with the epithet of "savior" being attached in any manner to his name. Yet, the Union had been preserved, and God had used a most unusual man to accomplish His eternal purposes.[1]

John Woodbridge

THE PUZZLING FAITH OF ABRAHAM LINCOLN

Where was God in this brutal national war? An unbaptized non-churchgoer came up with a profound answer.

The end of the Civil War in the spring of 1865 began a national discussion that has not stopped 135 years later. What did the war mean? What was its significance to the nation? More momentously, what was its significance to God?

MAKING NO BONES ABOUT IT

Such questions engaged many of those who lived through the bloody conflict. Among those who thought they knew what it meant were many clergymen, some of whom made no bones about saying so.

In the North, Henry Ward Beecher (1813–87) was the scion of the country's most prominent evangelical family. As pastor of Brooklyn's Plymouth Congregational Church, he enjoyed the most influential pulpit in the land. When he spoke at ceremonies marking the recapture of Fort Sumter, Beecher made clear what he thought the conflict meant in the eye of God: "I charge the whole guilt of this war upon the ambitious, educated, plotting leaders of the South. . . . A day will come when God will reveal judgment and arraign these mighty miscreants . . . . And then these guiltiest and most remorseless traitors . . . shall be whirled aloft and plunged downward forever and ever in an endless retribution."

In the South, Robert Lewis Dabney (1820–98) was almost as prominent as Beecher in the North. A Presbyterian defender of Scripture and of traditional confessions, he was even more orthodox than Beecher. During the war Dabney served on the staff of General Stonewall Jackson; afterward he presided over seminaries in South Carolina and Texas.

Yet from wherever Dabney viewed the conflict, his opinion was the same. The war, he thought, was "caused deliberately" by evil abolitionists who persecuted the South "with calculated malice." When fellow Southerners asked him to soften his views on denominational colleagues in the North, Dabney had only these chilling words: "What! Forgive those people who have invaded our country, burned our cities, destroyed our homes, slain our young men, and spread desolation and ruin over our land?! No, I do not forgive them."

THINKING THE UNTHINKABLE

In contrast to Beecher and Dabney—and the assumption that only one side enjoyed the blessing of God—

stands the odd figure of Abraham Lincoln. At least, he held an odd view in those heated days of sectional strife.

Ministers and theologians, who day and night studied the Scriptures, knew very well where God stood on the war (though, of course, they differed among themselves). We would expect Lincoln, as the Union's president, to be just as partisan as Beecher. We would assume Lincoln to be just as vituperative about Southern leaders as Dabney was about the North's. Yet Lincoln, though he pondered the ways of God almost as steadily as the professionals of religion, was not so sure.

Admittedly, in his first inaugural address, in March 1861, Lincoln had presented a fairly conventional view of God and the American nation. The "ultimate justice of the people," he said, would prevail, for there was no "better, or equal, hope in the world." Lincoln saw a solution to the national crisis in terms of civil religion: "Intelligence, patriotism, Christianity, and a firm reliance on Him, who has never yet forsaken this favored land, are still competent to adjust, in the best way, all our present difficulty." God, in other words, would stick with the Americans, whose own virtues would lead them out of trouble.

Soon, however, the vicious realities of war began to stir something else in the Northern president. As early as 1862 Lincoln began to think the unthinkable: Perhaps the will of God could not simply be identified with American ideals and the effort to preserve the Union.

In September that year, the North had suffered another disastrous reversal, this time at the Second Battle of Bull Run. Lincoln was considering the radical step of proclaiming the emancipation of slaves in the South. In those circumstances, at one of the darkest moments of the war, he penned the following "Meditation on the Divine Will." It was written, as his secretaries, Nicolay and Hay, said, "while his mind was burdened with the weightiest questions

of his life. . . . It was not written to be seen of men." Here is what Lincoln wrote about the religious meaning of the war:

> The will of God prevails. In great contests each party claims to act in accordance with the will of God. Both may be, and one must be, wrong. God can not be for and against the same thing at the same time. In the present civil war it is quite possible that God's purpose is something different from the purpose of either party—and yet the human instrumentalities, working just as they do, are of the best adaptation to effect His purpose. I am almost ready to say this is probably true—that God wills this contest, and wills that it shall not end yet. By His mere quiet power, on the minds of the now contestants, He could have either saved or destroyed the Union without a human contest. Yet the contest began. And having begun He could give the final victory to either side any day. Yet the contest proceeds.

Like a figure from Israel's ancient history, Lincoln was arguing with God. But it was no longer a domesticated deity, an American God, but the ruler of the nations. The truth had begun to dawn to Lincoln that this God was not at the nation's beck and call, but the nation at His. His thinking was beginning to diverge from the paths followed by Beecher, Dabney, and the overwhelming majority of his contemporaries.

THE STUNNING SECOND INAUGURAL

These notions developed more profoundly as the lists of casualties grew. They reached their climax in words Lincoln prepared for his second inauguration as president in March 1865. That address stands as the most remarkably biblical public statement by any American president.

The critical section of the address, complete with citations from Matthew 18:7 and Psalm 19:9, deserves to be quoted in full:

> Neither [side] anticipated that the cause of the conflict

[i.e., slavery] might cease with, or even before, the conflict itself should cease. Each looked for an easier triumph, and a result less fundamental and astounding. Both read the same Bible, and pray to the same God; and each invokes His aid against the other. It may seem strange that any men should dare to ask a just God's assistance in wringing their bread from the sweat of other men's faces; but let us judge not that we be not judged. The prayers of both could not be answered; that of neither has been answered fully. The Almighty has His own purposes. "Woe unto the world because of offences! For it must needs be that offences come; but woe to that man by whom the offence cometh." If we shall suppose that American Slavery is one of those offences which, in the providence of God, must needs come, but which, having continued through His appointed time, He now wills to remove, and that He gives to both North and South this terrible war as the woe due to those by whom the offence came, shall we discern therein any departure from those divine attributes which the believers in a Living God always ascribe to Him? Fondly do we hope—fervently do we pray—that this mighty scourge of war may speedily pass away. Yet, if God wills that it continue, until all the wealth piled by the bondman's two hundred and fifty years of unrequited toil shall be sunk, and until every drop of blood drawn with the lash, shall be paid by another drawn with the sword, as was said three thousand years ago, so still it must be said, "the judgments of the Lord are true and righteous altogether."

★ ★ ★ ★ ★ ★ ★ ★ ★ ★

ABRAHAM LINCOLN WAS THE FIRST PRESIDENT TO USE THE PHRASE, "THIS NATION UNDER GOD." IT INSPIRED PRESIDENT EISENHOWER, IN 1954, TO ADD THE WORDS "ONE NATION UNDER GOD" TO THE PLEDGE OF ALLEGIANCE.

★ ★ ★ ★ ★ ★ ★ ★ ★ ★

How could Lincoln point to the commanding sovereignty of a great God, while professional clerics spoke almost exclusively of a "house god" completely in league with the North or the South? How could such a profound grasp of God's grandeur come from an ordinary lawyer and politician, who during his lifetime was scorned for lack of culture?

There can be no final answers to these questions. But a brief look at the debate over Lincoln's religion, and at the circumstances of his life, can at least provide hints.

PUZZLING, UNCONVENTIONAL RELIGION

Confusion about Lincoln's religion arises from the multiple ambiguities of his life. On the one hand, Lincoln was, in the words of biographers James Randall and Richard Current, "a man of more intense religiosity than any other President the United States has ever had." On the other hand, Lincoln's faith was not conventional.

As a young man in Illinois, he eagerly read free thinkers like Tom Paine. At the same time, he was a kind of "frontier spiritualist" who believed that signs, dreams, and portents foretold the future. He had no use for Christian creeds or statements of faith, and little use for formal theology. At least early on, Lincoln was probably also a Universalist who believed in the eventual salvation of all people.

He spoke of God often and in many different ways—William J. Wolf counted thirty-three different expressions, like "Almighty Being" or "Father of Mercies," in Lincoln's Collected Works. Yet Lincoln rarely referred to Jesus.

After the death of his four-year-old son, Edward, in 1850, he regularly attended Presbyterian churches in Springfield and Washington, pastored by doctrinal conservatives. Yet he never became a member of any congregation.

MAKING RELIGION A POLITICAL ISSUE

An incident early in his political career highlights the unconventional character of Lincoln's faith. In 1846 he stood for election to Congress from Illinois's Seventh Congressional District.

The rumor began to spread that Lincoln mocked Christianity and scoffed at religious practice. This amounted to a vital issue since Lincoln's opponent was a preacher, Peter Cartwright.

To quiet the alarm, Lincoln published a broadside on his religion that denied any wrongdoing. Significantly, however, it made little claim to anything positive. Here is the key passage of the circular:

> That I am not a member of any Christian Church, is true; but I have never denied the truth of the Scriptures; and I have never spoken with intentional disrespect of religion in general, or of any denomination of Christians in particular.

★ HEADED FOR HEAVEN OR HELL?

How would Lincoln answer that question? His political opponent, a famous frontier preacher, wanted to know. Abraham Lincoln ran for Congress in 1846, and he faced a formidable opponent: Peter Cartwright. Cartwright, a raw-boned, circuit-riding Methodist preacher, was known throughout Illinois. During his sixty-five years of riding the circuit, he would baptize nearly ten thousand converts.

During the intense 1846 congressional campaign, some of Cartwright's followers accused Lincoln of being an "infidel." In response, Lincoln decided to meet Cartwright on his own ground and attended one of his evangelistic rallies.

Carl Sandburg, in *Abraham Lincoln: The Prairie Years,** tells the story this way:

In due time Cartwright said, "All who desire to lead a new life, to give their hearts to God, and go to heaven, will stand," and a sprinkling of men, women, and children stood up. Then the preacher exhorted, "All who do not wish to go to hell will stand." All stood up—except Lincoln. Then said Cartwright in his gravest voice, "I observe that many responded to the first invitation to give their hearts to God and go to heaven. And, I further observe that all of you save one indicated that you did not desire to go to hell. The sole exception is Mr. Lincoln, who did not respond to either invitation. May I inquire of you, Mr. Lincoln, where are you going?"

And Lincoln slowly rose and slowly spoke. "I came here as a respectful listener. I did not know that I was to be singled out by Brother Cartwright. I believe in treating religious matters with due solemnity. I admit that the questions propounded by Brother Cartwright are of great importance. I did not feel called upon to answer as the rest did. Brother Cartwright asks me directly where I am going. I desire to reply with equal directness: I am going to Congress."

He went.

*Carl Sandburg, *Abraham Lincoln: The Prairie Years and the War Years*, vol. 1 (Harcourt Brace, 1954).

I do not think I could, myself, be brought to support a man for office whom I knew to be an open enemy of, and scoffer at, religion. Leaving the higher matter of eternal consequences between him and his Maker, I still do not think any man has the right thus to insult the feelings, and injure the morals, of the community in which he may live.

Even as Lincoln recognized the importance of religious propriety for public officials, he made clear that his religion was his own business.

Long-Standing Debate

Lincoln's manifest trust in God alongside his unconventional piety confounded his contemporaries. A popular early biography by Joseph Gilbert Holland, published in 1866, described Lincoln as a model evangelical gentleman. This greatly upset Lincoln's law partner in Springfield, Illinois, William Herndon, who thought he knew what Lincoln was really like. The portrait in Herndon's biography was much saltier. Lincoln was depicted as a prairie "infidel" who got along very well without the church; an ambitious, even scheming, politician; a man more fond of the bawdy than the Bible, more given to introspective melancholy than to Christian holiness.

Modern studies continue the contrast. In G. Frederick Owen's *Abraham Lincoln: The Man and His Faith* (published in 1976 and reprinted several times), Lincoln appears as a Christian prophet who sustained evangelical convictions throughout his life. By contrast, in Gore Vidal's historical novel Lincoln (1984), Christianity is a superfluous veneer that Lincoln occasionally parades for political purposes.

The greatest difficulty in coming to a clearer picture of Lincoln's faith is the fact that his religion does not fit into modern categories. He was not an orthodox evangelical, "born-again" Christian striving toward the "higher life" (as these terms have been used since the 1870s). But neither was he a skeptical "modernist" with a prejudice against the supernatural and an aversion to the Bible.

Consequently, many conflicting stories about Lincoln lack concrete historical verification. In one, for example, Lincoln made a definite profession of faith; in another he was voicing agnostic opinions to the end of his days in the White House.

Three Key Influences

But three historical circumstances help explain the nature of Lincoln's religion—with its unusual belief in God's sovereign power—that came to fullest expression in the Second Inaugural Address.

First, Lincoln grew up in a poor dirt-farming family in the upper South and lower Midwest without privilege, position, or much formal education. The world of his upbringing was much closer to the culture of Puritanism than the culture of narcissism.

Common people were often deeply religious, believing without question in God and the unseen world. Yet they were not much troubled about doctrines, ecclesiastical affairs, or the glorious prospect of the millennium, which then preoccupied some of America's religious elite. Rather, the common people tried to accept their fate, to overcome guilt, to enjoy the fleeting comforts of love and family, to survive the uncertainties of birth, to eke out existence on an often-brutal frontier, and to come to terms with the ever-present reality of death.

As with many other such families, the Lincolns had very few books. But they did have the Bible, which Lincoln evidently read with great care. His later speeches and ordinary conversation were peppered with biblical quotations and allusions.

This family history provided the backdrop of Lincoln's religion. It had nothing to do with modern ideas about "finding oneself" or about "God's wonderful plan" for life.

The second circumstance was Lincoln's experience with denominations in the Indiana and Illinois of his youth. He found the harsh infighting among Methodists, Baptists, Presbyterians, Disciples, Universalists, and "village atheists" repulsive. As a consequence, Lincoln several times professed willingness to join a church that required nothing of its members but heartfelt love to God and to one's neighbors. The competing creeds of the churches were not for him.

The third circumstance was instruction in reality by the coldest master—death. The passing of his mother when he was nine, the death of a beloved sister shortly after her marriage, the death of two sons (in 1850, and at the White House in 1862), the death of several close friends in the early days of the Civil War (*his* Civil War), and increasingly, the heart-wrenching lists of casualties from the battlefields—these left him no taste for easy believism, no escape from the mysteries of God and the universe.

The truly remarkable thing about Lincoln's religion was how these circumstances drove him to deeper contemplation of God and the divine will. The external Lincoln, casual about religious observance, hid a man of profound morality, an almost unbearable God-consciousness, and a deep belief in the freedom of God to transcend the limited vision of humanity.

Such religious qualities are unusual in any age. They were even more rare in the period of the Civil War when, for almost every one else, partisan passion transformed God from the Lord of nations into the servant of North or South.[2]

★ *Mark Noll*

THANKSGIVING

★ ★ ★ ★ ★ ★ ★

Abraham Lincoln's name will forever be tied to the saving of the Union and the ending of slavery. These formed the two principal achievements of the American Civil War, those brutal years of horror and glory, cowardice and heroism, selfishness and sacrifice. Without that liberty and that Union, America and the world would be a very different place today. In the crucible of war Americans grow spiritually; therefore, these accomplishments remembered Lincoln's relationship with God, helping lead the people more toward a life of freedom.

Named after the first of the biblical patriarchs, Lincoln really learned that the will of God prevails. At Gettysburg, he intended to say that "this nation shall have a new birth of freedom and that government of the people, by the people, for the people, shall not perish from the earth." Yet, in an inspired moment, he said instead, "this nation, under God, shall have a new birth of freedom . . . ."

It is not surprising that Lincoln is responsible for creating the one completely American national holiday that included God in a fundamental way. Until 1863, Americans had two nationwide celebrations: Washington's birthday and July Fourth. Then, Lincoln proposed Thanksgiving Day.

Of course, showing gratitude for the harvest goes back to ancient times. In the New World, too, thanksgiving prayers reach back to the beginning of the settlements. After the founding of the United States, presidents Washington, John Adams, and James Madison issued occasional appeals for the people to give thanks and prayers to God. They designated days that ranged from

January to November. But after them, presidents stayed silent until Lincoln.

In the decades between, local leaders and governors of the states issued numerous proclamations calling for thanksgiving prayers. Under the leadership of Sarah Josepha Hale, the "Editress of the *Lady's Book*," as she called herself, many states and territories came together to celebrate Thanksgiving Day on the last Thursday of each November. Hale, a poet and writer, grew into a highly influential person in the antebellum decades editing *Godey's Lady's Book*, a magazine aimed at women and the home. In September 1863, she wrote to Lincoln, requesting to have the annual Thanksgiving Day made a national and fixed Union festival. "For the last fifteen years," she explained, "I have set forth this idea. . . . If Lincoln would now act, by the noble example of the President of the United States, the permanency and unity of our Great American Festival of Thanksgiving would be forever secured."

But, Lincoln did more than set an example. Immediately upon the receipt of Hale's letter, he issued a proclamation calling for a national thanksgiving. Though chances are that he did not himself compose the document, his signature made it Lincoln's own. The proclamation asked "the whole American People . . . to set apart and observe the last Thursday of November next, as a day of Thanksgiving and Praise to our beneficent Father who dwelleth in the Heavens." It noted the terrible Civil War and asked people to "implore the interposition of the

"Abraham Lincoln and his Emancipation Proclamation" by The Strobrige Lithograph Co.

Almighty Hand to heal the wounds of the nation and to restore it as soon as it may be consistent with the Divine purposes to the full enjoyment of peace, harmony, tranquility and Union."

It also highlighted the blessings received in spite of the war. The battles "have not arrested the plough, the shuttle, or the ship; the axe had enlarged the borders of our settlements, and the mines . . . have yielded even more abundantly than heretofore. Population has steadily increased, not withstanding the waste that has been made in the camp, the siege and the battle-field; and the country, rejoicing in . . . strength and vigor, is permitted to expect continuance of years with large increase of freedom." The people understood: Lincoln had issued that year his Emancipation Proclamation. But Lincoln gave God the glory. "No human counsel hath devised nor hath any mortal hand worked out these great things. They are the gracious gifts of the Most High God, who, while dealing with us in anger for our sins, hath nevertheless remembered mercy."

Sarah Josepha Hale, who had urged Lincoln to act, explained her request this way: "The last Thursday in November was suggested because then the agricultural labors of the year are generally completed; the elections are over; the autumnal diseases which usually prevail more or less at the South have ceased, and the summer wanderers are gathered to their homes. . . . Let the last Thursday in November be consecrated by gratitude to God for His wonderful blessings on our people, the crowning glory of which is our National Union."

America has changed a great deal since Lincoln's day. Working the land occupies a small portion of the people. The seasonal diseases that ravaged the folks of the southern part of the country are no more. The changes since then have indeed been unprecedented in human history. And now in the twenty-first century, Americans have more to be thankful for than ever before. They know it and have known it all along. Steadily since 1863, when Lincoln first called, they have remembered to give thanks every year. "The whole American People . . . to set apart and observe the last Thursday of November . . . . In testimony whereof, I have hereunto set my hand and caused the Seal of the United States to be affixed. Done at the city of Washington, this Third day of October, in the year of our Lord one thousand eight hundred and sixty-three, and the Independence of the United States the Eighty-eighth."

God willing, the American people will never forget our Lord God, who is the one to be utterly thankful for the most.

★ *Gabor S. Boritt*

Sarah Josepha Hale, the editor of the magazine Godey's Lady's Book, *wrote this 1863 letter, which influenced Abraham Lincoln to make Thanksgiving a national holiday to be celebrated on the fourth Thursday of November.*

ACTOR, ASSASSIN, MADMAN
JOHN WILKES BOOTH

It was Good Friday, April 14, 1865. President Lincoln was having breakfast with his wife Mary and his twenty-one-year-old son, Robert. Robert had just returned from the war where he was known by all, in a "safe" position on the staff of General Grant. He excitedly told of having been on the porch at Appomattox where General Robert E. Lee had agreed to surrender his Confederate army. As a souvenir, Robert had come away with one of Lee's visiting cards, which was engraved with the general's likeness. Looking long at it, President Lincoln remarked, "It's a good face. It is the face of a noble brave man. I am glad the war is over at last." During this time, Mary Lincoln told her husband she had been given tickets to a new play at Grover's Theatre but would prefer to attend the production of *Our American Cousin* at Ford's.

One of the men who sought an audience with Lincoln early that same day was John Hale of New Hampshire, who had recently been defeated for reelection after sixteen years in the U.S. Senate. Lincoln had appointed him to be the next ambassador to Spain. More important than the salary of twelve thousand dollars a year, Senator Hale hoped that by taking his daughter Lucy to Spain, he could break up her infatuation with John Wilkes Booth. As with most actors, Booth was thought of as a scoundrel and, in this case, with good reason.

John Wilkes Booth was born twenty-seven years earlier, the ninth of ten children, to Junius Brutus Booth (named for Caesar's assassin), a British-born actor who abandoned a wife and son there for a young actress named Mary Ann Holmes. Junius and Mary Ann immigrated to the U.S. in 1821 to the Baltimore area. The couple were passionately devoted to each other although they did not marry until 1851.

Junius Booth graced and disgraced the American stage. Once a theater manager, warned of the actor's fondness for spirits, locked him in his dressing room to keep him sober before a performance. Junius bribed a boy to bring a bottle and hold it outside the door. There he suckled the liquor to his heart's content through a straw stuck through the keyhole.

A dabbler in religion, Junius insisted his children be schooled in the combined tenets of both the Talmud and the Koran. He imagined that every animal was a former human with an immortal soul, and he taught his children to never harm any wild or domesticated creature. On one occasion he purchased some wild pigeons that had been shot by a hunter, bought a cemetery plot, and employed a Unitarian minister to conduct a funeral for the deceased birds.

John Wilkes Booth grew up roaming the fields of the Bel Air farm with his best friend and sister Asia (named by their father because Asia was "that country where God first walked with man"). His mother, Mary Ann, was the only stable presence in the Booth family. She admitted that John was her favorite child and the most handsome. With dark lustrous eyes, black hair, and delicate skin, he was the most striking of the Booths and became irresistibly attractive to women, old and young.

He was consumed at an early age by a desire for fame. His older brothers, Junius Brutus Jr. and Edwin, had followed their father onto the stage. To surpass or at least rival his father and brothers became a passion of John Wilkes's.

His acting debut came in 1855 at the age of seventeen in *Richard III* at Baltimore's St. Charles Theatre. He was hissed and booed because, petrified by stage fright, he

forgot his lines. His voice was not an actor's, but whatever his oral deficiencies, Booth more than made up for them with his boundless energy. He acted with such gusto that audiences eventually loved him, and he soon became one of American theaters' most popular performers, especially in Richmond and other cities in the South.

John Wilkes Booth

He stood only five-foot-eight, but his lithe 160-pound frame and chiseled features soon rivaled his brother Edwin. Some thought John Wilkes would one day outshine his brother. "Doubtless he would have been," said manager John Ford, "the greatest actor of his time had he lived." In the early 1860s, the youngest of the acting Booths drew large audiences and commanded fees of five hundred to one thousand dollars a week—princely sums for the time.

His greatest virtue came from those who thought they knew him best—he was totally without conceit. Despite his accessible manner and his illegitimate birth, John Wilkes Booth considered himself a member of one of Maryland's first families, and a Southern one at that.

By 1850, when war talk was rampant, he sympathized strongly with the South and argued heatedly with his brother Edwin, who had Union sympathies. He took the position that the South had a right to secede from the despotic government in Washington.

As chance would have it, in November 1859, while walking to a Richmond theater, he saw marching men in uniform. They were volunteer militia—the Richmond Grays—on their way to Charlestown in Western Virginia. Their task: to rescue John Brown, the arch-abolitionist, who had been captured at Harper's Ferry and condemned to death in Charlestown after failing to inspire an uprising of slaves. Booth somehow borrowed a uniform and, armed with a pistol and knife, talked his way on board the militiamen's ten-coach train.

So it was that when John Brown was hanged, John Wilkes Booth—a zealot for the Southern cause—was among the guards near the scaffold. Booth was deeply affected. Although he despised the abolitionist's ideals, he was fascinated by the aged man's audacity and by his single-handed attempt to alter history. Booth was most impressed by Brown's courage in the face of death, his Bible in his hand. The hanging itself, however, revolted him.

That was the first and only time Booth wore a military uniform. During the war, by any standard, including his own, he was a slacker. He used the excuse he had promised his mother he would never go to war. Others thought the reason might be that he was obsessed by fear of suffering a wound that might disfigure his handsome face.

He softened his guilt over not becoming a soldier for the South by purchasing drugs and other medical supplies and helping to smuggle them South. Still, by mid-1864, he was a deeply troubled man.

The South was losing, and Booth suffered pangs of conscience about the inactive role he had played. He decided to do something. Like many Southern sympathizers, as well as many of Lincoln's opponents, he viewed the president as a loathsome tyrant. He believed Lincoln was bent not only on wrecking the South and its way of life but also on destroying the liberties of all Americans through the suspension of habeas corpus and other wartime measures. Booth turned again to his childhood fantasy: He would make a place for himself in history by bringing down Lincoln.

The North's large manpower pool gave it an overwhelming advantage over the Confederacy. Grant, newly appointed chief of "all" Union armies, decided in mid-1864 to stop exchanging prisoners of war. At the time, there were about fifty thousand Southerners held by the Federals. Before the year's end there would be thousands more, all desperately needed to fill the depleted ranks of the Confederacy.

To Booth, the solution was simple. Kidnap Lincoln and carry him to Richmond. There he would be held hostage for the release of Southern prisoners, who could return to the fronts.

Booth, not known for meditation or having a personal relationship with God, went into action in late August or early September of 1864. The kidnapping would have to take place in a Washington theater, which appealed to Booth's sense of drama. He knew well the locations of boxes, back corridors, and behind-the-scenes passageways. It was well known that the Lincolns frequented the theaters.

On one of these occasions while the play was in progress, Booth and a fellow conspirator would attack the president in his box and hold him at gunpoint while binding and gagging him. If the theater had no stairs, they would lower the president by rope onto the stage and, with the help of others, carry the president out of the theater and on to Richmond.

Thinking an entire theater audience would remain quiet while the president of the U.S. was being kidnapped was insane. To carry out this plan Booth needed another accomplice, someone who would turn off the gaslights, so the theater would be dark, and open the right door at the right time to allow escape.

After many attempts to execute, the kidnapping failed for one reason or another, and Booth's grandiose plots were in tatters. Half of his coconspirators deserted him.

April 3, 1865: Richmond fell.

April 9, 1865: At 9 o'clock in the evening the war department received a telegram from Grant: "General Lee surrendered the Army of Northern Virginia this afternoon on terms proposed by myself."

Two nights later, after much celebration, thousands gathered in front of the White House. It was some time before Lincoln came out on the balcony above the main entrance with a candle in his hand. A chant of "Lincoln! Lincoln!" rose from the thousands. Finally Lincoln began to speak on many subjects. One passage concerned whether voting should be extended to Negroes; Lincoln said, "I would myself prefer that it were now conferred on the very intelligent and on those who serve our cause as soldiers."

For at least one man in the audience the president had just sealed his fate. Standing beside a large tree on the White House lawn, John Wilkes Booth whispered to Lewis Payne, a fellow conspirator: "That is the last speech he will ever make."

⭐ *"Miss Johnnie" Capell*

A DREAM COME TRUE

★ ★ ★ ★ ★ ★ ★ ★ ★ ★ ★

When actor John Wilkes Booth stopped by Ford's Theater at noon on April 14, he was delighted to see a group of carpenters busily preparing box 7 with the presidential regalia. Now that the war was over, President and Mrs. Lincoln were going to spend an evening out to attend the play *Our American Cousin*, and Booth, who had failed at his prior attempts to kidnap the president, could now carry out his more drastic plan to single-handedly assassinate him.

Only days before, Lincoln had confided to his friend Ward Lamon that he was haunted by a dream in which he had awakened to the sounds of sobbing in the White House. Following the sounds to the East Room, he described the scene. "Before me was a catafalque, on which rested a corpse. 'Who is dead in the White House?' I demanded of one of the soldiers. 'The president,' he replied. 'He was killed by an assassin.'"

Lincoln's dream was about to become a reality. At 9:30 that evening, Booth arrived at the Star Saloon next door to Ford's Theater, ordered a drink, and then sauntered over to the theater. Booth made his way up to box 7 where the Lincolns were enjoying the play with their guests, Major Henry Rathbone and his fiancée Miss Clara Harris. Unaware that John Wilkes Booth was standing behind them, the foursome continued laughing hysterically at Harry Hawk, the actor on the stage below.

Drawing his derringer, Booth fired a lead ball into Lincoln's head, shattering his skull, the bullet lodging in his brain. In an attempt to make a dramatic landing on center stage, Booth tried to leap over the balustrade, but Major Rathbone apprehended him. When Booth slashed

Box in Ford's Theater where Lincoln was assassinated

Rathbone's arm with a dagger, Rathbone immediately recoiled. Trying to escape again, Booth caught one of his boot spurs on the decorative flag draping the box and landed clumsily next to Harry Hawk, surprising the actor.

Unaware of what had transpired, the crowd grew confused as they recognized the actor John Wilkes Booth on the stage. Ever the showman, Booth turned to the audience and eloquently delivered the motto of the State of Virginia: *Sic semper Tyrannis!* (Latin for "Thus may it be

Lithograph by Currier & Ives: "The assassination of President Lincoln: at Ford's Theatre, Washington, D.C., April 14th, 1865"

ever to tyrants!" With his leg obviously broken in the fall, Booth then hobbled out of the theater into the darkness.

Lincoln was transported to the boarding house across the street where he lay in grave condition. Throughout the night, a crowd gathered outside to pray for the president, as his close friends, including the vice president, stopped by to bid their comrade good-bye. Robert Lincoln tried to console his mother, Mary Todd Lincoln, who despite her sedation grieved inconsolably in a nearby room. Sadly, the following morning, April 15, 1865, at 7:22, Abraham Lincoln died.

Booth, who had expected the South to rally around him, was shocked to learn that they were weeping for Lincoln instead. Hunted down by the Cavalry, John Wilkes Booth soon became the most hated man in America. The last entry Booth penned in his diary reads: "I am in despair. And why? For doing what Brutus was honored for—what made Tell a hero? And yet I, for striking down a greater tyrant than they ever knew, I am looked upon as a common cutthroat. My action was purer than either of theirs . . . . I hoped for no gain. I knew no private wrong. I struck for my country and that alone. A country that groaned beneath this tyranny . . . and yet now behold the cold hand they extend me . . . . I bless the entire world. Have never harmed or wronged anyone. This last was not a wrong, unless God deems it so."

Refusing to surrender, weeks later, Booth was shot and killed by the army who discovered him hiding inside a tobacco shed at a farm in Virginia.

Susan Huey Wales

No human counsel hath devised nor hath any mortal hand worked out these great things. They are the gracious gifts of the Most High God, who, while dealing with us in anger for our sins, hath nevertheless remembered mercy.

—Abraham Lincoln

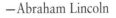

5
"As Safe in Battle As Bed"

"STONEWALL" JACKSON

★ ★ ★ ★ ★ ★ ★ ★ ★ ★ ★ ★ ★ ★ ★ ★ ★ ★ ★

Actor Stephen Lang as
General Thomas J. Jackson

General Stonewall Jackson

I seek to show the humanity of the leaders of the Civil War. . . . I want people to get to know the full person of Stonewall Jackson, a very important historical figure that, when not left completely out of history lessons taught in most schools, is simply glossed over. My goal is to show him as the full, complex man that he was . . . . Faith in God was a huge part of their lives—for both the leaders of the North and the South. Yet, it is the element most frequently discarded by historians and educators when teaching about the war.

—Ron Maxwell, director of Gods and Generals

STONEWALL JACKSON: THE GENERAL WHO LOOKED TO GOD

★ ★ ★ ★ ★ ★ ★ ★ ★ ★

Thomas Jonathan Jackson's interest in the Christian faith began in his early years. As a teenager, he would sometimes walk three miles on a Sunday to hear a sermon and during those years he was regarded by many as a promising biblical scholar. In his early twenties, while participating in the Mexican War, he began a more serious spiritual pursuit. He made a careful study of the Roman Catholic faith, and although there was much that impressed him, as exemplified by Mexico's devout parishioners, he knew that a more simple faith was what he wanted.

There is no record of an abrupt or startling transformation in Jackson's life. Although the change was slow, almost imperceptible, it was decisive. In 1848, on Sunday, April 29, Jackson publicly declared his faith by baptism at St. John's Episcopal Church in New York City, while he was stationed at Fort Hamilton, New York. Still unsure about which denomination he favored, he wanted it understood that he was not joining the Episcopal Church; he was committing his life to the known will of God. It was a commitment he struggled to keep for the rest of his life.

DEACON JACKSON

In 1851 Jackson began a ten-year term as an instructor at the Virginia Military Institute in Lexington. He was not a popular teacher at VMI. Most students regarded him as overly pious, rigid, and inflexible. He became the object of cadet pranks and derisive poetry. He joined the Presbyterian Church of the community after being assured by the pastor that he did not have to accept all points of Presbyterian theology. The sincerity and intensity of Jackson's spiritual devotion caused his fellow church members to feel that they were backsliders. He became a deacon in the church, and for the rest of his life he was often referred to as "Deacon Jackson." He also adopted a strict code of personal conduct. Dancing, theater-going, card playing, smoking, and drinking were eliminated from his life.

On August 4, 1853, he married Elinor Junkin. It was a beautiful relationship, and Elinor was instrumental in cracking the shy and aloof wall her husband had built around his life. In October of the following year, Jackson's newly found joy turned to devastation when Elinor died in childbirth. His shield of faith had its first real test.

Jackson in younger years

Jackson reconsecrated himself to Christ. His belief in the providence of God assured him that there was a purpose in his loss and that lessons could be gained from his bereavement. He asserted that he could suffer any misfortune if he were sure it was the will of God. More attention and time were given to matters of faith and duties in the church. Slowly but surely, the clouds began to part. In 1857 a new joy came to his life when he married Mary Anna Morrison. Both of his wives were daughters of Presbyterian ministers. Morning family prayers, with servants in attendance, were a daily feature in the Jackson household.

Jackson was not opposed to slavery. He believed the institution, for some unknown reason, was established by God. At various times throughout his life, Jackson owned slaves. Unlike some owners, however, he believed that blacks were human beings who had a right to be treated with kindness and respect. For Jackson, slaves were children of God with souls to be saved. In the autumn of 1855, Jackson began a Sunday school class for local blacks, most of whom were slaves. Initially, he taught the class himself. Later, while fighting with the Confederate army, he sent back funds to assure the continuance of the class.

"AS SAFE IN BATTLE AS IN BED"

In 1861, when Virginia seceded from the Union, Jackson resigned his commission in the United States army in order to fight for the Confederacy. Though certain friends and a few family members urged him not to desert the Union, Jackson was convinced that the South's cause was God's cause. His military exploits on behalf of that cause are well known. The part played by his faith in his battlefield experiences and in his military life is less known.

Early on in the war, after Jackson had demonstrated extraordinary courage in battle, another officer asked him how he could remain so calm while shells and bullets rained about his head. Jackson, with a serious look, replied, "Captain, my religious belief teaches me to feel as safe in battle as in bed. God has fixed the time for my death. I do not concern myself about that, but to always be ready, no matter when it may overtake me." Then he added, "Captain, that is the way all men should live, and then all would be equally brave."

Jackson was a strong believer in the providence of God. God ordained war. God brought about battlefield victories and administered defeats. Therefore, when Jackson was victorious in battle, he always gave credit to God. Following the Second Battle of Bull Run, when someone suggested that victory had been achieved as a result of brave fighting, Jackson replied, "No, it has been won by nothing but the blessing and protection of Providence." After he had won yet another victory, he confided to a friend, "Without God's blessing, I look for no success, and for every success my prayer is, that all glory may be given unto Him to whom it is properly due." He fought hard against the "sin of ambition."

SPEAKING TO HEAVEN'S KING

Prayer played an essential role in Jackson's life and career. All who were associated with him knew that Jackson prayed passionately before making major decisions, and on the eve of battle he would arise several times during the night to ask for God's blessings and guidance. After hearing Jackson pray, one minister said, "He did not

★ ★ ★ ★ ★ ★ ★

"I would like to see no questions asked . . . as to what denomination a chaplain belongs, but let the question be, 'Does he preach the Gospel?'"

—Thomas J. Jackson

★ ★ ★ ★ ★ ★ ★

pray to men, but to God. He seemed to realize that he was speaking to Heaven's King."

Jackson regarded the ministry as life's highest calling. During the war years, he would often invite pastors and chaplains of nearby churches to his tent to debates and discussions on biblical and theological matters. The general could more than hold his own in such conversations, and they seemed to exhilarate him. Jackson was also instrumental in establishing a chaplain's association to work with his troops. When selecting chaplains, he declared, "I would like to see no questions asked . . . as to what denomination a chaplain belongs, but let the question be, 'Does he preach the Gospel?'"

Jackson's seriousness about matters of faith, his emphasis upon religious observances, his opposition to Sunday mail, his often stern demeanor, and his abstinence from various "joys" of life caused some of his soldiers to regard him as an extremist. Some coined an alternative nickname, "Old Blue Light," but all of his troops respected their general too much to ever laugh at him.

As Jackson's faith sustained him in life, so it upheld him as he approached death. Wounded by gunfire from his own men on May 2, 1863, he lingered for a few days. His left arm needed amputation. As his condition became worse, Jackson made the following remark: "I see from the number of physicians that you think my condition dangerous, but I thank God, if it is His will, that I am ready to go." On May 10 he uttered his final words: "Let us cross over the river, and rest under the shade of the trees." It was Sunday—for many years it had been his desire to die on a Sunday.[1]

★ *John Woodbridge*

Standing Like a Stone Wall

★ ★ ★ ★ ★ ★ ★ ★ ★

The life of Thomas J. Jackson (1824–63) was one of the epic, bittersweet sagas of the nineteenth century. Hardly anyone would have appeared less likely bound for fame and greatness than young Tom Jackson of the western (now West) Virginia mountain country.

Tragedy struck his life early and it struck often. He lost his beloved elder sister when he was three, his father a week later, his mother when he was six, and his brother while Tom was still a teenager.

But it was his mother, Julia, on her deathbed, who uttered the immortal line that helped cast the little child's destiny: "You may be whatever you resolve to be." The words would stay with the orphaned boy his whole life, and he would need them as almost every conceivable obstacle and calamity presented themselves against him.

Jackson received an appointment to West Point almost on a fluke, and his backwoods education and demeanor rendered him the ill-equipped object of his classmates' scorn when he arrived at the college. Though he finished dead last in his class his first year, the fact that he did not flunk out was a harbinger of the iron will and unshakable determination that would mark him all his life.

By the end of Jackson's fourth year and graduation, one classmate remarked to another—who happened to be George McClellan, second man in the class academically—that had they one more year of school, Jackson would have finished top in the class!

Jackson went almost immediately to the 1846–48 Mexican War. It was this war where he first earned fame.

In a legendary feat, he, one other man, and one cannon turned a Mexican assault into the charge up Chapultepec Hill, the capture of the fabled "Halls of Montezuma," and the sealing of Mexican emperor Santa Anna's fate.

After returning from the war, Jackson took an instructor's position at the Virginia Military Institute in 1851. He taught there for a decade, earning a well-deserved reputation as one of the worst instructors the school ever had because of his rote, wooden lectures. But he also gained growing respect from those students and professors who got to know him.

The first and greatest love of his life was beautiful, Pennsylvania-born Elinor Junkin, daughter of Washington College president George Junkin. She and Jackson married in 1853, but barely a year later, the greatest blow of his life struck. Ellie died in childbirth, along with the baby.

"She has left me such monuments of her love to God," Jackson wrote, "and deep dependence upon her Savior's merits, that were I not to believe in her happiness, neither would I believe, though one were to rise from the dead and declare it. God's promises change not. She was a child of God, and as such she is enjoying Him forever."

Thomas Jackson

★ OVERCOMING THE ODDS

Stonewall Jackson is regarded as one of the outstanding tacticians in military history. His victories on the battlefield, as well as in his life in general, are an account of continually overcoming superior odds.

Because of a limited education in his early years, Jackson's dreams of entering West Point Military Academy seemed impossible. However, after he barely passed the entrance exams, he eventually graduated seventeenth in a class of fifty-nine cadets at the Point. He fought with distinction in the Mexican War, and during the 1850s he taught at Virginia Military Institute.

In 1861 Jackson joined the Confederate army. At the first Battle of Bull Run (Manassas), he won his famous nickname when his brigade stood firm "like a stone wall" before a Union attack. Following Bull Run, Jackson rendered significant military leadership in battles where Confederate forces were greatly outnumbered.

In the Valley Campaign, Second Bull Run, Antietam, Fredericksburg, and Chancellorsville, Jackson defeated Federal troops whose combined strength was several times his own. Only in the Peninsular Campaign, due to physical exhaustion, was Jackson's performance ineffective. At Chancellorsville, after another brilliant victory, Jackson was wounded by gunfire from his own men, who mistook him for the enemy. When he died a few days later, chances of a Confederate victory died with him.

Still, his grief threatened to overwhelm him. "The dearest of earth's spots," he wrote, "the grave of her who was so pure and lovely—but she is not there. Even so, I fight viciously an urge to dig up her coffin and take one last look at Ellie's dear ashes!"

"But religion is all that I desire it to be," he soon wrote Ellie's older sister, Maggie. "I am reconciled for my loss and have joy and hope of a future reunion, that you and I will soon join her, and that she will escort us to that heaven of which Melville speaks so beautifully."

The loss of his wife and baby, along with many contributions to his life by Ellie, aided Jackson's growing religious devotion. He and Maggie became best friends, and she played the piano for his black Sunday School classes. The two eventually fell

Jackson's second wife, Mary Anna Morrison Jackson

strongly in love, but a hard trial ensued here as well. The Presbyterian doctrine to which both subscribed prohibited a person marrying his dead spouse's sibling. Though neither Tom nor Maggie agreed with the stricture (which was shortly thereafter expunged from Presbyterian teaching), they chose to honor what they viewed as the God-sanctioned authority over them, as opposed to their own feelings.

In 1857, wedded bliss returned to Jackson as he married Mary Anna Morrison, the daughter of another Presbyterian clergyman and college president. They lost one child in infancy, but had another, Julia, who survived.

Jackson wrote his spiritually-struggling sister, Laura, many times concerning the need for salvation and obedience to God:

"You speak of your temptations. God withdraws His sensible presence from us to try our faith. When a cloud comes between you and the sun, do you fear that the sun will never appear again? O, pray for more faith."

In another letter he wrote,

You know I am concerned about your hopes in relation to the eternal future, Sister. So let's look at it logically. Suppose two persons, one a Christian and the other an infidel, are closing their earthly existences. And suppose the infidel is right, and the Christian wrong; they will then after death be upon equal footing. But suppose the infidel to be wrong, and the Christian right; then will the state of the latter after death be inestimably superior to that of the other. And if you will examine the history of mankind, it is plain that Christianity contributes much more to happiness in this life than the way of the infidel. Oh Sister, do pray to God for His mercy and eternal life through our Redeemer, Jesus Christ!

By the onset of the war in 1861, Jackson was a successful businessman, happy family man, and a devout deacon in the Lexington Presbyterian Church.

When his pro-Union first father-in-law decried the South's secession from the Union, Jackson respectfully replied, "I believe Christians should not be disturbed about the dissolution of the Union. It can come only with God's permission, and will only be permitted if for His people's good. I cannot see how we should be distressed about such things, whatever be their consequences."

"I greatly desire to see peace, blessed peace, and I am persuaded that if God's people throughout our Confederacy will earnestly and perseveringly unite in imploring His interposition for peace, that we may expect

Jackson's beloved sister, Laura

it," he wrote Maggie and her husband, VMI cofounder John T. L. Preston. "Oh! that our country was such a Christian, God-fearing people as it should be. Then might we very speedily look for peace."

"The only thing which gives me any apprehension about my country's cause is the sin of the army and people," Jackson said.

Despite having a brigade, then a division, then a corps to lead, Jackson was perhaps the single greatest engine behind what history calls the Great Revival in the Southern armies. This massive spiritual awakening particularly transformed the Army of Northern Virginia in which Jackson served.

Recognizing the worldliness of Confederate army camps in the war's early months, Jackson fired a letter to his denomination's governing body, the Southern Presbyterian General Assembly:

Each branch of the Christian Church should send into the army some of its most prominent ministers who are distinguished for their piety, talents and zeal; and such ministers should labor to produce concert of action among chaplains and Christians in the army. These ministers should give special attention to preaching to regiments which are without chaplains, and induce them to take steps to get chaplains, to let the regiments name the denominations from which they desire chaplains selected, and then to see that suitable chaplains are secured.

Denominational distinctions should be kept out of view, and not touched upon. And, as a general rule, I do not think that a chaplain who would preach denominational sermons should be in the army. His congregation is his regiment, and it is composed of various denominations. I would like to see no question asked in the army of what denomination a chaplain belongs to; but let the question be, "Does he preach the Gospel?"

Originally a non-Sabbatarian, Ellie's influence on him in that regard proved so profound that he lamented the lack of heed paid the Sabbath by the Confederacy. "How can a nation that defamed the Sabbath by choosing to deliver the mails that day expect the blessing of God on its pursuits?" he asked.

When a Catholic priest, with whom "Old Jack" would have had enormous theological differences, heard Jackson had ordered all soldier's tents left behind during a campaign march, the priest requested that one tent be taken so that he could receive private confessions from the (few) Catholic soldiers in that corps. Jackson permitted that one tent on the campaign.

His fame on many fields is well known. In July 1861, the Federals were in the process of routing the outnumbered Confederates in the conflict's first major battle, and perhaps ending the war that day.

Mortally wounded South Carolina general Barnard Bee gasped, "There stands Jackson like a stone wall," as he spotted his old Mexican War comrade mounted amidst the twenty-five hundred men of his Virginia brigade. They stood directly in the path of the Federal tidal wave. Seconds before he died, Bee choked, "Rally behind the Virginians, men!"

As Federal bullets began to fly all about him, Jackson, now forever baptized by Bee as "Stonewall," raised his arms, face, and silent prayers to heaven, beseeching the blessing of God on his men and his cause, which he considered to be the defense of his Virginia homeland.

Then one bullet tore off part of Jackson's finger, another struck his horse, and, his face twisted in fury, he shouted, "Reserve your fire till they come within fifty yards, then fire and give them the bayonet; and, when you charge, yell like furies!"

And so was born the Rebel Yell.

Jackson's men indeed turned the day for the Confederacy at what Northerners would call the First Battle of Bull Run and Southerners the First Battle of Manassas. The Federal assault was blunted, stopped, and reversed, and the initiative passed to the Confederates.

There were many such days. In the spring 1862 Shenandoah Valley Campaign, he defeated three Federal armies, all larger than his own, in a half-dozen battles, and helped save Richmond from McClellan's powerful host. At Sharpsburg his outnumbered corps prevented a Federal rout. At Second Manassas, or Bull Run, his men again held off a vastly larger force and prepared the way for James Longstreet's crushing assault.

Camp at Manassas, Va.

He commanded the Confederate right during the devastating victory at Fredericksburg, and at Chancellorsville, he electrified the world with one of the most stunning large-scale ambushes in military history. Again commanding a force only a fraction the size of his foe, Stonewall stampeded the Federal Corps of fellow-devout-Christian

Oliver O. Howard for three miles, and vanquished Fightin' Joe Hooker's plans to annihilate the Army of Northern Virginia with his colossal 134,000-man army.

But the unsearchable hand of Providence again intervened. At the zenith of his success and worldwide fame, and at the very point of cutting off the Federal retreat across the United States Ford of the Rappahannock River and perhaps destroying the entire Army of the Potomac, he was mistakenly shot down by his own men. Jackson alone had perceived the apocalyptic opportunity of sealing off the Federal retreat. Renowned for his secrecy and discretion in military matters, he told only A. P. Hill of his plan. When both men fell from serious wounds, no one was able to communicate Jackson's plan.

Confederate General James Longstreet

Gen. Joseph Hooker of the Federal army

J. E. B. Stuart took over Jackson's command and consummated the smashing Confederate victory the next day. Smashing but not fatal. "On such agate points do the balances of the world turn," wrote Winston Churchill years later of this dramatic sequence of events—and their later consequences.

Jackson survived his bullet wounds; however, he died eight days later, probably from pneumonia brought on when stretcher-bearers carrying him from the field at Chancellorsville dropped him and he landed hard on a tree stump, evidently puncturing a lung.

When the long-triumphant Army of Northern Virginia next took the field two months later at Gettysburg, they suffered their first major defeat of the war. The mistakes they made in that campaign, especially during its climactic stages, read like a catalog of all the miscues that seemed not to occur when Jackson rode with the army.

The Confederacy would never again field an army capable of visiting destruction on the Federals of a magnitude that would win Southern independence. And Jackson, along with World War II General George Patton, would be the only American military commander whose tactics and strategy were studied in depth by the Red Army of the twentieth-century Soviet Empire.

Jackson would have held in contempt the notion that military fame is a praiseworthy enterprise. About the Mexican War he wrote Laura, "My friends dying around me and my brave soldiers breathing their last on the bloody fields of battle, deprived of every human comfort—even now I can hardly open my eyes after entering a hospital, the atmosphere of which is generally so corrupted as to make the healthy sick." And years later he

Ambulance crew removing wounded soldiers from the field. Jackson died from injuries sustained from being dropped from a stretcher, causing a lung to puncture.

told Anna that those clamoring for war did not know for what they asked. He had seen enough of it—in Mexico—to consider it "the sum of all evils."

Rather than employing his battlefield successes and fame for his own career advancement, social advantage, or carnal gain as did many of his peers in that and subsequent generations, Stonewall spent his discretionary time laboring to fuel great religious revival in the Confederate armies. Thus upon the South was bestowed a legacy singular in the world that endures to this day—"The Bible Belt."

Not everyone, even on his own side, celebrated Jackson. Often stern and rigid, he failed to work harmoniously with many high-ranking officers who were directly subordinate to him. He court-martialed more subordinates than any other general in the war.

Comparisons to the mighty English Puritan warrior Oliver Cromwell came frequently—in regard to both Jackson's ambition and his devout faith.

But despite his tenacity in battle, Jackson carried his Christianity with him there too. When he recaptured Winchester, Virginia, from the Federals in the spring of 1862, he found that the invaders had treated the town and its merchants roughly. He also found they had emptied out one of the town's main buildings to use as their own hospital.

Eyewitness accounts suggest an adjacent Federal depot may have held more medicine and medical supplies than could be found in the whole of the Confederate nation, which Abraham Lincoln had blockaded. Jackson told his men to make sure the hospital had sufficient food and water, then to leave it alone.

Stonewall Jackson's last days, in which he experienced acute physical suffering, were observed by a host of eyewitnesses, including family, physicians, clergy, and soldiers. They chronicled a number of remarkable comments

★ ★ ★ ★ ★ ★ ★ ★ ★ ★ ★ ★ ★ ★ ★ ★

Many Civil War generals stood so committed to observing the Sabbath that it influenced their military operations. Stonewall Jackson would fight only "more ordinary battles" on Sunday, and William Rosecrans refused to pursue a fleeing enemy force on a Sabbath day. Other generals attributed defeats to the fact they had violated the Sabbath by fighting on that day.

★ ★ ★ ★ ★ ★ ★ ★ ★ ★ ★ ★ ★ ★ ★ ★

by the famed general and devout Presbyterian deacon. He told renowned Presbyterian pastor Tucker Lacy:

You see me severely wounded, but not depressed; not unhappy. I believe that it has been done according to God's holy will, and I acquiesce entirely in it. You may think it strange; but you never saw me more perfectly contented than I am today; for I am sure that my Heavenly Father designs this affliction for my good. I am perfectly satisfied, that either in this life, or in that which is to come, I shall discover that what is now regarded as a calamity, is a blessing. And if it appears a great calamity (as it surely will be a great inconvenience, to be deprived of my arm), it will result in a great blessing. I can wait, until God, in his own time, shall make known to me the object he has in thus afflicting me. But why should I not rather rejoice in it as a blessing, and not look on it as a calamity at all? If it were in my power to replace my arm, I would not dare to do it, unless I could know it was the will of my Heavenly Father.

"I know you would gladly give your life for me, but I am perfectly resigned," he told his wife Anna. "Do not be sad. I hope I may yet recover. Pray for me, but always remember in your prayers to use the petition, 'Thy will be done.'"

In the presence of Lacy, Jackson's physician and staff officer Hunter McGuire, and others, he discussed his favorite topics of practical religion:

The Christian should carry his religion into everything. Christianity makes man better in any lawful calling; it equally makes the general a better commander, and the shoemaker a better mechanic. In the case of the cobbler, or the tailor, for instance, religion will produce more care in promising work, more punctuality, and more fidelity in executing it, from conscientious motives. So, prayer aids any man, in any lawful business, not only by bringing down the divine blessing, which is its direct and prime object, but by harmonizing his own mind and heart. In the commander of an army at the critical hour, it calmed his perplexities, moderated his anxieties, steadied the scales of judgment, and thus preserved him from exaggerated and rash conclusions.

Famed theologian Robert L. Dabney, who also served in key campaigns of the war as Jackson's military chief of staff, recalled: "Again, (Jackson) urged, that every act of man's life should be a religious act. He recited with much

★ ★ ★ ★ ★ ★ ★ ★

In his last letter to me he spoke of our precious Ellie, and of the blessedness of being with her in heaven. And now he has rejoined her, and together they unite in ascribing praises to Him who has redeemed them by His blood.

—Margaret Junkin Preston about her brother-in-law, Thomas Jackson

★ ★ ★ ★ ★ ★ ★ ★

pleasure, the ideas of Doddridge, where he pictured himself as spiritualizing every act of his daily life; as thinking when he washed himself, of the cleansing blood of Calvary; as praying while he put on his garments, that he might be clothed with the righteousness of the saints; as endeavoring, while he was eating, to feed upon the Bread of Heaven."

"Before this day closes, you will be with the blessed Saviour in His glory," Anna told him on his last day, May 10, 1863, as Robert E. Lee and nearly the entire Army of Northern Virginia prayed for him.

Jackson said, "I prefer it." The final words of his life, as he lay comatose, were: "Let us cross over the river and rest under the shade of the trees."

In the end, Stonewall Jackson's most lasting impact on the world will likely prove to be a spiritual rather than a martial one. His simple unvarnished piety and humility stand in stark contrast to the brutal take-no-prisoners vanity and machismo that mark so much of the contemporary military.

It was Dabney who penned perhaps the most appropriate epitaph for his erstwhile commander. He wrote how the "virtue of the Sacred Scriptures" produced the true greatness of Jackson:

May it not be concluded then, that this was God's chief lesson in this life and death! He would teach the beauty and power of true Christianity as an element of national life. Therefore He took an exemplar of Christian sincerity and formed and trained it in an honorable retirement. He set it in the furnace of trial at an hour when great events and dangers had awakened the popular heart to most intense action;

He illustrated it with that species of distinction which, above all others, fires the popular enthusiasm, military glory; and held it up to the admiring inspection of a country grateful for the deliverances it had wrought.

Thus God teaches how good, how strong a thing, His fear is. He makes all men see and acknowledge, that in this man Christianity was the source of those virtues which they so rapturously applauded; that it was the fear of God which made him so fearless of all else; that it was the love of God which animated his energies; that the lofty chivalry of his nature was but the reflex of the spirit of Christ.

Even the profane admit, in their hearts, this explanation of (Jackson's) power, and are prompt to declare that it was his religion which made him what he was. His life is God's lesson, teaching that "it is righteousness that exalteth a nation."

John J. Dwyer

His life is God's lesson, teaching that
"it is righteousness that exalteth a nation."
—Robert L. Dabney, writing about Jackson

Drawing of General Jackson praying, author unknown

A MAN OF PRAYER:
STONEWALL JACKSON

★ ★ ★ ★ ★ ★ ★ ★ ★

Stonewall Jackson was a man of prayer. It was jokingly said of him that he was always praying when not fighting, but in reality, he often prayed while he was fighting as well. Jackson prayed each morning and every night, before each decision and every fight. He prayed more for his men's conversions than for their victories. He prayed that they would be an army of the living God and of their country.

Before the war, when he was a professor at Virginia Military Institute in Lexington, Virginia, Jackson really began to grow as a Christian. With a strong sense of duty and almost military obedience, he looked up to his pastor, Rev. Dr. William White, as a kind of spiritual superior officer. He regularly reported his religious views and actions to the minister. One Sunday Dr. White encouraged the congregation to regularly attend prayer meeting and stated that church officers and even the regular members should lead in prayer. Jackson took this as an order to be obeyed, and he came to discuss with Dr. White if he should lead in prayers. This was something he was unaccustomed to do and didn't really know how, but Jackson told Dr. White, "You are my pastor, and the spiritual guide of the church; and if you think it my duty, then I shall waive my reluctance and make the effort to lead in prayer, however painful it may be." The next prayer meeting Dr. White called on Jackson to pray, and he was so frightened and obviously ill at ease that the whole congregation was embarrassed for him. Dr. White didn't call on him again. After a time, Jackson again visited his pastor and asked him if he had refrained from calling on him to pray because he had been so uncomfortable when first asked. When White admitted that was the case, Jackson replied, "My comfort or discomfort is not the question; if it is my duty to lead my brethren in prayer, then I must persevere in it, until I learn to do it aright; and I wish you to discard all consideration for my feelings in the matter."[2] So, Dr. White continued to call on Jackson to lead in public prayer, and gradually it was no longer an ordeal for him.

Though public prayer was at first difficult for Jackson, private prayer had become a way of life with him. Once a friend asked him how he understood the Bible's command to "pray without ceasing." Jackson said that the habit of prayer had become like breathing with him: "I have so fixed the habit in my own mind that I never raise a glass of water to my lips without lifting my heart to God in thanks and prayer for the water of life. Then, when we take our meals, there is grace. Whenever I drop a letter in the post-office, I send a petition along with it for God's blessing upon its mission and the person to whom it is sent. When I break the seal of a letter just received, I stop to ask God to prepare me for its contents, and make it a messenger of good. When I go to my class-room and await the arrangement of the cadets in their places, that is my time to interceded with God for them. And so in every act of the day I have made the practice [of prayer] habitual."[3]

After Lincoln's election and the resulting swelling tide of secessionist feeling in the South, Jackson approached Dr. White about trying to unite the Christian people of the nation in a prayer for peace: "Do you not think that all the Christian people of the land could be induced to unite in a concert of prayer, to avert such an evil? It seems to be, that if they would unite thus in prayer, war might be prevented, and peace preserved."[4]

Dr. White carried on a correspondence with Northern Christians to try to arrange this, and a date of January 4, 1861, was set for prayer. Jackson felt that prayer was all the Christian could do to avert war. The final outcome for peace or war was in God's hands.

When war did come and Jackson became an officer in the Confederate army, his disciplined habits seemed eccentric to some, and some men even thought he was crazy. In 1861, when Rev. Dr. William Brown was visiting the army around Centreville, a friend told him that "'Old Jack' is crazy. I can account for his conduct in no other way. Why, I frequently meet him out in the woods walking back and forth muttering to himself incoherent sentences and gesticulating wildly, and at such times he seems utterly oblivious of my presence and of everything else."

That evening, when Jackson and Dr. Brown were having a long conversation on how to promote a Christian spirit among the soldiers, Jackson said: "I find that it greatly helps me in fixing my mind and quickening my devotions to give utterance to my prayers, and hence I am in the habit of going off into the woods, where I can be alone and speak audibly to myself the prayers I would pour out to my God. I was at first annoyed that I was compelled to keep my eyes open to avoid running against the trees and stumps; but upon investigating the matter I do not find that the Scriptures require us to close our eyes in prayer, and the exercise has proven to me very delightful and profitable."[5]

From this conversation the Reverend Brown learned the truth behind the conduct his friend had used to cite Jackson was "crazy."

At the beginning of Jackson's campaign in the Shenandoah Valley, General Ewell also thought Jackson was crazy; by the end of the campaign, however, he thought he was inspired. Jackson's prayer life eventually led to Ewell's conversion. One night at a council of war,

Jackson listened to the views of the officers, then said he would announce his plan in the morning. As they were leaving, General A. P. Hill joked to Ewell, "Well, I suppose Jackson wants to pray over it." Ewell soon realized he forgot his sword and had to return to Jackson's tent. There he found Jackson on his knees praying to God for guidance in the military movements. Ewell was so deeply impressed by Jackson's religious faith and example that he said, "If that is religion, I must have it."[6]

During his stay at Winchester, Jackson became friends with Rev. James Graham, the Presbyterian pastor. Rev. Graham found Jackson the most sincere Christian he had ever known: "He was simply an humble, earnest, devout, consecrated Christian man. Whatever was remarkable about his religion was due to its absolute possession of him—its thorough power over him. He was a man of God first, last, and always. He feared God and tried to serve Him. He loved his Saviour and tried to glorify Him."[7]

Before Rev. Graham had come to know Jackson well, he was moved by his prayer. November 15, 1861, was appointed a day of fasting and prayer by the Confederacy, and a special service was held at the Presbyterian church. General Jackson had quietly entered during the singing of the first hymn, and at the conclusion of the hymn, Graham asked Jackson to lead the congregation in prayer. Though Jackson was surprised and somewhat embarrassed by the request, he rose and led the congregation to the throne of grace:

> Beginning with words of adoring reverence, which immediately impressed and subdued every heart, he asked to be heard for the sake of our divine redeemer; and then,

★ ★ ★ ★ ★ ★ ★ ★

In the whole course of his prayer he did not forget for one moment that he was one of a company of sinners deserving nothing of God, yet pleading with Him, for Christ's sake, to be merciful to us and bless us.

—Rev. James Graham

★ ★ ★ ★ ★ ★ ★ ★

as if pouring out his soul before God, in the most simple manner, yet with deep fervor, he made confession of our utter unworthiness as sinners and of our absolute dependence on divine mercy. In words borrowed from Scripture, and uttered in most earnest tones, he besought God to bless our afflicted country and give success to our arms. In the whole course of his prayer he did not forget for one moment that he was one of a company of sinners deserving nothing of God, yet pleading with Him, for Christ's sake, to be merciful to us and bless us. Not a single word did he utter inconsistent with the command to love our enemies. Not once did he venture to tell God what He ought to do in that great crisis in our country. But while he did importunately ask that our arms might be crowned with victory and our country obtain its independence, he was careful to ask it in humble deference to divine wisdom, and only if it would be for God's glory and our good.[8]

Rev. Graham always remembered that prayer because it had such an effect on the entire community. By his very example, Jackson seemed to teach the people of Winchester how to pray.

Since Jackson's military plans were made with prayer, to him any victories won were clearly from the Lord. Repeatedly in his military reports he acknowledged God as the true source of victory and encouraged the soldiers to return thanks to Him for victories won. On May 12, 1862, after the victory at McDowell and the retreat of Milroy and Fremont to Banks, Jackson issued the following congratulations to the army:

> Soldiers of the Army of the Valley and the North West:
> I congratulate you on your victory at McDowell:
> I request you to unite with me, this morning, in thanks-

giving to Almighty God, for thus having crowned your arms with success, and in prayer that He will continue to lead you on from victory to victory, until our independence shall be established, and make you that people whose God is the Lord. The Chaplains will hold Divine service at two o'clock, A.M., this day, in their respective Regiments.[9]

As Jackson rode through the camps seeing that services were under way, he saw a captain along the road smoking a pipe. Jackson asked him if divine service was going on in his camp, and the captain stammered that he didn't know. Jackson asked where the colonel's headquarters were, and the captain offered to take him there. As they approached, Jackson could see services going on and told his guide, "Captain, the next time I order divine service to be held, won't you promise me to attend?" Jackson then removed his hat and went to the services. Though it began to rain, the captain watched Jackson continue in prayer for some time.

Frequently in his letters and correspondence Jackson asked for prayers or expressed the importance of prayer for the success of Southern independence. Typical is the following, written to his sister: "Do not forget to remember me in prayer. To the prayers of God's people I look with more interest than to our military strength. In answer to them God has greatly blessed us thus far, and we may sanguinely expect Him to continue to do so, if we and all His people but continue to do our duty."[10] These were not empty words to Jackson but expressed his deep conviction of the importance of prayer and trust in God for the great national struggle.

After his command rejoined the Army of Northern Virginia and was stationed for a time at Gordonsville, Virginia, Jackson enjoyed family worship in Rev. Ewing's household, where he was sometimes asked to lead in prayer. Rev. Ewing later wrote: "There was something

very striking in his prayers. He did not pray to men, but to God. His tones were deep, solemn, tremulous. He seemed to realize that he was speaking to Heaven's King. I never heard any one pray who seemed to be pervaded more fully by a spirit of self-abnegation. He seemed to feel more than any man I ever knew the danger of robbing God of the glory due for our success."[11]

Even though participating in a battle to establish an earthly nation, Jackson's eyes and heart were ever on eternity and God's glorious throne.

In the winter of 1862–63, as the Army of Northern Virginia camped near Fredericksburg, Jackson worked not only to strengthen his corps for the spring and summer campaign, but also to improve the spiritual condition of his soldiers. His strongest desire was to lead a "converted" army. He was often in prayer for God's direction and guidance and always completely trusted the outcome to be from the Lord. One of his favorite sayings was, "Duty is ours; consequences are God's."

Shortly before the battle of Fredericksburg, a chaplain came across an officer lying in the rear of a battery wrapped in an overcoat, quietly reading his Bible. The chaplain entered into a conversation with the officer about the prospects of the upcoming battle, but the officer soon turned the conversation to spiritual matters. The chaplain then thought he was speaking with a fellow chaplain, and asked what regiment he was from. How surprised he was to find out that the Bible reader and man most interested in spiritual conversation was General Jackson.

On the opening of the campaign of Chancellorsville, which was to be Jackson's last, before he ordered his tent struck, Jackson dismounted his horse and went into his tent for a private time of prayer. The men outside were bustling around preparing to leave when Jim, Jackson's servant, raised his hand in warning and with a loud whisper said, "Hush! . . . The general is praying." Silence immediately came to the camp until the praying soldier came out of his tent. The day had been clothed in prayer, and whether it brought victory or death, Jackson had placed all in the Lord's hands.

Steve Wilkins and Diana L. Severance

JACKSON'S MISSION FIELD

★ ★ ★ ★ ★ ★ ★ ★ ★

Jackson was ever devoted to the spread of the gospel, and this concern extended to the slaves as much as to the freemen of his community. Although he did not oppose slavery (he simply assumed there was some purpose in God's providence for slavery), he did recognize slaves as human beings who should be treated with decency and respect. His own family servants included the cook, Amy; Hetty, Anna's maid and nurse since she was an infant; Hetty's two boys, Cyrus and George; and Anna, another housemaid. Cyrus and George were full of mischief, but Jackson exercised a firm hand, taught the boys to read, and made certain they received a religious education. Morning and evening Jackson included the servants in the family devotions. During the war, when Jackson's servants were hired out to others, Jackson wrote the masters to make certain the servants were cared for properly and were faithful in their church attendance.

Jackson's burden for the spiritual welfare of the slaves even prompted him to start a Sunday school class for the children and young people of his community. This was not an entirely new thing. Rev. Dr. William White of Lexington's Presbyterian church, where Jackson was a deacon, had himself taught slaves the tenets of Christianity, and in 1845, the Lexington church had actually started a class for blacks. These efforts gradually ended primarily because the numbers had dwindled. More were turning to the Baptists and Methodists, whose services were more boisterous than the Presbyterians'. Jackson studied the earlier failure of the Sunday school class and believed he saw how to set up a successful program.

Hand-tinted ambrotype, made in the 1850s. This portrait of a black housemaid and her charge illustrates the value the family placed on her, similar to Jackson's fondness for his slaves.

The new class began in the autumn of 1855 in the church building of Lexington Presbyterian. Characteristically, Jackson threw himself wholeheartedly into the work. His burden for the slave children was plain and obvious to all. One of his student assistants noted,

"Their neglected condition excited his sympathy, and a sense of duty impelled him to make an effort to redeem them from the slavery of sin."

Jackson's efforts bore more fruit than even he had anticipated. Soon, more than one hundred students were enrolled in the black Sunday school class, except during the summers when Major Jackson was absent on his vacations. Jackson enlisted twelve students to assist him, and each Lord's Day afternoon the church bell rang for the faithful to gather. Jackson established strict rules for the school, and punctuality was one of them. When at first people wandered in throughout the session, Jackson announced school would begin promptly at 3:00 p.m. He rang the bell a quarter of an hour before school, then closed and locked the doors promptly at 3:00 p.m. When he opened the doors at the conclusion of the school, a number of servants and even teachers were waiting on the streets. They were never late again.

The meeting followed a strictly prescribed order, never varying. As soon as the door was closed, Major Jackson said, "Let us pray." One of the student assistants noted that "his prayer was striking for its beautiful simplicity. It was the petition of one conscious of his own weakness and praying for strength. There was the true contrition of heart, accompanied by a faith which took a sure hold on the promises."

After concluding the prayer, Jackson led the class in "Amazing Grace." Though totally tone deaf, he had learned the tune well enough for the students to learn it from him and sing it with enthusiasm. Bible readings followed, with Jackson's simple explanations. Next came a prayer, usually offered by Jackson; then the assembly broke into small groups for catechism. On the first Sunday of each month, New Testaments and Bibles were awarded to those who had shown outstanding progress.

The class concluded promptly at 3:45 with the singing of "Amazing Grace" one final time.

Jackson's concern for the well-being of the slaves was deep and sincere. He took the trouble to learn all their names and addressed them by their names in class and out. They in turn affectionately called him "Marse Major." He always treated them with the respect they were due as human beings. One of Jackson's friends noted that "it was pleasant to walk about the town and see the veneration with which the Negroes saluted him, and his unfailing courtesy towards them." Monthly Jackson called on the plantation owners to give a report on their children's progress. He also visited the children's homes; if the children misbehaved, he talked the situation over with the parents.

After the slaves were freed, many were forced to stay and work cotton on their former master's plantation because of limited opportunities.

Richmond, Va. First African Church

When Anna Morrison married Jackson and moved to Lexington, she planned to work in the Sunday school for white children, but Jackson encouraged her to work with the Negro Sunday school. It was his mission field—to him the Negro children were human beings with souls to be saved, and he rejoiced to see the youngsters become Christians. Watching her husband among the young people, Anna realized that "never did his face beam with more intelligence and earnestness than when he was telling the colored children of his Sabbath-school the story of the cross."[12]

Jackson taught the class until he left for the war in 1861. (He remarked that one of the greatest privations the war brought to him was that it took him away from his work in the colored Sunday school.) Even during the war, Jackson's thoughts were often with the class. Whenever anyone came to camp from Lexington, Jackson's first question was often about the Sunday school.

Shortly after the Battle of First Manassas a letter came from Jackson to Dr. White. The Lexington community was eager for details of the Southern victory and was sure the letter would give them the latest news of the battle.

Dr. White opened the letter and read: "My dear pastor, in my tent last night, after a fatiguing day's service, I remembered that I had failed to send you my contribution for our colored Sunday school. Enclosed you will find my check for that object. T. J. Jackson."[13] There was not one word of the great victory just won, only Jackson's concern for his Sunday school.

Jackson's efforts on behalf of the Negro Sunday school bore fruit for many years after the war. The class continued until the late 1880s. No less than three black churches were started by the graduates of Jackson's Sunday school class, and one of these churches still stands in Roanoke, Virginia. On one wall is a stained glass window in honor of Jackson—showing him kneeling in prayer.

⋆ *Steve Wilkins and Diana L. Severance*

Duty, in a way, was indivisible. When Deacon Jackson made his contribution to his Negro Sunday school, he was doing part of his Christian work, just as he was doing another part in war. Duty was living for God. And living for God might require various things—praying, giving, fighting, and very possibly dying.

Part of duty, too, lay in subordination to authority—ecclesiastical, civil, or military. Subordination at times might be hard, but it came easier as it was recognized as God's way of working for the good of a Christian. Obedience tempered ambition, and in turn, the tempering of ambition made obedience less difficult.

—Frank Vandiver, author of Mighty Stonewall

"Nothing but a Poor Sinner"

Robert E. Lee

★★★★★★★★★★★★★★★★★★★

Actor Robert Duvall as
General Robert E. Lee

Lee . . . loved and believed in the union. In the end, he loved Virginia more. He felt that by invading Virginia, by invading part of your own country, you were in effect dissolving the union yourself. He felt that secession was one thing, but it was a point of fact that the union had been dissolved by the actions of the president. . . . I think that there are some histories that probably get to your heart far more than others. Certainly, the Civil War is such a passionate . . . complicated and deeply felt part of our history. —actor Stephen Lang

"AN EPISTLE, WRITTEN OF GOD"

★ ★ ★ ★ ★ ★ ★ ★

Robert Edward Lee (1807–70) learned responsibility early. By the time he was seven years old, bad business dealings had disgraced his father, the famed "Light Horse Harry" Lee, who had long ago left his home and family, then died. Disaster beset the Lee financial fortunes, the family had to sell their home place, and young Robert was left to tend his devout but very ill mother.

Kind, sensitive, and dutiful from the beginning, he began to work to make something of himself and restore the honor of the Lee family name. Later, with the family fortune blasted, pressure weighed upon him to provide even the most basic living for himself and those for whom he would be provider.

MILITARY MAN

Lee received an appointment to the United States Military Academy at West Point, where he excelled. He finished second in his class, and to this day is the only cadet ever to complete the school's four-year program without receiving a demerit.

His West Point accomplishments gained him a choice assignment in the army's elite engineer corps. For more than fifteen years, he set about construction and preservation tasks great and small, such as saving the city of St. Louis from the encroachments of the Mississippi River.

His accomplishments landed him a staff position with American commander in chief Winfield Scott when the Mexican War came. Like Lincoln, U. S. Grant, and many others, Lee lamented that controversial conflict because of its dubious, expansionist objectives. Still, he performed a series of reconnaissance missions on horseback that resulted in a string of American flanking maneuvers and defeats of larger Mexican forces.

Lee's legendary nighttime solo rides back and forth through the volcanic field of the Pedregal in a howling storm, which other crack soldiers had failed to accomplish, death looming every foot of the way, gained him so exalted a status that Scott called him "the greatest soldier in the American army."

After the war, Lee remained with the army. He gained high marks for his leadership and innovation as West Point superintendent for three years in the early 1850s. Then he commanded the prestigious 2nd U.S. Cavalry in Texas. In 1859, it was Lee whom President James Buchanan called upon to defeat the looming rebellion led by a man named John Brown.

Lee succeeded famously in that endeavor.

FAMILY MAN

Though he spent many years of his military career prior to the War Between the States in lonely isolation from his family, Lee and his wife, Mary, had seven children. For extended periods of time, when he served at remote army posts, his family remained at the beautiful Arlington plantation, across the Potomac River from Washington City, that Mary had inherited from her family. Lee visited them as often as he could.

Throughout his many separations from his family, Lee penned a steady stream of letters. They offered not only counsel and instruction but also love. "I long to see you through the dilatory nights," he wrote his fourteen-year-old daughter Annie from his lonely Texas post. "At dawn when I rise, and all day, my thoughts revert to you in expressions that you cannot hear or I repeat. I hope you will always appear to me as you are now painted on my heart, and that you will endeavour to improve and so conduct yourself as to make you happy and me joyful all our lives. Diligent and earnest attention to *all* your duties can only accomplish this."

Lee has received criticism, probably with some justification, for continuing in a career that long separated him from his family. However, he viewed his responsibility to provide for them as paramount in importance. All his training and qualifications were for the military, whereas he believed himself ill-equipped to run a large plantation such as Arlington.

Withal, his influence on his own children proved profound. Letters he wrote to his family following Annie's death in 1862 amidst the storms of war illustrate both his tenderness toward them and the Christian faith that guided his convictions and his leadership of them. "In the quiet hours of the night, when there is nothing to lighten the full weight of my grief, I feel as if I should be overwhelmed," he wrote daughter Mary Custis. But he reminded her that "the Lord gave and the Lord has taken away: blessed be the name of the Lord."

He wrote wife Mary, "I cannot express the anguish I feel at the death of our sweet Annie. To know that I shall never see her again on earth, that her place in our circle, which I always hoped one day to enjoy, is forever vacant, is agonizing in the extreme. But God in this, as in all things, has mingled mercy with the blow, in selecting that one best prepared to leave us. May you be able to join me in saying 'His will be done!'"

He again wrote Mary in 1863 following the death of their daughter-in-law and her infant children:

It has pleased God to take from us one exceedingly dear to us, and we must be resigned to His holy will. She, I trust, will enjoy peace and happiness forever, while we must patiently struggle on under all the ills that may be in store for us. What a glorious thought it is that she has joined her little cherubs and our angel Annie in Heaven. Thus is link by link the strong chain broken that binds us to earth, and our passage soothed to another world. Oh, that we may be at last united in that heaven of rest, where trouble and sorrow never enter, to join in an everlasting chorus of praise and glory to our Lord and Saviour! I grieve for our lost darling as a father only can grieve for a daughter, and my sorrow is heightened by the thought of the anguish her death will cause our dear son and the poignancy it will give to the bars of his prison. May God in His mercy enable him to bear the blow He has so suddenly dealt, and sanctify it to his everlasting happiness!

Lee's children loved him intensely and held him in the highest regard. His youngest daughter, Mildred, cried out to her mother after he died, "To me he seems a hero—and all other men small in comparison."

Apparently her sentiments never changed because neither she nor any of her three sisters ever married.

The residence of General Robert E. Lee in Richmond, Va.

LOYAL VIRGINIAN

In April 1861, Northern hopes must have been high when President Lincoln authorized still Commander in Chief Scott to offer his fellow Virginian, Lee, command of all Federal armies in the field against the Confederacy after war broke out.

Lee's loyalty to the United States ran deep. His father had been governor of Virginia, and before that, one of Washington's cavalry chiefs in the American War of Independence. Other relatives, such as Henry Lee, also had played leading roles in the formation of the United States. Lee's wife Mary's great-grandmother was Martha Custis Washington, wife of George Washington.

Also Lee supported neither the institution of slavery, which he considered a moral crime against the black race and a greater one against the white, nor, initially, the idea of Southern secession.

Nonetheless, after an evening spent on his knees in prayer, reading his Bible and pacing the floor of his room, Lee declined the offer and resigned from the army.

Ending a thirty-two-year career and knowing his beloved Arlington estate must soon be overrun by the Federals, whose capital lay just across the Potomac River from it, Lee wrote his Unionist sister: "With all my devotion to the Union, and the feeling of loyalty and duty of an American citizen, I have not been able to make up my mind to raise my hand against my relatives, my children, my home."

Two days later he accepted a rather less spectacular command—the armed forces of a single state, his native Virginia, against that Federal army of Lincoln's.

Even after Federal generals such as John Pope and Benjamin Butler had savaged the Southern homeland and civilian population, when Robert E. Lee took the Army of Northern Virginia north on the Gettysburg campaign midway through the war, he issued his famous General Order No. 73 to all his soldiers:

> It must be remembered that we make war only upon armed men, and that we cannot take vengeance for the wrongs our people have suffered without lowering ourselves in the eyes of all whose abhorrence has been excited by the atrocities of our enemies, and offending against Him to whom vengeance belongeth, without whose favor and support our efforts must all prove in vain.

> The commanding general therefore earnestly exhorts the troops to abstain with most scrupulous care from unnecessary or wanton injury to private property, and he enjoins upon all officers to arrest and bring to summary punishment all who shall in any way offend against the orders on this subject.

Indeed, during the campaign at least six Confederate soldiers were executed by firing squads for vandalism, one of them for taking fence railing to kindle a fire.

SPIRITUAL REVIVAL IN LEE'S ARMY

The sweeping religious revivals in the Confederate armies, particularly Lee's Army of Northern Virginia, comprise one of the great overlooked chapters of the war, and one of the preeminent spiritual awakenings in American history.

Historically, the rough surroundings of wartime military camp life prove spawning grounds for every conceivable vice man can imagine. But Lee's devout leadership spurred contrary developments in his army. He facilitated an atmosphere where Christian belief and practice flourished. What did that spiritual movement look like?

Well, a frightened sixteen-year-old Confederate army volunteer entering the camp of his unit in Lee's army would have found a very different scene from what he expected.

Many of the card decks he saw were tossed aside by repentant soldiers marching the trail to war—and were often replaced by prayer books, pocket testaments, or catechisms.

Not only was the imbibing of alcoholic spirits frowned upon by many in the army, but when stores of enemy liquor were captured, they were poured out onto the ground or burned—and that by order of the boy's own commanding officers.

Unlike most any other army of the day, women of ill repute were not welcome in the van that followed the army, and if it became known that a soldier of the South, ranker or officer, was being unfaithful to a wife or causing a wife's unfaithfulness with his own actions, he risked cashiering.

The boy would learn, to his surprise, that aside from himself and his fellow greenhorn volunteers, gambling and profanity were uncommon in this fearsome army.

★ ★ ★ ★ ★ ★ ★ ★ ★ ★ ★ ★ ★ ★ ★

A "Great Revival" occurred among Robert E. Lee's forces in the fall of 1863 and winter of 1864. Some tens of thousands of soldiers were converted. Revivals also swept the Union army at that time. Sometimes preaching and praying continued twenty-four hours a day, and chapels couldn't hold the soldiers who wanted to get inside.

★ ★ ★ ★ ★ ★ ★ ★ ★ ★ ★ ★ ★ ★ ★

Soon, he might be one of those whose captain professed belief in Christ after one of the camp's soul-searching sermons, then called his company together, told them they had followed him into many hard-fought battles, as well as into sin, and that he now wished them to follow him into the blessed service into which he had just enlisted.

He might see a log chapel to his left built by a Mississippi regiment for its own worship activities, men streaming in and out of it seven days a week, twenty-four hours a day. In that chapel, he learned that those Mississippians, half-starved already, had emerged from a time of extended prayer with the decision to give the entire rations allotted to them every tenth day to the hungry civilians of Richmond, a city most of them had never seen.

Up ahead, on a hillside to his right, the boy might hear the chorus of more than two thousand manly voices echoing off the surrounding hills as they sang General Lee's favorite hymn, "How Firm a Foundation," in an open-air amphitheater built by a Virginia brigade:

How firm a foundation, ye saints of the Lord,
Is laid for your faith in His excellent Word!
What more can He say than to you He hath said,
To you who for refuge to Jesus have fled?
The soul that on Jesus hath leaned for repose
I will not, I will not desert to His foes;
That soul, though all hell should endeavor to shake,
I'll never, no, never, no never forsake!

Through the months the young man would witness the sermons and teaching of the greatest preachers in the South—Presbyterians like Robert L. Dabney, Beverly Tucker Lacy, James Henley Thornwell, Moses Drury Hoge, and Benjamin Palmer; Baptists like John Broadus, Robert Ryland, W. F. Broaddus, and J. William Jones; and Episcopalians like Brigadier General William Nelson Pendleton.

Their common message despite denominational distinctives: the proclamation of Christ, and Him crucified.

And the once-frightened teenager, callow and acne-faced, would likely join the large proportion of that company professing their own conversion in the next months, following their captain as he followed Christ, especially after the boy was handed a gospel tract one afternoon while slipping through the muddy camp, perhaps by none other than Stonewall Jackson himself.

If the boy later doubted the wisdom of his new path, he might be confirmed in it upon overhearing a chaplain tell Robert E. Lee of the many fervent prayers offered on his behalf and hear Lee respond in a choked voice, "Please thank them for that, sir. And I can only say that I am nothing but a poor sinner trusting in Christ alone for my salvation, and need all of the prayers they can offer for me."

Perhaps only Oliver Cromwell and his Puritan army of "Roundheads" in the seventeenth-century English Civil War against King Charles I even approached the degree of orthodox devoutness of Lee's army.

A sampling of the abundant contemporaneous accounts of the historic spiritual movement reveal its impact during and after the war. From 1861–65, Lee and the Southern armies accomplished a cavalcade of legendary deeds (First Manassas, the Seven Days, Second Manassas, Fredericksburg, Chancellorsville, Spotsylvania, the Wilderness, and Cold Harbor, among many others) while outmatched to the extremity in nearly every way. Whilst doing so, they exhibited, from the most senior commanders to the commonest foot soldiers, in a conspicuous and consistent manner, many of the primary attributes of Christian manhood.

They exhibited them as well in what they did not do as in what they did. Despite suffering at the hands of the Federals the most brutal prosecution of total war given high government sanction by a Christian country in at least 250 years, never did the Confederate States' military or governmental high command approve like behavior. The instances where it occurred were isolated and/or unsanctioned.

Tens of thousands of Southern soldiers drew strength and consolation from their faith to endure the many horrors of war while Southern fortunes prospered, and they did so all the more after events turned against the South.

The benefits of the Great Revival in the Southern armies continued after the war as thousands of Southern soldiers emulated the example of Lee, John Gordon, and others, and applied their energies and talents productively to provide for their dependents and rebuild their land. Though some former Confederate soldiers resorted to unlawful and even violent behavior following the war, no doubt many more would have done so without the profound influence that Lee and the Christian faith had had on them.

General Lee with his soldiers.

PEACEMAKER

Ironically, Robert E. Lee's greatest legacy is perhaps as a peacemaker rather than a warrior. Following the war, the South lay in rubble, its manhood decimated, a harsh Federal troop occupation further crushing it, and financial opportunists descending upon it from across the United States.

If Abraham Lincoln alone held the power to end or continue North-South hostilities before and after the war commenced, not even he possessed that power once it ended. Only Lee did. Many Northerners desired the utter destruction of the South as a recognizable culture. Bitterness and hatred filled most former Confederates. Lee recognized that the issue was nothing less than the survival of the Southern people and their civilization.

But wisdom seasoned his thoughts and actions. He rebuked younger officers who advocated continuing the war with guerilla tactics; he refused to countenance or support large scale emigration of Confederates to foreign lands; he urged Southerners to work lawfully and cheerfully within the existing laws of the United States to rebuild their fortunes and their land; and most of all, he beseeched them to forgive and forget wrongs committed against them by Federals past and present.

He counseled one of his many lovely, but bitter, young female admirers in this way: "I want you to take a message to your friends. Tell them from me that it is unworthy of them as women, and especially as Christian women, to cherish feelings of resentment against the North. Tell them that it grieves me inexpressibly to know that such a state of things exists, and that I implore them to do their part to heal our country's wounds."

All the while, offers and opportunities cascaded in

from around the South, across the United States, and even other nations. Railroads, insurance companies, and corporations of every stripe offered Lee positions of leadership. One wealthy Englishman offered him a sprawling estate in the land of his forefathers, for life, at no cost. Leaders of the Democratic Party, most of them former Federal military officers, campaigned him to accept their party's nomination for president and oppose Republican nominee U. S. Grant—in fact, some of the North's most powerful newspapers cheered him on in print!

But as he often did, despite his simple dignity and guileless ways, he surprised nearly everyone. He took the helm of tiny, war-ransacked Washington College in the backwater Virginia mountain village of Lexington, where Stonewall Jackson spent the decade before the war.

With no assistant, scant budget, and beset by the burgeoning health problems of his aging body, Lee set about rebuilding the school, placing special emphasis on what curricula would best prepare the young men of the South to rebuild their land.

Yet many times, in many ways, he voiced his primary concern. Rev. Dr. Thomas J. Kirkpatrick, professor of moral philosophy at Washington College, recalled Lee's words: "Oh, Doctor! if I could only know that all the young men in this college were good Christians, I should have nothing more to desire!"

Time and again he counseled forbearance and forgiveness on the part of his students, friends, family, and people across the South toward mercenary Northern carpetbaggers, self-serving Southern scalawags, black freedmen, occupying Federal occupation forces, and the Radical Republicans' corrupt, crushing "Reconstruction" in general.

★ ★ ★ ★ ★ ★ ★ ★ ★ ★

Oh, Doctor! if I could only know that all the young men in this college were good Christians, I should have nothing more to desire!

—Robert E. Lee

★ ★ ★ ★ ★ ★ ★ ★ ★ ★

"The gentleman does not needlessly and unnecessarily remind an offender of a wrong he may have committed against him," he wrote. "He can not only forgive, he can forget; and he strives for that nobleness of self and mildness of character which imparts sufficient strength to let the past be but the past. A true man of honor feels humbled himself when he cannot help humbling others."

No one ever tabulated how many thousands of letters Lee received—and answered—from Southerners seeking his counsel on what to do.

"My whole trust is in God, and I am ready for whatever He may ordain," he said.

Lee was not without opposition, even until he died. Many of the radical Republican leaders wanted him hanged for treason. An austere congressional committee grilled him more than once in Washington, seeking evidence with which to prosecute him. They failed at every turn, as the constitutional course of Lee's actions became obvious even to those who despised both him and the Constitution.

Abolitionist leader and *Liberator* publisher William Lloyd Garrison decried Lee's place at the head of a college: "Who is . . . more obdurate than himself? He at the head of a patriotic institution, teaching loyalty to the Constitution, and the duty of maintaining that Union he so lately attempted to destroy! Has Lucifer regained his position in Heaven? . . . If the South could reasonably hope to succeed in another rebellious uprising, and should make the attempt, who can show us any ground for believing that Gen. Lee would not again act as generalissimo of her forces?"

But as Lee's peaceable, forbearing example became manifest, as well as the fruits of his leadership at resurgent Washington College, his legion of admirers grew, even in the North.

GODLY EXAMPLE

Accounts of Lee's charity and kindness after the war are legion. Two months after Appomattox, a black man boldly strode forward to take communion with the white members of St. Paul's Church in Richmond. Always before, the black parishioners took communion after the whites. The entire assembly sat in stunned silence. Then Lee stood from his pew, walked alone to the communion rail, and knelt—within feet of the black man.

This photograph of St. John's Church in Richmond, Va. shows an African American man and little girl with white children. White churches were slow to welcome blacks.

A singular demonstration for its place and time of the Christian principle of "neither Jew nor Greek . . . bond or free . . . neither male nor female," Lee's action led the rest of the congregation to move forward and receive their own communion with their black brother.

At another time, years after the war, Pastor J. William Jones, Lee's wartime chaplain, saw Lee give money to a stranger in Lexington. When he asked who it was, Lee said, "One of our old soldiers." Jones then asked which Confederate command the man served under, and Lee replied, "Oh, he was one of those who fought against us. But we are all one now, and must make no difference in our treatment of them."

Lee established a ritual in Lexington wherein every year at Christmastime he would ride through the town, handing down presents from a large bag to the often-impoverished children.

The night before his fatal stroke in September 1870, Lee and the vestry of his church realized they were far short of meeting the paltry salary required for Rector William Pendleton to continue in his position. When all looked hopeless, Lee, already donating much of his own meager subsistence to the church, announced, "I will give that sum."

By the time of his death, most Southerners had followed Lee's example—remaining in their homeland, pursuing peaceable ways, and putting their hand to the plow of rebuilding their country.

"I have never so truly felt the purity of his character as now, when I have nothing left me but its memory," the person who knew him better than anyone else, his wife, Mary, wrote a close friend. "God knows the best time for us to leave this world, and we must never question either His love or wisdom. This is my comfort in my great sorrow, to know that had my husband lived a thousand years he could not have died more honored and lamented even had he accomplished all we desired and hoped."

"He is an epistle, written of God," Edward Gordon, Lee's former assistant at Washington College, wrote, "and designed by God to teach the people of this country that earthly success is not the criterion of merit, nor the measure of true greatness."

After all the suffering, all the disappointment, all the loss and death and heartbreak, the following words, spoken by Lee near the end of his life, should offer great encouragement to moderns who believe the world is spiraling downward from now until some supposed cataclysmic destruction: "The march of Providence is so slow and our desires so impatient; the work of progress so immense and our means of aiding it so feeble; the life of humanity is so long, that of the individual so brief, that we often see only the ebb of the advancing wave and are thus discouraged. Just as the dominant party cannot reign forever, and truth and justice will at last prevail, in a larger way—it is history that teaches us to hope."

⭐ *John J. Dwyer*

LEE: Mr. President and Gentlemen of the Convention: Profoundly impressed with the solemnity of the occasion, for which I must say I was not prepared, I accept the position assigned me by your partiality. I would have much preferred had your choice fallen on an abler man. Trusting in almighty God, an approving conscience, and the aid of my fellow citizens, I devote myself to the service of my native state, in whose behalf alone will I ever again draw my sword.

—*Lee accepts commission
from Virginia House of Delegates;
from the script of* Gods and Generals

THE WORLD'S GREAT SOLDIER

⭐ ⭐ ⭐ ⭐ ⭐ ⭐ ⭐ ⭐

Renowned as the General of the Confederate army in the War Between the States, Robert Edward Lee is a premier example of noble character produced by the grace of God through great trial and sorrow.

Robert E. Lee's own notable sense of duty came early, for his father died while Robert was a boy. The brilliant and energetic performance of Lee's father, Richard Henry Lee, in the Revolutionary War gained him a popularity that seated him in the Virginia House of Delegates in 1785 and in the governor's chair for three one-year terms. His funeral oration for George Washington in 1799 included the now famous characterization: "First in war, first in peace, and first in the hearts of his countrymen." Nevertheless, he ran through the fortune of two wives, including that of Robert E. Lee's mother, his second wife, Ann Hill Carter. His debts and depression, combined with the injuries he had received from a melee in Baltimore, drove him to the West Indies in 1814 when Robert was still six years old. His family never saw him again because he returned to America only in time to die on March 24, 1818, in the home of Nathanael Green in Georgia.

Richard Lee's death may have released the Lees from his debts, but it also left Robert responsible for managing the house, servants, marketing, and horse and carriage. Childhood diversions vanished as Robert cared for his invalid mother and found ways to make her laugh through her profound sadness. When her son finally left for West Point in June 1825, Ann Lee confided in her sister-in-law, "You know what I have lost. He is son, daughter, and everything to me!"

Southern Aristocrat

His pre–West Point education included significant work in classic literature (Homer and Cicero as well as "all the minor classics") and advanced mathematics. Just as valuable, however, were the lengthy periods spent in company with his mother and her social contacts. The best graces of Southern aristocracy became his.

No less central was Robert Lee's regular attendance at Christ Church, Alexandria, which still maintained George Washington's pew and used Washington's Bible for public Scripture reading. The sermons and catechizing from Bishop Meade instilled biblical truth into Lee's discerning mind. His appreciation of the impact of Meade's influence is seen in a letter of May 16, 1861. Lee had attended the church convention in which Meade preached his fiftieth-anniversary sermon. "It was most impressive," Lee had written, "and more than once, I felt tears coursing down my cheeks. It was full of humility and self-reproach." Meade's own estimation of Lee was very laudatory: "It is a great relief to me that in the Providence of God so important a station has been assigned to you, as I believe that by natural and acquired endowments and by the grace of God you are better qualified for the same than any other of our citizens of Virginia."

Full-length wartime portrait of General Robert E. Lee in 1863.

In God's Hands

For many years, this sense of providence and utter dependence on God had grown in Lee.

In 1857, sensing some danger from Indians in Texas, he wrote, "I know in whose powerful hands I am and on Him I rely and feel that in all our life we are upheld and sustained by Divine Providence, and that providence requires us to use the means He has put under our control." Later, in a letter to his son Rooney, he declared, "May Almighty God have you in His holy keeping. To His Merciful Providence I commit you, and will rely upon Him, and the Efficacy of the prayers that will be daily and hourly offered up by those who love you." He was not slow in seeing calamities as a demonstration of the "justice of His afflictions" and even the "scourge of God . . . to repress the sins of our people."

Using "the beautiful funeral service" in the Episcopal prayer book, Lee officiated at the funerals of two children who died in Texas. He empathized with the anguish of the parents, yet fully believed, "It was done in mercy to both—mercy to the child, mercy to the parents. The former has been saved from sin and misery here, and the latter have been given a touching appeal and powerful inducement to prepare for hereafter. May it prove effectual, and may they require no further severe admonition."

Lee loved the Bible. He led his family in daily devotions and read it every day when away. After the war he served as president of the Rockbridge County Bible Society to assist in "extending the inestimable knowledge of the priceless truths of the Bible."

THE UNIVERSAL BALM

Robert Lee's moral character was beyond reproach. Not only did he abstain from personal vices, but he also practiced and encouraged the love of one's enemies. He advised Rooney that he "always be distinguished for [his] avoidance of the 'universal balm,' whiskey, and every immorality"—words from a man who carried a gift bottle of "fine old whiskey" all the way through the Mexican War and, in the end, returned it to its donor to demonstrate that he could "get on without liquor." On hearing that Rooney was smoking, Lee admonished him with the following words: "it was dangerous to meddle with" and he had "much better employment for [his] mouth." He should reserve it for legitimate pleasure and not "poison and corrupt it with stale vapors or tarnish your beard with their stench." Alexander Stephens, having known of Lee only by his reputation as the consummate soldier, assumed that he shared all the vices of his companions and was surprised that "he used no stimulants, was free even from the use of tobacco, and that he was absolutely stainless in his private life."

Lee viewed slavery as a "moral and political evil in any country" and was resolved to aid its abolition with his prayers and all "justifiable means in our power." He shared the views of some Southerners, however, that Providence would accomplish God's purposes slowly. The abolitionist must recognize that "he has neither the right nor the power of operating except by moral means and persuasion; and if he means well to the slave, he must not create angry feelings in the master." He viewed this as neither a happy or defensible situation but as analogous to the progress of Christian faith in the world. "The doctrines and miracles of our Saviour have required nearly two thousand years to convert but a small part of the human race, and even among Christian nations what gross errors still exist!"

★ ★ ★ ★ ★ ★ ★ ★ ★ ★ ★ ★ ★ ★ ★

I prefer the Bible to any other book. There is enough in that to satisfy the most ardent thirst for knowledge; to open the way to true wisdom; and to teach the only road to salvation and eternal happiness. It is not above human comprehension, and is sufficient to satisfy all its desires.

—Robert E. Lee

★ ★ ★ ★ ★ ★ ★ ★ ★ ★ ★ ★ ★ ★ ★

NO BITTER SPIRIT

The grace of a nonembittered spirit testified to the genuineness of Lee's Christian character. In the years that followed the war, Lee lived as a paroled prisoner of war. This was accomplished under the terms of surrender, written by U. S. Grant. In spite of guarantees in those terms, Lee was indicted for treason in June 1865. He expressed no desire "to avoid trial" and was "ready to meet any charges," but did desire that the provisions of the surrender be attended to. Through the intervention of Grant, the charges were dropped, although Lee's application for reinstatement as an American citizen, including an oath of loyalty, was ignored.

The notarized document, including a pledge to "abide by and faithfully support all laws and proclamations which have been made during the existing rebellion with reference to the emancipation of slaves," was found in an old file drawer in Washington in the mid-1970s. It was at this time that the United States House of Representatives voted unanimously to restore the citizenship of Robert E. Lee. In spite of personal recriminations in his own time, Lee never stopped admonishing all in the South "to unite in the restoration of the country and the reestablishment of peace and harmony." In pursuit of those goals, he personally intended to learn from the experience "under the guidance of an ever-merciful God."

Nor did Lee harbor bitterness. When Lee was indicted, a minister friend of his expressed bitterness and indignation within a small group gathered in Lee's home; Lee diverted the subject to other topics by responding, "Well, it matters little what they may do to me. I am old and have but a short time to live anyhow." Later he followed the minister to the door and said, "Doctor, there is a good old book which I read, and you preach from, which says, 'Love your enemies, bless them that curse you, do good to them that hate you, and pray for them which despitefully use you.' Do you think your remarks were quite in the spirit of that teaching?" After some apology came from the minister, Lee added, "I have fought against the people of the North because I believed they were seeking to wrest from the South dearest rights. But I have never cherished toward them bitter or vindictive feelings, and have never seen the day when I did not pray for them."

Perhaps Lee's humble, forgiving spirit arose out of the profound sense he had of his own sin. Though viewing an infant in "purity and innocence, unpolluted by sin, and uncontaminated by the vices of the world," when he felt his own sin he would say, "Man's nature is so selfish. So weak. Every feeling every passion urging him to folly, excess & sin that I am disgusted with myself & sometimes with all the world." When told by a Confederate chaplain of the fervent prayers which had been offered on his

behalf, he responded with a flushed face and tears in his eyes, "Please thank them for that, sir. And I can only say that I am nothing but a poor sinner, trusting in Christ alone for salvation, and need all of the prayers they can offer for me."

Looking unto Jesus

His concern for gospel salvation extended to others, and he was elated by the great revival that swept the Army of Northern Virginia with fifteen thousand conversions in the last two years of the war. As president of Washington College, Lee rejoiced when the preaching of John A. Broadus "gave our young men the very marrow of the Gospel, and with a simple earnestness that must have reached their hearts and done them good." To a supporter of the college he confided, "I shall fail in the leading object that brought me here, unless these young men become real Christians." And at a Concert of Prayer for Colleges, Lee told one of the speakers, "Our great want is a revival that shall bring these young men to Christ." J. W. Jones, a leading Baptist pastor in Virginia, who had closely observed the general, gave a fitting assessment of the Christian, Robert E. Lee: "If I have ever come in contact with a sincere, devout Christian—one who, seeing himself to be a sinner, trusted alone in the merits of Christ—who humbly tried to walk the path of duty, 'looking unto Jesus the author and finisher of our faith,' and whose piety was constantly exemplified in his daily life, that man was the world's great soldier, and model man, Robert Edward Lee."[1]

General Lee used frequently to attend preaching at Jackson's headquarters; and it was a scene which a master hand might have delighted to paint—those two great warriors, surrounded by hundreds of their officers and men, bowed in humble worship before the God and Saviour in whom they trusted.

—Rev. J. William Jones

★ *John Woodbridge*

R. E. LEE
AND FATHERHOOD

★ ★ ★ ★ ★ ★ ★ ★ ★ ★

The Puritans used to say, "The father is the mirror by which the child dresses himself." This reality was impressed upon thirty-three-year-old father Robert Lee one winter's day eight years after the birth of his first-born son, Custis. Lee was now the father of four: Custis, who was eight; Mary, six years; Fitzhugh, who was approaching his fourth birthday; and Annie, who was yet in the cradle. One afternoon Lee took Custis for a walk in the snow, holding him by the hand. When they had walked for a short way, Custis dropped his father's hand and fell behind. In a few minutes Lee looked back over his shoulder and saw Custis imitating his every movement—walking as his father walked, head and shoulders erect, with all the grace and dignity the eight-year-old could muster, and struggling to walk in the very footprints his father had left behind in the snow.

Lee would later say, "When I saw this, I said to myself, 'It behooves me to walk very straight, when this fellow is already following in my tracks.'"

Even though he was often called away from home by the exigencies of war and service in the army, Lee was not a detached, out-of-touch father. He wrote home regularly, addressing each of the children with specific concerns, encouragements, admonitions, and exhortations to faithfulness. He called upon them to be diligent and conscientious in their studies. He exhorted them to honor their mother. He encouraged them to be good examples to those around them. And most of all, he reminded them of his love for them and their duties to God.

"I shall not feel my long separation from you," he once wrote the two older boys on his way to Mexico, "if I find that my absence has been of no injury to you, and that you have both grown in goodness and knowledge, as well as stature. But, ah! How much I will suffer on my return if the reverse has occurred! You enter all my thoughts, into all my prayers; and on you, in part, will depend whether I shall be happy or miserable as you know how much I love you. You must do all in your power to save me pain."

General Robert E. Lee with his son, Custis (George Washington Custis Lee).

On March 31, 1846, he wrote: "I cannot go to bed, my dear son, without writing you a few lines to thank you for your letter, which gave me great pleasure. I am glad to hear you are well, and hope you are learning to read and write, and that the next letter you will be able to write yourself. I want to see you very much, and to tell you all that has happened since you went away. I do not think that I ever told you of a fine boy I heard of in my travels this winter. . . ."

After relating the story of this young man whose father was killed by a falling limb in the woods and was found by his son who manfully brought his father's body home, Lee continues: "You and Custis must take great care of your kind mother and dear sisters when your father is dead. To do that you must learn to be good. Be true, kind, and generous, and pray earnestly to God to enable you to 'keep his commandments, and walk in the same all the days of your life.'"

When Lee was stationed in Texas in June 1860, he received word from home that Robert was preparing for confirmation. In a letter Lee wrote to Mrs. Anna Fitzhugh, we see something of his holy desires for the spiritual well-being of his children: "I know you will sympathize in the joy I feel at the impression made by a merciful God upon the youthful heart of dear little Rob. May He that has opened his eyes to the blessing of Salvation, taught him the way, and put in his heart the good resolution he has formed, enable him to do all things to secure and accomplish it."

LEE AND DUTY

It is probable that Lee never made the statement so often attributed to him: "Duty is the sublimest word in the English language." But there is no question that his view of duty was equal to this sentiment. Faithfulness to duty dominated his life wherever you look: at home as a child caring for his mother; at West Point never incurring a single demerit; in the army of the United States serving with nobility and grace; at the head of the Southern forces leading with boldness and fortitude; as president of Washington College, quietly molding the lives of young men—"duty" echoes all around.

After the fall of Mexico City, when the army was celebrating the victory with great joy and relief in the emperor's palace, one arose to propose a toast to the captain of the engineers who had found a way for the army to take the city. It was only then that the men noticed that Robert E. Lee, the captain of the engineers, was not present. Major John Magruder was immediately dispatched to find the captain and bring him to the hall to receive his honors.

After an extended search, Magruder finally found Captain Lee in a remote, quiet room in the palace, busily working on a map! It was his responsibility to make maps of the area, and he had not yet finished this task. Magruder reproached Lee for ignoring the festivities. Lee calmly responded by pointing to his instruments. Magruder was incredulous.

"But this is mere drudgery! Make somebody else do it and come with me."

"No," replied Lee, "no, I am but doing my duty."

Magruder knew Lee well enough to know that this was indeed his strict view of the matter and no amount of words would sway him.

It was said of Lee as a young student that his "specialty was finishing up." He completed what he began and fulfilled his responsibilities to the full. It later became a maxim with him: "You cannot be a true man until you learn to obey."

★ *Steve Wilkins*

THE FAITH AND VALUES OF ROBERT E. LEE

★ ★ ★ ★ ★ ★ ★ ★ ★ ★

Lee in later years

Robert E. Lee survives as the most exemplary hero of the Civil War to both sides. What was it about this soft-spoken nobleman that inspired such respect and awe among his contemporaries? Was it his military genius to defeat repeatedly the superior numbers sent against him? Was it his thirty-one years of distinguished service in the United States army? Was it his turning down the command of the Union forces by President Lincoln to defend his home state in a lost cause? The consensus seems to indicate that the unique feature that guaranteed Lee his prominence in history was his character. His deep-seated integrity and concern for individual soldiers coupled with a brilliant and well-disciplined military mind that displayed extraordinary leadership skills elevated Lee to a revered position.

His character stemmed in part from good stock. His mother, Ann Hill Carter, personified the generosity and purity of the Virginia Carters, especially when forced through difficult times by her husband's financial and political troubles. General Henry Lee earned a spectacular reputation in the American War for Independence as "Light Horse Harry" Lee, but turned afterward to politics and land speculations. His compounding debts, despite three terms as Virginia governor, sent him to debtors' prison on two occasions. His opposition to the War of 1812 with the British and failing health drove him to live the last years of his life in the Caribbean. His letters home, however, were preserved by his youngest son in a biography of General Henry Lee, which was published in Robert's last year. Although Robert did not see his father after age six, clearly he carried these written lessons throughout his life. Here is a sampling:

From Port-au-Prince, St. Domingo, June 26, 1816:

You know my abhorrence of lying, and you have been often told by me, that it led to every vice and cancelled every tendency to virtue.

From Nassau, New Providence, December 1, 1816:

Fame in arms or art, however conspicuous, is naught, unless bottomed on virtue. . . .

It is hard to say whether too much drinking or too much eating most undermines the constitution. . . .

Cleanliness of person is not only comely to all beholders, but it is indispensable to sanctity of body. Trained by your best of mothers to value it, you will never lose sight of it.

Many . . . fall into another habit which hurts only themselves and which certainly stupefies the senses—immoderate sleeping.

From Nassau, New Providence, May 5, 1817:

Self command is the pivot upon which the character, fame, and independence of us mortals hang. . . .

From Nassau, New Providence, September 3, 1817:

Avoid debt, the sink of mental power and the subversion of independence, which draws into debasement even virtue, in appearance certainly, if not in reality. "A man ought not only to be virtuous in reality, but he must always appear so," thus said to me the great Washington.

From Nassau, New Providence, November 20, 1817:

[Quoting St. Pierre] "Religion places all on a level. She

humbles the head of the mighty by showing the vanity of their power, and she raises up the head of the unfortunate by disclosing the prospect of immortality. . . ."

From Nassau, New Providence, January 24, 1818:

In all my letters I urge you to the habits of virtue in mind and body as the only path to happiness in this life, and as the most probable security to happiness in another world. But . . . What is happiness? Hoc opus, hic labor est. Peace of mind based on piety to Almighty God, unconscious innocence of conduct with good will to man; health of body, health of mind, and prosperity in your vocation; a sweet, affectionate wife; sana mens in corpore sano; children devoted to truth, honor, right, and utility, with love and respect to their parents; and faithful, warm-hearted friends, in a country politically and religiously free;—this is my definition.

When Robert was six, the family left his birthplace at Stratford, now owned by his oldest half brother, to move to Alexandria. There he grew up in the shadow of Mount Vernon, home of Lee's hero and model who had only recently passed away. There, too, he cared for his increasingly invalid mother, who guided his studies through two excellent schools before his admission to West Point. His diligence in study and his exemplary conduct placed him second in his class without earning a single demerit in four years. Choosing the Corps of Engineers, he served two years on the Georgia coast before reassignment to Virginia.

Back in Virginia, he pursued and captured the heart of a childhood sweetheart, Mary Custis, the daughter of Washington's adopted son. Looking back on their June 1831 wedding from the defenses of Petersburg during the war, he wrote her: "Do you recollect what a happy day thirty-three years ago this was? How many hopes and pleasures it gave birth to! God has been very merciful and kind to us, and how thankless and sinful I have been. I pray that He may continue His mercies and blessings to us, and give us a little peace and rest together in this world, and finally gather us and all He has given us around His throne in the world to come."

The Lees were blessed with seven children, who due to his distant military assignments, depended largely on their mother for rearing. Nevertheless, his four girls and three boys played frequently with their father when he was the superintendent at West Point. Later his letters from distant outposts to each child carried fatherly instruction, like these letters to his oldest son at West Point:

To George Washington Custis Lee, May 4, 1851:

The full play of your young and growing parts, the daily exercise of all your energies, the consciousness of acquiring knowledge, and the pleasure of knowing your efforts to do your duty, will bring you a delight and a justification far surpassing all that idleness and selfishness can give. Try it fairly and take your experience. . . . Hold yourself above every mean action. Be strictly honorable in every act; and be not ashamed to do right. Acknowledge right to be your aim and strive to reach it.

To George Washington Custis Lee, April 5, 1852:

You must study to be frank with the world. Frankness is the child of honesty and courage. Say just what you mean to do on every occasion, and take it for granted you mean to do right. . . . Never do a wrong thing to make a friend or to keep one. . . . Above all, do not appear to others what you are not. . . . We should live, act and say nothing to the injury of anyone. . . .

Going off to fight in the Mexican War in 1845, Lee won commendations for bravery under fire and bold scouting work behind the enemy positions. Serving alongside him there were many officers whose new skills would be turned soon against each other: Meade, McDowell,

McClellan, Burnside, and Grant from the North, and Johnston, Early, Longstreet, and Jackson from the South. Writing home to his wife, Lee spoke of the beauty of the countryside and the horrors of war, saying after Cerro Gordo, "The papers cannot tell you what a horrible sight a field of battle is, nor will I. . . ."

Lee personally avoided alcohol, tobacco, and other vices throughout his life, warning his son of the dangers in a letter.

To W. F. Lee, May 30, 1858:

I hope you will always be distinguished for your avoidance of the "universal balm," whiskey, and every immorality. Nor need you fear to be ruled out of society that indulges in it, for you will acquire their esteem and respect. . . . I think it better to avoid it altogether, as its temperate use is so difficult. . . . You see I am following my old habit of giving advice, which I dare say you neither need nor require. But, you must pardon a fault which proceeds from my great love and burning anxiety for your welfare and happiness. When I think of your youth, impulsiveness, and many temptations, and your distance from me, and the ease (and even innocence) with which you might commence an erroneous course, my heart quails within me, and my whole frame and being tremble at the possible result. May Almighty God have you in His holy keeping! To His merciful providence I commit you, and will rely upon Him, and the efficacy of the prayers that will be daily and hourly offered up by those who love you.

Perhaps it was a spirit of concern that made his namesake son recollect: "I always knew that it was impossible to disobey my father. I felt it in me. I never thought why, but was perfectly sure when he gave an order that it had to be obeyed."

The years leading up to the Civil War found Lee stationed in Texas while the country debated the slavery issue. Lee's attitude favored gradual emancipation, and he had already granted in his will in 1846 that the half-dozen slaves his father-in-law had given him would be freed at his death. He, in fact, granted them manumission during the war. In an 1856 letter to his wife, he shared his views:

In this enlightened age there are few, I believe, but will acknowledge that slavery as an institution is a moral and political evil in any country. It is useless to expatiate on its disadvantages. I think it, however, a greater evil to the white than to the black race, and while my feelings are strongly interested in behalf of the latter, my sympathies are stronger for the former. The blacks are immeasurably better off here than in Africa, morally, socially and physically. The painful discipline they are undergoing is necessary for their instruction as a race, and, I hope, will prepare them to better things. How long their subjection may be necessary is known and ordered by a wise and merciful Providence. Their emancipation will sooner result from a mild and melting influence than the storms and contests of fiery controversy. This influence, though slow, is sure.

★ ★ ★ ★ ★ ★ ★ ★ ★ ★ ★ ★ ★ ★ ★ ★

The doctrines and miracles of our Saviour have required nearly two thousand years to convert but a small part of the human race, and even among Christian nations what gross errors still exist!

—Robert E. Lee

★ ★ ★ ★ ★ ★ ★ ★ ★ ★ ★ ★ ★ ★ ★ ★

The doctrines and miracles of our Saviour have required nearly two thousand years to convert but a small part of the human race, and even among Christian nations what gross errors still exist! While we see the course of the final abolition of slavery is onward, and we give it the aid of our prayers, and all justifiable means in our power, we must leave the progress as well as the result in His hands who sees the end and who chooses to work by slow things, and with whom a thousand years are but as a single day; although the abolitionist must know this, and must see that he has neither the right nor the power of operating except by moral means and suasion; and if he means well to the slave, he must not create angry feelings in the master. That although he may not approve the mode by which it pleases Providence to accomplish its purposes, the result will never be the same; that the reasons he gives for interference in what he has no concern hold good for every kind of interference with our neighbors when we disapprove their conduct. Is it not strange that the descendants of those Pilgrim Fathers who crossed the Atlantic to preserve the freedom of their opinion have always proved themselves intolerant of the spiritual liberty of others.

When pressed by the election of Lincoln and the secession of several states to take clear-cut stands on the issues, the formerly nonpolitical Lee felt his ultimate allegiance would be to his state. But he wrote his son Custis on January 23, 1861, that he feared the breakup of the Union:

> The South, in my opinion, has been aggrieved by the acts of the North, as you say. I feel the aggression, and am willing to take every proper step for redress. It is the principle I contend for, not individual or private benefit. As an American citizen, I take great pride in my country, her prosperity and institutions, and would defend any State if her rights were invaded. But, I anticipate no greater calamity for the country than dissolution of the Union. It would be an accumulation of all the evils we complain of, and I am willing to sacrifice everything but honor for its preservation. I hope, therefore, that all constitutional means will be exhausted before there is a resort to force. Secession is nothing but revolution. . . .

At the same time, he wrote his cousin, Martha Custis Williams ("Markie"):

> God alone can save us from our folly, selfishness & shortsightedness. The last accounts seem to show that we have barely escaped anarchy to be plunged into civil war. What will be the result I cannot conjecture. I only see that a federal calamity is upon us & fear that our country will have to pass through for its sins a fiery ordeal. I am unable to realize that our people will destroy a government inaugurated by the blood & wisdom of our patriot fathers, that has given us peace & prosperity at home, power & security abroad, & under which we have acquired a colossal strength unequalled in the history of mankind. I wish to live under no other government, & there is no sacrifice I am not ready to make for the preservation of the Union save that of dishonor. If a disruption takes place, I shall go back in sorrow to my people & share the misery of my native state, & save in her defense there will be one less soldier in the world than now. I wish for no other flag than the "Star Spangled Banner," and no other air than "Hail Columbia." I still hope the wisdom & patriotism of the nation will yet save it.
>
> I am so remote from the scene of events & receive such excited & exaggerated accounts of the opinions & acts of our statesmen, that I am at a loss what to think. I believe that the South justly complains of the aggressions of the North, & I have believed that the North would cheerfully redress the grievances complained of. I see no cause for disunion, strife & civil war & I pray it may be averted.

When Texas seceded, Lee was called back to Washington and commissioned a full colonel in the U. S. Cavalry. However, after learning of Virginia's secession, he formally resigned from the army in a letter to General Winfield Scott, saying, "Save in the defense of my native state, I never desire again to draw my sword."

Within two days, he would be called from his mansion

in Arlington to Richmond to accept command of the forces of Virginia as a Major General. It was his father, "Light Horse Harry" Lee, who had set the standard in a 1798 speech over the Virginia Resolutions opposing the Federalist sedition acts: "Virginia is my country; her will I obey, however lamentable the fate to which it may subject me."

In the early days of the war, after the Lee family fled the Custis-Lee mansion overlooking Washington, Brigadier General Lee was busy with advising President Davis, challenging the Union troops in western Virginia, and overseeing coastal defenses in the Carolinas and Georgia as an army engineer. From Savannah, he wrote his daughter, Annie, on March 2, 1862:

> I hope you are all well, and as happy as you can be in these perilous times for our country. They look dark at present and it is plain we have not suffered enough, laboured enough, repented enough to deserve success. But, they will brighten after a while, and I trust that a merciful God will arouse us to a sense of danger, bless our honest efforts, and drive back our enemies to their homes. Our people have not been earnest enough, have thought too much of themselves and their ease, and instead of turning out to a man, have been content to nurse themselves and their dimes, and leave the protection of themselves and their families to others. To satisfy their consciences they have been clamourous in criticizing what others have done, and endeavoured to prove that they ought to do nothing. This is not the way to accomplish our independence.

The very next day, Lee was called back to Richmond. On May 31, both Lee and President Davis observed the Southern attack against McClellan at Seven Pines outside Richmond in which commanding General Joseph E. Johnston was badly wounded. The responsibility of defending the capital fell upon Lee, who was given command of the Army of Northern Virginia.

Building up the defense of the city and sending the cavalry under J. E. B. Stuart completely around McClellan's 115,000 troops in forty-eight hours without losing a man, Lee took the offensive and, helped by Jackson's Valley Army, succeeded in driving McClellan away. The Federal forces were no more fortunate in battles at Cedar Mountain and Manassas, although McClellan did stop Lee's advance into the North at Sharpsburg (Antietam). A new Lincoln nominee for commanding general, Ambrose Burnside, challenged Lee foolishly at Fredericksburg in December 1862. As the rebels repelled bloodily another assault on their lines at Marye's Heights, Lee observed to Longstreet, "It is a good thing that war is so terrible; or we would grow to fond of it." In that two-day battle, the Union lost 12,647 men and the Confederates lost 5,309. That Christmas, after dinner with Jackson at Moss Neck, Lee wrote his wife:

> My heart is filled with gratitude to Almighty God for His unspeakable mercies with which He has blessed us in this day, for those He has granted us from the beginning of life, and particularly for those He has vouchsafed us during the past year. What should have become of us without His crowning help and protection? Oh, if our people would only recognize it and cease from self-boasting and adulation, how strong would be my belief in final success and happiness to our country! But what a cruel thing is war; to separate and destroy families and friends, and mar the purest joys and happiness God has granted us in this world; to fill our hearts with hatred instead of love for our neighbors, and to devastate the fair face of this beautiful world! I pray that, on this day when only peace and good-will are preached to mankind, better thoughts may fill the hearts of our enemies and turn them to peace. . . . My heart bleeds at the death of every one of our gallant men.

The following spring, when hostilities quickened again, Lee caught his new adversary, General Joe Hooker, without protection of his flank at Chancellorsville. Boldly dividing his force and sending Jackson's Corps hastily around the exposed Union troops, Lee scored another smashing victory against superior numbers. Unfortunately, in the twilight Stonewall Jackson was mistaken for the enemy and wounded by his own troops. To save his life, his left arm was amputated. To this Lee responded, "Tell him to make haste and get well, and come back to me as soon as he can. He has lost his left arm, but I have lost my right." When infection and pneumonia began to threaten the life of Jackson, Lee exclaimed to his aides, "Surely General Jackson must recover! God will not take him from us, now that we need him so much. Surely he will be spared to us, in answer to the many prayers which are offered for him." Later, he sent this word through his staff: "When a suitable occasion offers, give him my love, and tell him that I wrestled in prayer for him last night, as I have never prayed, I believe, for myself." When Jackson died, the official announcement came from Lee's hand:

> With deep grief the commanding general announces to the army the death of Lieutenant-General T. J. Jackson, who expired on the 10th instant quarter-past three P.M.
>
> The daring, skill, and energy of this great and good soldier, by the decree of an All-wise Providence, are now lost to us. But, while we mourn his death, we feel that his spirit still lives, and will inspire the whole army with his indomitable courage and unshaken confidence in God, as our hope and strength. Let his name be a watchword to his corps, who have followed him to victory on so many fields. Let his officers and soldiers emulate his invincible determination to do everything in the defense of our beloved country.

Over the next month, while Richmond and Lexington were mourning Jackson, Lee moved the Army of Northern Virginia north through Maryland into

General Robert E. Lee with General Ulysses S. Grant.

Pennsylvania. His hope, expressed in a letter to Jefferson Davis, was to give the peace voices in the North added relevance and to encourage enlistments from Maryland. The high-tide mark of the Confederacy can be measured on the slopes of Cemetery Ridge at Gettysburg, on July 3, 1863. On the same day that Vicksburg fell, opening up the Mississippi and dividing the South, Lee's attack was bloodily repulsed, reducing his threat to the North. His dispatch to Davis about Gettysburg displayed the true leader's sense of ultimate responsibility:

To President Davis, from Camp Culpepper, July 31, 1863

No blame can be attached to the army for its failure to accomplish what was projected by me, nor should it be censored for the unreasonable expectations of the public—I am alone to blame, in perhaps expecting too much of its prowess & valor. It however in my opinion achieved under the guidance of the Most High a general success, though it did not win a victory.

Later that summer, a day was proclaimed by President Jefferson Davis as a national day of prayer and fasting. The official dispatch from Lee's hand provoked an evangelistic movement among the army that led the chaplains to convert more than fifteen thousand soldiers to faith:

Soldiers! Let us humble ourselves before the Lord, our God, asking through Christ, the forgiveness of our sins, beseeching the aid of the God of our forefathers in the defense of our homes and our liberties, thanking him for his past blessings, and imploring their continuance upon our cause and our people.

★ ★ ★ ★ ★ ★ ★ ★ ★ ★

Knowing that intercessory prayer is our mightiest weapon and the supreme call for all Christians today, I pleadingly urge our people everywhere to pray.

—Robert E. Lee

★ ★ ★ ★ ★ ★ ★ ★ ★ ★

Knowing that intercessory prayer is our mightiest weapon and the supreme call for all Christians today, I pleadingly urge our people everywhere to pray. Believing that prayer is the greatest contribution that our people can make in this critical hour, I humbly urge that we take time to pray—to really pray.

Let there be prayer at sunup, at noonday, at midnight—all through the day. Let us pray for our children, our youth, our aged, our pastors, our homes. Let us pray for our churches.

Let us pray for ourselves, that we not lose the word "concern" out of our Christian vocabulary. Let us pray for our nation. Let us pray for those who have never known Jesus Christ and redeeming love, for moral forces everywhere, for our national leaders. Let prayer be our passion. Let prayer be our practice.

Afterward, when his chaplain, J. William Jones, and Jackson's chaplain, B. T. Lacy, called on him in his tent to tell him that all the chaplains were praying daily for him, Lee's eyes filled with tears. "Please thank them for that, sir—I warmly appreciate it." Jones's diary preserved Lee's words: "And, I can only say that I am nothing but a poor sinner, trusting in Christ alone for salvation, and need all of the prayers they can offer me."

Lee's humility seemed genuine indeed. Foreign visitors were always struck by the sheer simplicity of his staff and headquarters almost completely devoid of any pretension when compared to a European staff. Only three stars designated his rank, and a clean uniform and well-groomed horse characterized his appearance. Yet the word would sweep through the troops when he rode regularly: "Here comes Marse Robert." The men would stand in reverence, would touch him and occasionally—to his embarrassment—break into the famed Rebel yell.

When a soldier once commented that he wished all the enemy were dead, Lee retorted, "Now I wish that they were all at home attending to their own business, and leaving us to do the same." Once a general complained that Grant had hindered their supplies so that there was not enough food to feed both the troops and the Yankee prisoners, suggesting that the latter should suffer. Lee bristled in his response: "The prisoners we have here, General _____, are my prisoners; they are not General Grant's prisoners, and as long as I have any rations at all, I shall divide them with my prisoners."

After offering his sword to Grant at Appomattox on April 9, 1865, Lee's final order to his army stated: "I have determined to avoid the uscless sacrifice of those whose past services have endeared them to their countrymen. By the terms of the agreement, officers and men can return to their homes. . . . I earnestly pray that a merciful God will extend to you His blessing and protection."

When indicted for treason in June of 1865 by a grand jury in Norfolk, some of Lee's friends protested angrily. Lee's own statement was calmer: "I have fought against

McLean house where General Lee surrendered. Appomattox Court House, Va., April 1865

the people of the North because I believed they were seeking to wrest from the South dearest rights. But, I have never cherished toward them bitter or vindictive feelings, and have never seen the day I did not pray for them."

Robert E. Lee's funeral at his home, Arlington House, Va.

Without housing or income, and barred from federal office, Lee was in need of a post-war career. Offered the presidency of Washington College in Lexington, he accepted in August 1865, and spent his last five years among the students and faculty. His old chaplain recalled his comments from one visit when he spoke:

Oh, Doctor: if I could only know that all the young men in this college were good Christians I should have nothing more to desire.

I wish, sir, to thank you for your address. It was just what we needed. Our great want is a revival which shall bring these young men to Christ.

I should be disappointed, sir, and shall fail in the leading object that brought me here, unless these young men all become Christians; and I wish you and others of your sacred profession to do all you can to accomplish it.

We poor sinners need to come back from our wanderings to seek pardon through the all-sufficient merits of our Redeemer. And we need to pray earnestly for the power of the Holy Spirit to give us a precious revival in our hearts and among the unconverted.

The body of Robert E. Lee rests quietly now in the crypt of the chapel at what is today Washington and Lee University, his name joined with his boyhood hero and model. No memorial marks his greatness except the two-hundred-foot likeness carved in the "Southern Rushmore" at Stone Mountain, Georgia—reminding one of the prediction of General Winfield Scott that if Lee joined the Southern cause it would be like adding ten thousand men to their ranks. In retrospect, Lee's unique greatness eclipses virtually all of the other leading combatants. The source of his strength of character this humble sinner would credit to the all-merciful Creator.

★ *Dorsey M. Deaton*

★ ★ ★ ★ ★ ★ ★ ★ ★ ★ ★ ★ ★ ★

I have fought against the people of the North because I believed they were seeking to wrest from the South dearest rights. But, I have never cherished toward them bitter or vindictive feelings, and have never seen the day I did not pray for them.

—Robert E. Lee

★ ★ ★ ★ ★ ★ ★ ★ ★ ★ ★ ★ ★ ★

7
BEHIND EVERY GOOD MAN
WOMEN IN THE WAR

In the movie *Gods and Generals*, Jeff Daniels and Mira Sorvino are Joshua Lawrence Chamberlain and his wife Fanny.

Fall of Richmond, Va., on the night of April 2, 1865

THE GENTLE WARRIOR
MRS. GENERAL LEE IN RICHMOND, 1863

★ ★ ★ ★ ★ ★ ★ ★ ★

It was as miserable a winter as anybody could remember. Snow, sleet, and rain pelted the city in endless succession, making the cold that much more chilling, the mud that much more inescapable. Mud was heaped along the sidewalks, strewn through the hotel lobbies, and clotted on the front steps of houses up and down Clay Street, carried by a ceaseless progression of soldiers' boots, which, like the soldiers themselves, were worn and patched to the point it was impossible to imagine them ever having been new and fresh and hopeful.

The first of January 1863 was the second New Year's Day of the war. This time last year there were still people in Richmond who believed the Union would sue for peace any minute, that great European powers—England, France, and Russia—would recognize the Confederacy, and that they would then take their rightful place at the table of sovereign nations, supplying cotton to the world's spinning mills at a satisfying profit and telling their grandchildren stories of the second War for Independence around the fireplace on crisp autumn nights.

Recognition hadn't come, nor victory, and now the period of political and military uncertainty in the North was long past. Outgunned, outmanned, and outprovisioned, the Confederacy was sacrificing its resources at a desperate rate to maintain battlefield momentum long enough to convince President Lincoln, either directly or through his advisors and constituents, that holding onto the rebels was more trouble than it was worth.

Added to the miserable weather and the wearying tension of war was the near impossibility of running a household. Richmond was one of the oldest and wealthiest cities in America, a center for commerce, for society, and now the capital of the Confederate States. But the war economy had brought stark shortages and unfamiliar hardship: flour was twelve dollars a barrel, tea twenty-five dollars a pound, and sugar and coffee unavailable at any price. The Spottswood Hotel sold drinking glasses to its guests for twenty-five dollars each; broken or stolen, they were irreplaceable.

In the midst of all the cold and depravation of a capital at war in winter, a simply but elegantly dressed woman sat in the upstairs parlor of a house at the corner of Clay and Eleventh. People who saw her without knowing who she was would scarcely have suspected her identity, but they would have sensed in her an extraordinary presence.

The parlor where she sat was an oasis of warmth and hospitality in a city hardened to the absence of both. At almost anytime of the day there were likely to be callers, ladies who felt sorry for her for losing so much these last twenty months, who pitied her for the crippling pain that had confined her to a wheelchair even longer. And yet anybody who came to comfort and encourage Mary Custis Lee invariably came away comforted and encouraged themselves. As Mrs. General Lee saw it, her blessings were manifold and her burdens few.

She was in her late middle years, hair almost completely gray and pulled back severely, her features both

★ THE FALL OF RICHMOND

The "Burnt District" in Richmond was a pitiable sight for the various photographers who scrambled to record the Confederate capital in the last days of the Civil War. As the government collapsed and people rioted, the fires—meant to destroy the arsenal, bridges, and anything of military value—spread to a large part of the city's prime commercial districts. Richmond's weary and long-suffering inhabitants searched for missing friends and relations and combed the ashes for what could be saved. Photographs such as this, of two soldiers and three young boys with piles of cannonballs in the foreground, serve as a reminder to posterity of the terror and devastation of the war.

sharpened by constant pain and illuminated by a spirit that refused defeat or despair. Her dainty feet rested on the footstand of her wheelchair, her ankles and knees swollen and misshapen by the arthritis that required her to be carried up and down stairs like a child.

Even so, Mary's eyes still shone in the firelight with the intellect and joy of life that had impressed the elegant old Marquis de Lafayette on his triumphal return to America a generation after the Revolution; her smile still radiated the appeal that brought a proposal of marriage from a dashing young Tennessee congressman named Sam Houston when she was only sixteen.

But God had meant her for other things. She knew that as surely as she knew God was watching over her family scattered as it was to the four winds here in this second winter of the war. She had felt God's hand on her ever since the day when, twenty-one and newly engaged to her cousin Robert Edward Lee, she was driven to her knees by the presence of her Creator in an encounter that was as real as the fire now dancing in the grate, as solid as the knitting needles she worked with practiced ease though her fingers were too crippled to hold a pen.

The summer of 1830 was a time when war or arthritis or a twelve-dollar barrel of flour was unimaginable. Mary Anna Randolph Custis wondered excitedly what it would be like to marry a soldier, and what it would be like to leave Arlington. It was the only home she'd ever known, built by her father, George Washington Parke Custis, as a memorial to his foster father and namesake, President George Washington. Mr. Custis filled the Arlington mansion with furniture and keepsakes from Mount Vernon where he grew up, and Mary was surrounded by these trappings of history as long as she could remember: Washington's uniforms, silver, furniture, paintings, even his campaign tent, which little Mary had used as a playhouse.

That was the summer her Uncle William Fitzhugh died, leaving Aunt Maria the Ravensworth plantation, an estate of twenty-two thousand acres—ten times the size of Arlington—and a fortune in cash and other property. And yet Aunt Maria was devastated, transformed from a gracious and effervescent society figure into a broken shell.

All the money and connections and social standing in the world were worthless. There must be something more, Mary thought, more than worldly wealth and even more than the love of family and tradition and belonging. They have been tested and they have failed.

Seeing her aunt's misery, Mary started praying for her, never suspecting how dramatically God would answer her plea. She wrote of her experience soon afterward in a prayer journal that would preserve the privacy of her tender spiritual awakening for 170 years:

> The view of Aunt Maria's utter wretchedness impressed me with the vanity of earthly things, and one night I prayed fervently that God would comfort her. I do not recollect whether I prayed for myself—I returned home still thirsting after the world & its honours.
>
> We went to Ravensworth where I had spent my happiest hours—there all was desolation and woe—there I first prayed to my God to change my heart & make me His true & faithful servant until my life's end. I was led on by His blessed spirit from day to day more & more to desire His favour, to see my base ingratitude & unworthiness to Him who so loved us as to give His only son to die for us, to see my utter helplessness, to cast all my hopes upon my Saviour, to feel a willingness to give up all I had formerly delighted in for His sake & afterwards through His grace not to desire them, to feel my heart melted with love to God.

Within days the transformation was complete. "Peace, peace that the world knows not of. I was reading the Commandments & felt that I had certainly broken them all except one & yet the pardon of Jesus is free & sweet. He is faithful who promised. He will support me when flesh & heart fail for His word is truth."

God had kept her close to Him since that time, through thirty-one years as an army wife raising seven children alone and managing household business affairs for months, sometimes years, at a stretch. Now one of those children, gentle Annie, was dead of typhoid fever, and all three sons were soldiers at war. The Arlington estate, hers since her father's death, had been confiscated by Union soldiers, depriving her not only of her home, but of her livelihood and legacy. Her parents were buried on a hillside behind the house in a place she herself had chosen; soon their graves would be hidden by the tombstones of thousands of Union dead buried at Arlington on orders of Quartermaster General Montgomery Meigs, "encircling the house and as close to it as possible."

At least the Arlington mansion was still standing. White House, another family estate where the widow Martha Dandridge Custis, Mary's great-grandmother, and Colonel George Washington were married more than a century before, was soon reduced to a pair of blackened chimneys.

Mary's faith had led her to hope there would be no war at all. Early in 1861 she wrote to her daughter Mildred at school that "the prospects before us are sad indeed. And as I think both parties are in the wrong in this fratricidal war there is nothing comforting even in the hope that God may prosper the right, for I see no right in

Richmond, Va. Street in the burned district

this matter. We can only pray that in His mercy He will spare us."

Mrs. General Lee left Arlington for Ravensworth in May, a month after the assault on Fort Sumter, expecting to stay a few weeks and return home. She sent several trunks of Washington's papers and silver to Lexington, Virginia, for safekeeping, and brought as much more as she could carry with her to Aunt Maria's.

But the Union kept coming, and when Ravensworth was threatened she joined her cousins at Chantilly plantation. Soon her presence there became a threat and she went on to Eastern View, then to Kinloch and on to Audley—stately homes, each with a lifetime of pleasant memories, now only way stations for refugees of war.

Caught behind enemy lines in spite of herself, Mrs. General Lee was passed through on personal orders from General McClellan on June 10, 1862, to rejoin her husband in Richmond. The capital in wartime had grown to four times its normal population and lodging was almost impossible to find. The Caskies, a family she knew from the mineral springs where she went for arthritis treatments, offered their home only a few blocks from General Lee's headquarters, and Mary accepted it gratefully.

God in His wisdom had denied her the use of her legs, but He gave her some movement in her hands: she could still knit like lightning. She set up a vigorous cottage industry in the Caskies' second floor parlor, encouraging her daughters Agnes and Mildred and all her neighbors to knit socks and gloves for Confederate soldiers. Mrs. Lee had them packed into boxes and sent to her husband in the field for distribution to the most needy. In one six-month stretch Mary and her helpers knitted 859 pairs of socks and 190 pairs of mittens. Cotton thread was four dollars a spool and knitting yarn available only by barter. Mrs. Lee sent out "yarn scouts" who combed the city for supplies.

"Tell the girls to send all they can," General Lee wrote his wife. "I wish they could make some shoes too."

Mary Chestnut, wife of former South Carolina senator James Chestnut, came to call and described Mrs. Lee's room in her diary as "like an industrial school: everybody so busy. Her daughters were all there plying their needles,

During the war, women knitted, sewed, and quilted clothing and blankets for the needy soldiers.

with several other ladies." Another visitor portrayed her as "always bright, sunny-tempered and uncomplaining."

Still others wrote with astonishment of Mrs. General Lee's indomitable spirit. "Almost unable to move," one of them recalled, "Mrs. Lee was busily engaged in knitting socks for sockless soldiers." A neighbor who dropped by noted that Mary "listened, and strengthened, and smiled even when her own heart ached. The brightness of her nature, amidst uncertainty and pain, was wonderful."

New Year's Day brought news of Lincoln's Emancipation Proclamation. Mrs. Lee had no use for Lincoln or his politics, but she had been a moral opponent of slavery all her life. By the time she inherited Arlington almost six years earlier—long before the war or thoughts of war—the slaves had already been promised their freedom and Mary saw that they received it. The day the president's proclamation was issued there were no slaves at Arlington: they were working for wages or long gone in search of other opportunities and adventures.

Another new law that winter affected her far more: An Act for the Collection of Direct Taxes in the Insurrectionary Districts within the United States that required her to pay a $92.07 levy on Arlington in person to Union authorities. Even if she hadn't been the wife of the Confederate general-in-chief, it would have been impossible to travel to the courthouse in Alexandria. Just getting downstairs to the street was an excruciating, dangerous, and time-consuming ordeal she seldom attempted. Within a year the estate would be sold on the courthouse steps for non-payment of a lawful tax.

Winter turning to spring brought soothing, cheerful mornings and temperate days. Mary sat at the window enjoying the view of rooftops and the intense blue Virginia sky, her knitting needles flashing in the sunlight. And yet there was a sinister side to the emerging dogwoods and apple blossoms. The same sun that nurtured them ripened the seeds of war: companies and battalions abandoned the safety of their winter encampments for another season of killing and being killed.

Overmatched as they were, General Lee's men continued to stand steadfast and even to gain ground. Against the worst odds of the war so far—134,000 United States troops under Fighting Joe Hooker to Lee's 60,000—the Confederates made a bold offensive at Chancellorsville, just west of Fredericksburg, before daylight on May 2. Within four days the Union army had retreated north across the Rappahannock.

It was a great victory but at a terrible price. The day of the attack General Stonewall Jackson, Lee's fearless and indispensable tactical mastermind, was accidentally shot by one of his own troops; eight days later he died of pneumonia despite the amputation of his shattered left arm in a desperate attempt to save his life. He died on the tenth, and the next day Mary heard church bells tolling all over Richmond to mourn his loss.

The next month brought the kind of news that every soldier's mother hoped never to hear. Brigadier General William Henry Fitzhugh Lee—"Rooney," her second son—was shot in the thigh at the battle of Brandy Station on June 9. She thanked God that the wound was not life threatening and rejoiced when Rooney received a furlough to recuperate at Hickory Hill, home of her husband's Uncle William Wickham.

There was no question in Mary's mind that she should nurse him back to health, and so she made the difficult trip by carriage to the plantation, a few miles north of Richmond on the Pamunkey River. Rooney was healing nicely and recovering his strength until the morning of June 26, when a posse of Federals rode up the drive to the plantation office that had been converted into Rooney's

quarters, claimed the bedridden officer as a prisoner of war, bundled him into old Mr. Wickham's carriage, and disappeared as fast as they'd come.

The news that summer continued grim, though it would be yet awhile before they realized July of 1863 marked the beginning of the end. On July 4 Vicksburg fell at last, starved and exhausted after forty-seven days, giving the Union undisputed control of the Mississippi from New Orleans to St. Louis and splitting the Confederacy in two. The same day back east, General Lee retreated in a thundering downpour from the hills of Gettysburg, the deepest penetration ever into enemy territory, despondent over opportunities lost but determined to carry on.

When Mary Custis Lee returned to Richmond it was to a small rented house at 210 East Leigh Street. There the mistress of Arlington House had not a chair or a spoon to call her own. But she borrowed odd pieces of furniture, found a cache of linens (this difficult because so much had been torn up for bandages) and carpets (likewise rare, cut up for army blankets), then set up her sock factory and resumed knitting day and night.

Early in December, one of Mary's most frequent and fervent prayers was answered when Robert arrived at Richmond on official business and came to be with her at the house on Leigh Street. It had been six months since they'd seen each other, and each was distressed by the other's appearance. Robert saw Mary's disability was worse than ever, the lines of pain and worry in her face chiseled deeper. Mary saw a man aged dramatically, his beard nearly white now, his figure so heavyset that he had had to order bigger uniform jackets, his energy and mobility impaired by the pain of angina and the burdens of an unwinnable war.

And yet there was so much to be thankful for. Mary and her husband hadn't spent Christmas together since

1859. The cramped and modest house on Leigh Street was far from the elegant ballroom at Arlington, appointed with Washington's favorite furniture and decorated every Christmas with garlands from Arlington Forest, dried fruits, lavish bows, the fragrance of roasted pheasants drifting in from the dining room and the Custis and Washington family silver polished to its utmost brilliance.

The great house and its contents were in the hands of strangers now, and what little silver Mary was able to save sat tarnishing, buried in the dirt somewhere far away. But it was Christmastime and Robert was here with her, as were all three of their daughters and oldest son, Custis. They'd heard, too, from Rooney in prison at Fort Lafayette, in good health and good sprits, his wound fully healed.

They decorated their small rooms with holly boughs and cranberries, built up the fires of scarce and expensive coal a little brighter in spite of the cost, and celebrated gifts that no war could take away: the gifts of love between husband and wife, between parent and child, and the unspeakable gift of God's only Son to a hopeless and fallen world.

Sitting quietly before the fire late on Christmas Day, Mary let her thoughts drift to the image of a young woman, newly engaged, standing straight and beautiful at a window overlooking her mother's vast rose garden and on toward the silvery Potomac River shimmering in the moonlight. Ancient oaks towered overhead. God had just entered her life and she couldn't sleep on account of it. She was too excited and couldn't make herself lie down until she captured her emotions on paper. They were too precious and intimate to put in a letter, much less talk to anybody about. And so she put them in a prayer journal, a letter to God:

I would not exchange the hope I have now in my Saviour for all that the world could give. I now solemnly dedicate myself & all that I have or may possess to His service.

Have I not the sweetest promise for the days of temptation & darkness? Why should I fear? Oh doubting soul, trust entirely to thy God for He will yet glorify thee! My prayer is for a stronger faith, though I sometimes shrink at the tribulation I may be called to endure for this purpose. But Jesus is all sufficient.

Separated from her home, her health, her heritage, her livelihood, her friends, her worldly riches, and even her beloved husband who had returned to his troops in the field, faith was about all Mary Custis Lee had left in these troubled times. But faith was all she needed.

Mary smiled and looked into the fire, her eyes dancing.

★ *John Perry*

MARY LEE
AND LOVE FOR OTHERS

★ ★ ★ ★ ★ ★ ★ ★ ★

Mary Custis had the good providence to have a godly mother who took care to train her not only in the womanly arts but also in the arts of the spirit. Mary had received from her mother a love for the Word of God and a reverence for the truth that leads to righteousness. Wealth and prestige are notorious for causing shipwreck in the lives of children, yet trained to understand that all things come from God, Mary never allowed her privileges to blind her to her responsibilities.

There was in her, as in her husband, Robert E. Lee, a humility born of grace. She never was known to despise those whom the world would view as "beneath her rank," and she cared for their best interests. After arriving at Fort Monroe with Robert, she found to her great distress that the room in which worship was held on the Lord's Day had no seats provided for the blacks of the community. She wrote to her mother, there "are no seats provided in the room for the blacks, consequently they never go." This Mary viewed as a serious omission and set about to double her efforts in the spiritual instruction of her maid Cassy. Mrs. Lee, like many other Christians in the South, was quite concerned to teach her servants to read in order that they might study God's Word on their own. She regularly reported on the progress of the servants in letters to her mother: "Margaret and Meniday get their lessons every week & Dick has gotten through the first reader."

While at West Point with her husband, she faithfully taught a "Sunday school" for blacks. She mentions in letters to her mother her desires for the conversion of those around her—the blacks, the soldiers, friends, and family. The nature of the sermons she heard were carefully recorded: "Dr. Ducachet preached two excellent sermons last Sunday. The one in the morning was particularly addressed to young officers. It was a faithful sermon, and the one at night more so, from the text 'What shall it profit a man if he gain the whole world and lose his own soul?' on what he gives in exchange for his soul. I was glad to see the house crowded and some very attentive hearers, particularly among the soldiers. I hope some good may have been done."

As a faithful mother, she did not overlook the spiritual welfare of her own children. Upon hearing of her daughter Annie's conversion, Mrs. Lee wrote joyfully to her:

It is very late my precious little daughter, but I cannot let another day pass without telling you the real happiness your letter afforded me, you for whom I have felt so anxious to hear that God had sent His spirit into your heart & drawn you to Himself. Remember what He says, "Those who seek me early shall find me." The promises of God are sure & cannot fail. Therefore seek Him with all your heart. You must pray for your sister & for your brothers who are out of the fold of Christ. Think what a happiness to your Mother to be able to present all her children at the throne of God & to be able to say, "Here I am Lord & the children Thou hast given me." Pray for your Mother that she may be more faithful in her prayers & example.

"There is no such thing as an indolent Christian!" Mrs. Lee loved to remind her daughters and friends. And she followed this maxim though afflicted severely with crippling arthritis. Throughout the war, Mrs. Lee kept herself and the girls of the household constantly busy knitting socks and other items for the destitute soldiers of the South. A lady visitor to her house during the war made this observation: "Her room was like an industrial school—everyone was busy. Her daughters were all there plying their needles, with several other ladies. When we came out someone said, "Did you see how the Lees spend their time? What a rebuke to taffy parties!" In one three-month stretch (March, April, and May of 1863) Mrs. Lee sent more than two hundred pairs of socks for distribution to the Stonewall Brigade. This, while she was confined to a wheelchair!

Though she was reared in the lap of privilege, Mary Lee never viewed it a sacrifice to live within the limits of a military officer's meager salary. No one would ever have known that she came from one of the most prominent

★ ★ ★ ★ ★ ★ ★ ★ ★ ★

There is no such thing as an indolent Christian!

—Mary Custis Lee

★ ★ ★ ★ ★ ★ ★ ★ ★ ★

families in the country. Though after the war provisions were slender, the bounty and abundance of prior days now only a memory, Mrs. Lee never complained. The same blessing was said before every meal regardless of its sparse nature: "God bless us and make us truly grateful for these and all thy mercies, and be pleased to continue them to us."

During the war and afterward, she suffered the loss of nearly all her earthly possessions, not least of which was her beloved home, Arlington, yet she was never known to complain. Her constant submission to the wise disposal of God had perhaps the greatest influence upon her husband and those around her. Most of her life was spent in crippling pain. Pain threw her into the arms of her heavenly Father: "I do not improve at all in walking & have to be lifted in & out of a carriage by 2 men & the physicians do not give me hope that I shall be any better—sad is it not to renounce all hope. I can only pray & strive for submission to God's holy will."

Her disappointments were many, and the defeat of her beloved Southland was high on the list. Here again, however, she willingly bowed before the wisdom of the Sovereign: "Tho' it has not pleased Almighty God to crown our exertions with success in the way & manner we expected, yet we must still trust & pray not that our will but His may be done in Heaven & in earth."

The loss of her faithful husband was the heaviest loss of all that she endured. Yet again we see the grace of God was sufficient: "God knows the best time for us to leave this world & we must never question either His love or wisdom." To General Butler, who had written to comfort her in "the untimely death" of her husband, she replied, "You speak of my husband's 'untimely death.' We must not deem that untimely which God ordains. He knows the best time to take us from this world; and can we question

either his love or wisdom? How often are we taken from the evil to come. How much of care and sorrows are those spared who die young. Even the heathen considers such the favorites of the gods; and to the Christian what is death but a translation to eternal life. Pray that we may all live so that death will have no terrors for us."

God has said that when two marry, they are no longer two but one. Each is used as instruments of His grace in the life of the other. It was this example of faith and love that stirred and encouraged General Lee throughout his life. He was a better man because of the companion God gave him.

✳ Steve Wilkins

MARY BOYKIN MILLER CHESTNUT

★ ★ ★ ★ ★ ★ ★ ★ ★

Born on March 31, 1823, in Statesburg, South Carolina, Mary Chestnut became one of the most insightful personal voices on the Civil War from a Confederate perspective. Her aristocratic, well-to-do family afforded her the opportunity to become well educated at an exclusive boarding school in Charleston. From her early childhood, her intelligence and razor-sharp wit became apparent, and she excelled in her studies.

At seventeen, Mary married James Chestnut, and the

Mary Chestnut

newlyweds moved onto his parent's plantation in Mulberry, South Carolina, near Camden. Her frustration began shortly thereafter when she found out she could not bear children, and this was compounded when her new mother-in-law would not give her anything to do. Feeling powerless and aggravated, she had little outlet for venting during the first twenty years of marriage.

The Chestnuts moved to Washington, D.C., in 1856 upon James winning a seat in the Senate. They began to become acquainted with another couple named Jefferson and Varina Davis. James resigned in 1861 to protest Lincoln being voted into office. That same year Mary began her diary, beginning with this entry: "I do not allow myself vain regrets or sad foreboding. This Southern Confederacy must be supported now by calm determination and cool brains. We have risked, and we must play our best for the stake is life and death."

A year later, the couple moved to Richmond, Virginia, when Confederate President Davis commissioned James to be his aide. Mary continued to write insatiably, commenting on the "Yankee interference" to praising Robert E. Lee in his victories. Politically and socially astute, she offered a wide viewpoint to all issues, from a high society woman's perspective to the effects on the common class.

She also wrote on her quasi-abolitionist sentiments, as she never intended parts of her diary to ever reach publication. Her diary shows the life of a privileged Southern woman and the centrality and dichotomy of her thinking on certain issues. While she wrote on her aversion to slavery, she enjoyed the fruits of such a society in her day-to-day life. She describes her interest in slavery as "narrowly self-interested," in that it helped her defy the stereotypes and social conventions thrust upon her. Slavery "threatened her position as a woman," where she comments on the servitude of women to their husbands. Mary operated

within the society, supporting the war and expressing her own ideas and beliefs by integrating them with prevalent issues of the time.

When 1864 rolled around, the Chestnuts moved back to South Carolina and then again to Lincolntown, North Carolina, to avoid the ever advancing Yankee troops. Once the war ended, they moved back to Mulberry, only to find their plantation in ruins from the Union march through the area. Now deeply in debt, the couple faced financial hardships and concerns that they never even had to think about before.

Throughout the Reconstruction until her death, Mary penned her diary. Upon her death, many versions of her diary existed, some clearly made for publication, some for her own personal keeping. The entire section from 1862–64 has never been recovered, possibly destroyed during the war.

In the postwar years, Mary filled in the gaps in a retrospective diary. She revised until the mid-1870s, resuming in 1881 only to be stopped again in 1885 by the death of her husband and her mother. In light of this event, Chestnut never picked up her pen to work on the piece again. She died in 1886, never to see her diary published as she hoped.

A first edition came into existence in 1905, entitled *Diary from Dixie*,[1] and in 1981, Mary Chestnut's *Civil War* hit the market with a newly edited and annotated version of her diary by C. Vann Woodward, having come into more pages of her personal diary. The latter book won a Pulitzer Prize in history that same year. While Mary herself never saw the fruits of her labor, many people have enjoyed her diary and through it have vicariously experienced the war through the eyes of one who lived it.

Mary's diary is peppered with strong faith, references to God, and Christian virtue. As she noted on December

21, 1860: "Mrs. Charles Lowndes was sitting with us today, when Mrs. Kirkland brought in a copy of the Secession Ordinance. I wonder if my face grew as white as hers. She said after a moment: 'God help us. As our day, so shall our strength be.' How grateful we were for this pious ejaculation of hers!"

Ted Baehr

Another prolific writer during the Civil War, Harriet Beecher Stowe became famous for her antislavery novel Uncle Tom's Cabin.

THE CORBIN WOMEN

During the winter following the Battle of Fredericksburg in December 1862, the Stonewall Brigade of the Army of Northern Virginia camped on the plantation of a famous Virginia family whose tragic suffering typified that of the Southern aristocracy. It was during their twelve weeks here that Stonewall Jackson's assistant adjuvant general, Sandie Pendleton, met, and ultimately married, one of the daughters of this prominent family. Here Robert E. Lee celebrated Christmas that year with Jackson and J. E. B. Stuart at the home of Lee's distant cousin, James Parke Corbin.

Corbin, orphaned at the age of eleven, lost two of the four plantations he inherited to pay off debts caused by his lifestyle and his guardian's mismanagement. After his marriage to Jane Catherine Wellford of Fredericksburg, to protect his legacy he transferred the deeds to his wife and five children. In 1843 he sold Laneville plantation, his second loss, and moved to Moss Neck Manor, ten miles south of Fredericksburg, where he built a modest home. The plantation there comprised more than two thousand acres and listed thirty-seven slaves in service. In 1856, he built a replica of the Laneville mansion and named it Moss Neck. Unfortunately, Jane died the year before they were to move in, and the ownership moved to the children. Corbin remarried within two years and settled with his new wife on the other remaining plantation, leaving Moss Neck under the control of his children.

Richard and Spottswood Wellford, the two oldest sons, had entered the University of Virginia in 1854, but neither completed their studies. Wellford married and settled next to his father—and his inheritance—at Farley

Vale. Richard also chose to marry and presided over the plantation with his wife, the lively and entertaining Roberta (Bertie) Cary, the orphaned daughter of a Lewisburg physician. They had one daughter, Jane, before Richard volunteered for the Confederate army as a private in the Ninth Virginia Cavalry.

Sharing the mansion were his younger Corbin siblings, Catherine (Kate) Carter, Fanny (Nettie) Nelson, and James Parke Jr. After schooling at home by tutors, the girls went off for a year at a private school for girls in Richmond.

Nettie Corbin later married W. H. (Bee) Dickinson and settled with him on his property, Echo Dell, in King George County. After Dickinson volunteered for service and the Federals occupied the area, Nettie and her three small children came to live at Moss Neck with Bertie, Kate, and James Parke Jr. In early 1862 the Union army under McDowell established itself on the Falmouth Heights across the Rappahannock from Fredericksburg, which the Confederates evacuated. The presence of the Union troops prompted the flight to freedom of many of the field slaves, and federal foraging parties vandalized the proud mansion and its furnishings. The family survived in the mutilated mansion with the help of their domestic slaves.

Early on December 12, 1862, Confederate troops began moving through the Moss Neck property at a fast pace through fences and fields, heading rapidly toward Fredericksburg. This was Stonewall Jackson's Second Corps that had only recently come to Guiney Station several miles further south. News of an impending battle prompted Kate and Bertie to ride off on their horses toward Fredericksburg to watch. Although warned of the danger, the girls rode even closer the next day to watch the federal defeat through a field glass.

Three days after the battle, General Jackson and his staff appeared at Moss Neck, looking for a winter head-

quarters. In the absence of her husband who was away on duty, Mrs. Corbin invited the general to use a wing of the house, but he protested that it was "too luxurious for a soldier, who should sleep in a tent." Jackson did sleep in a tent until his medical officer advised him to move into the small frame office of the plantation. Nevertheless Jackson and the staff took their meals in a tent, and the staff slept in tents nearby. Christmas Day Jackson hosted Generals Lee, Stuart, and Pendleton for dinner. The commanding General Lee was blessed with a kiss by the winsome daughter of Bertie, five-year-old Jane, who announced she also wanted to kiss General Jackson.

The often dour Professor Jackson was also swept up by the girl's charms, perhaps in part by the news that his only child, a girl, had been born only days before in Lexington. In a few weeks Mrs. Jackson and "Baby Stonewall" visited Moss Neck as guests of the Corbins, but daily Jackson could find diversion in childish amusements with little Jane.

For the next three months, Jackson and his staff prepared reports of the past and plans for the future. On most days the general rode or walked through his troops camped alongside the river, inspecting their defenses and visiting the wounded. On several occasions visitors from Richmond and even Europe called on Jackson there. While at Moss Neck the twenty-two-year-old assistant adjuvant general to Jackson, Sandie Pendleton, began a courtship with Kate Corbin, despite the competing interest of several other officers.

The three-month hiatus at Moss Neck came to a swift and shocking end. On March 19, Jackson moved his headquarters to the Yerby place at Hamilton's Crossing to be closer to General Lee. Before leaving Moss Point the general called on the convalescing little Jane in her sick bed to bid her farewell. Only moments after Jackson's departure, the child died from scarlet fever despite Dr. Hunter McGuire's attention. Bertie became uncontrollably hysterical, and Nettie caught Major Pendleton as he was leaving. The son of an Episcopal priest and artillery general, William Nelson Pendleton, Sandie described the tragedy in a letter to his mother:

I went back, and never have I witnessed such a scene. The grief of that young mother—just 24—at the death of her only child—and that too so sudden and unexpected—was it itself tearful enough. But since that young mother was a purely worldly woman, with no idea of religion in its real power—a bright butterfly nature that had lived only in the sunlight of life and never seen one of its storms before—under such circumstances, it was truly appalling to witness that heart-broken anguish.

When I entered the room, she was clinging to Miss Kate Corbin, almost frantic, uttering the most piercing cries I ever heard. I spoke to her & told her she must be calm, when she loosened her hold on Miss Kate & seized me, and began afresh with her wild lamentations. I soothed her, as best I could, and got her somewhat quieter by repeating, as I recalled them, such passages as "Suffer little children to come unto me," "the Lord gave and the Lord hath taken away," which seemed the best I could do. She would continually break in, "but why did the Lord take my child," which question would stagger me, and unused to such scenes I could answer nothing.

At last I asked her if she could pray. She said no, but asked me to pray for her. I could not refuse at such a time, and there standing by the bedside, the crushed, but almost frantic mother clinging to me for comfort & support, I offered up the most earnest prayer for her guidance and comfort from on High that she might be strengthened to bear the blow, and led to seek the Saviour & Comforter in consequence of it; then she being more quiet I left.

Upon hearing of Jane's death, Jackson was "moved and wept freely." Jane was joined in less than three days by two of Nettie Dickinson's small children, Parke and Gardiner. "Surely the angel of Death has spread his wings over this house," diaried Captain Henry Douglas. Richard Corbin had to be recalled from a cavalry outpost to bury the three children in the family graveyard. Tragically, Richard himself was killed the following summer in battle.

Following the war, the family fortunes continued to deteriorate, and Corbin's widow Bertie was forced to sell Moss Neck in December 1864, and James Parke Corbin Jr. struggled to subsist on his land as a hard-working farmer. After visiting her father, Kate, now the widow of Sandie Pendleton, found employment as a governess in Lexington, before marrying again in 1871. Bertie was remarried to a Christian minister.[2]

⭐ *Dorsey M. Deaton*

I have never studied the art of paying compliments to women; but I must say that if all that has been said by orators and poets since the creation of the world in praise of women were applied to the women of America, it would not do them justice for their conduct during this war. I will close by saying, God bless the women of America!

—Abraham Lincoln,
Closing of Sanitary Fair,
Washington, D.C., March 18, 1864

The Love Affair of Fanny and Lawrence Chamberlain

★ ★ ★ ★ ★ ★ ★ ★ ★ ★

Joshua Lawrence Chamberlain's stuttering may have opened the door to one of the great romances of the nineteenth century, proving true the Scripture in Romans 8:28 (KJV): "And we know that all things work together for good to them that love God, to them who are the called according to his purpose."[3] Although embarrassed over this affliction, Chamberlain joined the First Parish Church choir. It was soon after that he realized he didn't stutter when he sang! Chamberlain explained, "If you are coming to something which you can't speak, persuade yourself you are going to sing—feel the emotion of it and that will bear you on its motion—it is not necessary to do this so badly and unskillfully as to draw the attention of your hearers from the things you are saying to the way you are saying them . . . anything that is worth saying, is worth singing."[3]

Chamberlain was singing in the church choir when he first saw the attractive church organist, Frances Caroline Adams, three years his senior and affectionately known as Fanny. The adopted daughter of the Maine Congregationalist Church's pastor, Dr. George Adams, Fanny was born and raised in Boston, but when she was four, her elderly father had sent the girl to live with his childless cousin, believing the younger man and his wife could offer Fanny a much brighter future.

Educated in the arts and music, the strong-willed young woman, who refused to join her uncle's church in favor of her Unitarian beliefs, had also developed a fondness for beautiful clothes and fur, so she was not attracted to the young Bowdoin student named Joshua Lawrence Chamberlain. Nor did her guardian, the church's pastor, consider him to be worthy of his adopted daughter. But that didn't stop Chamberlain from falling madly and hopelessly in love with Fanny.

Eventually, the persistent and romantic Chamberlain won Fanny's hand, but because of her lack of attraction to him, she initially considered a platonic marriage. This notion quickly changed when the betrothed pair was forced to delay their marriage so Fanny could work to repay her guardians and Chamberlain could complete his education. While Fanny taught at a girl's school, gave private piano lessons, and played the organ for the Presbyterian Church in Milledgeville, Georgia, Chamberlain's love letters won her heart. The three-year separation was the first of many such partings, but it afforded future generations a rich history through a series of their beautiful letters.

Joshua Chamberlain

With her debt paid, Fanny returned from Georgia in August 1855 in time for her fiancé's graduation from Bangor Theological Seminary and the completion of a master's degree from Bowdoin College. Just prior to their marriage on December 7, 1855, Chamberlain wrote to Fanny: "I know in whom all my highest hopes and dearest joys are centered. I know in whom my whole heart can rest—so sweetly and so surely. Fanny, Dear Fanny, only tell me that YOU do love me as I DO love you."[4]

Married at First Parish Church by Dr. Adams, the newlyweds were deliriously happy as they began their wedded life together. Chamberlain wrote of their honeymoon night spent in Fanny's room at the minister's parish:

"When my fairy honeysuckle girl came to the arms that once lifted her up among the leaves roses, so sadly so tremblingly yet so calmly came laid her head in my bosom on that wedding night—that sweetest purest ever to be honored night."[5]

To the skeptics' surprise, the artistic and sophisticated Fanny quickly settled into the role of devoted wife. By October 1856, she gave birth to the couple's first child, Grace Dupee Chamberlain, a healthy baby affectionately called "Daisy." In October 1858, their son, Harold Wyllys, was born. Motherhood also came naturally to the young woman, who had often expressed slightly feminist views, but, sadly, three other children born to the couple did not survive a year.

In 1859 Chamberlain purchased a home for his growing family, a modest Federal style Cape surrounded by a beautiful garden. This home had once belonged to noted poet Henry Wadsworth Longfellow, who had brought his own bride to live there in 1829. Life was idyllic for Fanny Chamberlain, who was happily raising her daughter and son and enjoying her home and garden, as well as the role of a promising Bowdoin College professor's wife.

Fanny's euphoria ended soon, however, because following the 1860 election of Abraham Lincoln, eleven Southern states began to secede. They feared their way of life and their economy were about to end and declared themselves a new country: the Confederate States of America. On April 12, 1861, the guns of the state of South Carolina opened fire on the United States' Fort Sumter in Charleston harbor. The Civil War had begun. Immediately, several Bowdoin upperclassmen and alumni enlisted in the Union army. Fanny urged her husband to stay behind, and both believed the conflict would be short-lived.

Over the next year as the War Between the States escalated, Chamberlain had a change of heart. He confided in Fanny that he was going to offer his services to the Union army instead of taking an approved sabbatical to Europe. Poor Fanny was distressed at the thought of her husband's departure, as well as the possibility of not only losing her husband but the children's father and the family's sole supporter.

Surprisingly, her father-in-law, Joshua Sr., sided with Fanny. Chamberlain Sr. explained his opposition by saying, "Not our war," which seemed uncharacteristic based on the facts that he had earlier urged his son to enroll in West Point and had named him for James Lawrence, a hero of the War of 1812 whose famous dying words were, "Don't give up the ship!" The elder Chamberlain believed that the Southern states should be allowed to secede from the Union. His son, Lawrence, disagreed. Even the board at Bowdoin College expressed their discontent with Chamberlain's desire to join the war. They feared that if he didn't return he would be replaced by someone who didn't share their devout Congregationalist faith.

Despite the opposition of Fanny, his family, and his colleagues, duty called and Chamberlain enlisted. Governor Washburn offered Chamberlain the rank of colonel, but because of his lack of experience as a soldier, he declined. Chamberlain was assigned the rank of lieutenant colonel for Maine's 20th Infantry Regiment. Sadly, Fanny was forced to kiss her husband good-bye on August 8, 1862, when he was put in as second-in-command to Colonel Adelbert Ames, an army officer from Rockland, Maine.

Once her husband enlisted, Fanny vehemently supported his war efforts and even traveled to the battlefield to visit him. Rumors among the men even credited Fanny with the victory at Gettysburg because prior to the battle she had boosted the morale of her husband and his troops.

Chamberlain proved to be a great soldier. Wounded four times in battle, he was told that he would not survive the injuries he sustained during the siege of Petersburg and even sent a farewell letter to Fanny. General Ulysses S. Grant personally brevetted the rank of brigadier general upon Chamberlain, and on April 28, 1865, he had the distinguished honor of commanding the Union troops to receive the surrender of General Robert E. Lee's infantry at Appomattox Court House. Believing the Confederate army deserved some recognition, Chamberlain ordered his men to salute the defeated soldiers. This heartfelt gesture won the respect of many of the Confederates and prompted one soldier to write to Chamberlain that when the soldier had a perfect aim at him, God had divinely intervened on two different occasions and the soldier put his gun down. Perhaps this was in answer to Fanny's prayers for her husband.

When the war was over, Chamberlain went home a hero to Fanny, to his children, to the faculty at Bowdoin College, and to the citizens of Maine. Joking with a reporter after he returned to Brunswick, he quipped, "When I returned to Brunswick after the war, I found I was a great man—so I added another story to my house."[6] But he wasn't joking. Chamberlain had their home moved across the street from the Parish Church and Bowdoin College and raised the house eleven feet, installing a new first floor, which converted the story-and-a-half residence into a grand home with more than twenty rooms. The Brunswick, Maine, building is now home to the Joshua Lawrence Chamberlain Museum.

Following his wartime experiences, Chamberlain found teaching unfulfilling, and a year later he entered

Chamberlain as soldier

politics at the urging of the head of Maine's Republican party. In 1867, Fanny Chamberlain became First Lady of Maine when her husband was elected governor, but the family declined to move into the governor's residence in Augusta, preferring to remain in their own home in Brunswick. Chamberlain commuted to Augusta to serve four terms as governor from 1867 to 1871.

Influenced and fueled by Fanny's love, support, and respect, Chamberlain became known as a governor who was his own man, guided not by his party, or any man, but by his conscience. Although it had once appeared that the couple might continue on to Washington with Chamberlain a possible senatorial candidate, he irked the Republicans with several controversial stands, especially when he sided against the impeachment of President Andrew Johnson; Chamberlain believed he was innocent. This marked the end of Chamberlain's political aspirations.

Chamberlain returned to Bowdoin College to assume the presidency in 1871, where he became a successful leader. At times he accepted speaking engagements at veteran and civic groups throughout the country and even ventured abroad as the United States Commissioner of Education for the Universal Exposition in Paris.

Evidenced by his writing and actions, Fanny's influences on her husband were compelling. Although Bowdoin remained a male college until 1971, Chamberlain encouraged women to attend the summer programs and wrote, "Women too should have a part in this high calling. Because in this sphere of things, her 'rights,' her capacities, her offices, her destiny are equal to those of man. She is the Heaven, appointed teacher of man, his guide, his better soul. By her own right, however she inherits here, not as the sister of man, but as the daughter of God!"[7]

In deteriorating health and ordered to a milder climate, Chamberlain resigned as president of Bowdoin College in 1883. The couple spent time in Florida where Chamberlain convalesced and invested in real estate and other ventures with his son. They also visited their three grandchildren, daughter Daisy, and her husband, a successful attorney, in Boston and at their summer home in Maine.

The Chamberlains also purchased a summer home at Simpson's Point near Brunswick that they named Domhegan. Chamberlain enjoyed many hours there, riding his war-horse Charlemagne and sailing his schooner *Pinafore*. Because of Fanny's love of the arts, they also established an artists colony for an eight-week course at Domhegan every summer.

Throughout Fanny's life, she had suffered with eye problems, and by 1900 she was totally blind. Over her husband's and her son-in-law's protests, Fanny became reclusive, but Chamberlain remained devoted to her and would often read aloud to her in her later years. He included the love letters, which he still wrote to her. On her eightieth birthday, Chamberlain wrote, "Your husband and your children 'rise up and call you blessed'—as the old scriptures represent the crowning grace of a good woman."[8]

In 1900 President William McKinley appointed Chamberlain as the Surveyor of Customs of the Port of Portland, and he was reappointed by subsequent presidents Roosevelt and Taft. Shortly after accepting the position, Chamberlain suffered problems from his old war injury. Forced to recuperate in a milder climate, he traveled to the Mediterranean and Egypt, but because of her blindness, Fanny chose to stay at home.

By the summer of 1905, the great love affair was coming to an end when Fanny, after breaking her hip, became seriously ill. She passed from this life the following October. Her funeral was held in the First Parish Church where she had first met her husband. Chamberlain deeply grieved and had the words "UNVEILLED, October 18, 1905," inscribed upon her tombstone, referring to her blindness. He believed, as the Bible promised, her sight was restored in heaven. Chamberlain's deep faith sustained him through his grief. Subsequently, he wrote a beautiful tribute to Fanny in a war paper, the Last Review of the Army of the Potomac: "You in my soul I see, faithful watcher by my cot-side long days and nights together through the delirium of mortal anguish—steadfast, calm, and sweet as eternal love. We pass now quickly from each other's sight; but I know full well that where beyond these passing scenes you shall be, there will be heaven!"[9]

In 1914, nine years following his bride's death, Joshua Lawrence Chamberlain, at age eighty-five, finally succumbed to a serious relapse of the inflammation and infection of his old war injury. Both his son Wyllys and his daughter Daisy were at their father's side on February 24, 1914, as he peacefully took his last breath.

Even during their most difficult times, for better for worse (the separation and horror of war, frequent separations, and political challenges), in sickness and in health (the loss of their babies, Chamberlain's war injuries, and Fanny's failing eyesight), Chamberlain and Fanny's love for one another remained strong until they were parted by death. Their earthly remains were laid to rest, side by side in the family plot in Pine Grove Cemetery in Brunswick near the First Parish Church where Joshua Lawrence Chamberlain first laid eyes on his beloved Fanny.

★ *Susan Huey Wales*

"THOSE DREADFUL HOURS"
EXCERPT FROM THE DIARY OF CLARA BARTON

No one has forgotten the heart-sickness which spread over the entire country as the busy wires flashed the dire tidings of the terrible destitution and suffering of the wounded of the Wilderness whom I attended as they lay in Fredericksburg. But you may never have known how many hundredfold of these ills were augmented by the conduct of improper, heartless, unfaithful officers in the immediate command of the city and upon whose actions and indecisions depended entirely the care, food, shelter, comfort, and lives of that whole city of wounded men. One of the highest officers there has since been convicted a traitor. And another, a little dapper captain quartered with the owners of one of the finest mansions in the town, boasted that he had changed his opinion since entering the city the day before; that it was in fact a pretty hard thing for refined people like the people of Fredericksburg to be compelled to open their homes and admit these dirty, lousy, common soldiers," and that he was not going to compel it.

This I heard him say, and waited until I saw him make his words good, till I saw, crowded into one old sunken hotel, lying helpless upon its bare, wet, bloody floors, five hundred fainting men hold up their cold, bloodless, dingy hands, as I passed, and beg me in Heaven's name for a cracker to keep them from starving (and I had none); or to give them a cup that they might have something to drink water from, if they could get it (and I had no cup and could get none); till I saw two hundred six-mule army wagons in a line, ranged down the street to headquarters, and reaching so far out on the Wilderness road that I never found the end of it; every wagon crowded with wounded men, stopped, standing in the rain and mud, wrenched back and forth by the restless, hungry animals all night from four o'clock in the afternoon till eight next morning and how much longer, I know not. The dark spot in the mud under many a wagon, told only too plainly where some poor fellow's life had dripped out in those dreadful hours.

Barton fought to remedy the "terrible destitution and suffering of the wounded."

I remembered one man who would set it right, if he knew it, who possessed the power and who would believe me if I told him I commanded immediate conveyance back to Belle Plain. With difficulty I obtained it, and four stout horses with a light army wagon took me ten miles at an unbroken gallop, through field and swamp and stumps and mud to Belle Plain and a steam tug at once to Washington. Landing at dusk I sent for Henry Wilson, chairman of the Military Committee of the Senate. A messenger brought him at eight, saddened and appalled like every other patriot in that fearful hour, at the weight of woe under which the Nation staggered, groaned, and wept.

He listened to the story of suffering and faithlessness, and hurried from my presence, with lips compressed and face like ashes. At ten he stood in the War Department. They could not credit his report. He must have been deceived by some frightened villain. No official report of unusual suffering had reached them. Nothing had been called for by the military authorities commanding Fredericksburg.

Mr. Wilson assured them that the officers in trust there were not to be relied upon. They were faithless, overcome by the blandishments of the wily inhabitants. Still the Department doubted. It was then that he proved that my confidence in his firmness was not misplaced, as, facing his doubters he replied: "One of two things will have to be done—either you will send some one to-night with the power to investigate and correct the abuses of our wounded men at Fredericksburg, or the Senate will send some one tomorrow."

This threat recalled their scattered senses.

At two o'clock in the morning the Quartermaster-General and staff galloped to the 6th Street wharf under orders; at ten they were in Fredericksburg. At noon the wounded men were fed from the food of the city and the houses were opened to the "dirty, lousy soldiers" of the Union army.

Both railroad and canal were opened. In three days I returned with carloads of supplies.

No more jolting in army wagons! And every man who left Fredericksburg by boat or by car owes it to the firm decision of one man that his grating bones were not dragged ten miles across the country or left to bleach in the sands of that city.

★ ★ ★ ★ ★ ★ ★ ★ ★ ★ ★ ★ ★ ★ ★

A messenger brought him at eight, saddened and appalled like every other patriot in that fearful hour, at the weight of woe under which the Nation staggered, groaned, and wept.

—Clara Barton

★ ★ ★ ★ ★ ★ ★ ★ ★ ★ ★ ★ ★ ★ ★

8
THE BRIGHTEST
AND THE BEST

THE PENDLETONS

★ ★ ★ ★ ★ ★ ★ ★ ★ ★ ★ ★ ★ ★ ★ ★ ★ ★ ★ ★

Led by their fearless general, Stonewall Jackson, the Confederate army advances in the Battle at Chancellorsville.

The Confederate flag carried into battle.

While some people may doubt his effectiveness as a messenger of Christ because of his military allegiance, there can be no doubt that throughout his life he took the time to comfort those in need and share the love of Christ, loving those who needed it when times were grim.

—Ted Baehr on William Nelson Pendleton

"OLD ARTILLERY": WILLIAM NELSON PENDLETON

★ ★ ★ ★ ★ ★ ★ ★ ★ ★

As the Southern states one by one seceded from the Union, many had to face the decision of how to respond to the action taken by their native state and the threatened invasion of the Northern armies across their borders. Rev. William Pendleton of Virginia was one who faced this dilemma. An Episcopal priest in Lexington, Virginia, Pendleton had graduated from West Point and had artillery experience in the army. He was a loyal American, but how should he respond to secession and the impending war? On May 1, 1861, Pendleton spent a longer time than usual in his private devotions, praying for divine guidance in the course he should take. When he was offered command of the Rockbridge Artillery that day, he accepted.

After his death, among his private papers was found a document he had written that morning in 1861, summarizing his reasons for the decision he had made. His reasoning fell into four main points. First, defensive war was perfectly biblical. Government's main responsibility was the protection of its people. Since the North was planning an invasion of the seceding South, the states were justified in defending their people and lands. Second, Virginia had repeatedly appealed to the North in the last forty years not to violate the equal status of the states agreed to in the constitutional compact. Virginia had not hastily seceded with some of her sister states, but when the North called for seventy-five thousand men on her immediate borders, Virginia was compelled to defend herself. Third, the Northern governmental proclamations, press, and un-Christian pulpit had so inflamed the passions of the people that Virginia and other Southern states were threatened with murder and universal desolation by the multitude of the North. It was Pendleton's sacred duty to work for the protection of his own family and his countrymen. Fourth, he was personally called to lead the artillery, a job in which he was well trained. If he failed to respond to that call, he could cause men to feel that the gospel hope does not provide courage in a difficult time. He decided to be led by Providence, and if someone else should come along who was worthy to lead the artillery, he would prefer duties of a more spiritual nature. Pendleton concluded his thoughts with a prayer:

> Trusting that the Judge of all the earth will accept me in the covenant of His grace, help me to honor His holy name in the trying position, and restore me, if it be His holy will, in time to my family and ordinary duties; take care of the dear ones I leave behind, and deliver us all from the cruel tyranny impending, I go to the post of danger. Lord Jesus, go with me. Blessed Spirit, be my guide. Almighty Father,

spare the effusion of blood, frustrate evil counsels, order for our land conditions of peace, and make our people that happy people whose God is the Lord![1]

William Pendleton

Soon after, Pendleton wrote to a northern clergyman explaining his reasons for joining the army: "To take part in the dreadful work of death is to me the severest trial of my life. Loving peace, praying for peace, preaching peace from the bottom of my heart, I find myself, in the very name of the Prince of Peace, obliged to see my own dear country subdued, disgraced, ruined, and my wife and daughters exposed to brutal outrage worse than death, or to fight side by side with my only son, my son-in-law, my brothers, and dearest friends of every grade, in defense of our hearthstones. Do you blame me?"[2]

On May 12 the Rockbridge Artillery was mustered at Staunton, Virginia, with seventy-six men on the original roster. Once it was known Captain Pendleton had taken the company, men from all over the state came. Parents thought their sons would be well cared for under his direction and training. Pendleton had prayer every morning at reveille roll-call and in his quarters every night for those men and officers who wished to attend. In the beginning, the company had only four guns, which the boys quickly named Matthew, Mark, Luke, and John, after the Four Gospels.

On Sundays, Pendleton regularly preached. Since he was in active duty as well as being a minister, it seemed that the soldiers liked to hear him more than the chaplains. Most Sundays he preached three or four times in different sections of the army. General Lee often conferred with Pendleton on how Christianity could better be encouraged among the young men in the army, and he regularly led the various prayer and chapel services throughout the camps.

From First Manassas to Appomattox, Pendleton directed the artillery in every major battle fought by the Army of Northern Virginia. His Christian faith gave him calm and peace in the midst of the smoke, chaos, and terror of battle. In April 1862, he wrote his eighty-year-old aunt: "You wish to know the state of my mind in prospect of the bloody conflict impending. Of course, I feel the hazard, but have very little shrinking. God can cover my head as He has done before. If He sees fit to have my days cut short and your hearts smitten by such an affliction, He can make it work for good to us all, and will, I am persuaded.[3]

When the troops, North and South, were massing around Fredericksburg in the fall of 1862, Pendleton was busy preparing the defensive position of the artillery batteries. He took time to explain some of his feelings in a letter to his daughter:

When I contemplate my own part in the struggle here my feelings are solemn, yet trustful and hopeful. He who notes the fall of the sparrow holds in His hands my life on the battlefield as everywhere else. And I desire, harder though it then be, to realize this when the shells crash and the bullets whiz within a hair's-breadth as when all is quiet and peace around me. It is a strange position for a servant of the Prince of Peace and a minister of the Gospel of Peace. But as I do not delight in war, and would not hurt the hair of the head of any human being save under conviction of public duty; as by

Soldiers prepare artillery for battle.

126

prayer, pleadings, and expostulations I have earnestly tried for peace, so I trust the blessing of the peace-maker will not be denied me, though as a soldier of the Cross I follow the example of old Abraham in endeavoring to defend my kindred against cruel outrage.[4] . . . [The Lord] knows how truly I mourn over the wrongs which have compelled the best people of the South to resolve on resistance unto death, and how painful to me the alternative of seeing all that I most value on earth desolated. . . . He sees that I desire in all sincerity to be a faithful soldier of the Cross, while trying also to be a useful soldier of a much-wronged country. And He graciously accepts, I trust, my unworthy services, whatever error, whatever sin be chargeable against me in this as in other portions of my life. The blood of Christ cleanseth from all sin.[5]

The losses at Gettysburg and Vicksburg in July 1863 were a severe blow to the Confederate cause. The Army of Northern Virginia especially was not used to defeat. The earlier loss of Jackson at the battle of Chancellorsville had weakened the Confederate operations, and the army drew nearer to Richmond to protect the capital from General Meade. In the wake of such defeat, Pendleton steadfastly maintained his trust in the Lord and wrote his wife: "You are all well, I trust, and comfortable in reliance on God notwithstanding the unfavorable turn in our national affairs. It is undoubtedly a time to try our faith and fortitude. But God has not vacated His throne, nor will He, except for wise purposes, permit iniquity to triumph ultimately. And if, for such purposes, although impenetrable to us, He see fit to allow our enemies to triumph, we can, I hope, submit

★ ★ ★ ★ ★ ★ ★ ★ ★ ★

He who notes the fall of the sparrow holds in His hands my life on the battlefield as everywhere else.

—William Pendleton

★ ★ ★ ★ ★ ★ ★ ★ ★ ★

to Him even therein, as did our Saviour under the hands of His enemies—'Not my will, but thine, be done.'"[6]

As the war worsened for the South, Brigadier General Pendleton faithfully maintained his military and spiritual duties. In addition to overseeing the artillery, he continued to regularly preach several times on Sundays, hold prayer meetings, and provide spiritual counsel with individual soldiers. In the last year of the war he wrote his wife about a conversation with General Wise: "General Wise expressed himself very warmly to me about my sermon last Sunday night. He said the text did him good: 'That blessed hope.' He thanked me, and spoke at length of sins, struggles, and faith. Said he 'would not give up his faith in Jesus for all the world besides.' Yet he says the devil makes him kuss sometimes. A strange but interesting man. The war has greatly humbled him, he says. He finds himself a poor creature, whereas he thought a good deal of himself before."[7]

By April 1865, Robert E. Lee recognized that his Army of Northern Virginia was overwhelmed by superior numbers and resources. General Pendleton along with Generals Longstreet and Gordon were chosen the three Confederate commissioners to arrange the details of the surrender at Appomattox. The circumstances connected with the surrender were so painful that General Pendleton rarely spoke of it in later years. Whenever he began telling his daughter about Appomattox, his speech became choked with emotion and he would defer his tale to another time, which never came. Yet General Pendleton maintained his stalwart faith in his Lord. He returned to Lexington to resume the pastorate of Grace Episcopal Church, where Robert E. Lee was later a vestryman. He remained at the church until his death in 1883. At his funeral, the vestry recognized him: ". . . an humble, obedient, and devoted servant of God, a Christian of great sincerity and purity of character, a minister of the Gospel of our Lord Jesus Christ, 'thoroughly furnished unto all good works.'"[8]

     ⭑ *Diana L. Severance*

ELEVATED MULES

⭑ ⭑ ⭑ ⭑ ⭑ ⭑ ⭑ ⭑ ⭑

The Civil War brought many young men face to face with death as never before. The American Tract Society distributed numerous tracts among the soldiers to encourage them to turn to their Savior and face death with Christian peace and hope. Organized in 1825, the American Tract Society had quickly become a leader in the printing technology of the day. By the end of the decade, it was printing and distributing more than 5 million tracts annually. In 1832, William Pendleton, then a professor at West Point, took the opportunity while in New York of visiting the Tract Society offices. He described his visit in a letter to his wife:

> I must tell you of the great gratification I had in New York, and one which I hope you may one day have—in seeing the steam printing-presses at the house of the Bible Society, and the great number of cheap Bibles printed there. The house of the Tract Society is also very gratifying. It would do your heart good, and your mamma would be delighted to see the air of Christian benevolence about everything, and the extreme neatness of the little girls and the numerous women engaged there. It is curious to see the

great rapidity of execution in every department of both institutions, printing, folding, stitching, pasting, pressing and binding the Bibles and tracts. I was diverted to see two mules stabled in the fourth or fifth story of the Tract Society house. They were raised up by ropes and pulleys through trapdoors, for the purpose of working the presses, and, poor animals—or fat animals, for they were very fat— they are doomed to feel what many biped asses have felt before them—the miseries of an elevated station in life.[9]

     ⭑ *Diana L. Severance*

STONEWALL'S MAN: SANDIE PENDLETON

⭑ ⭑ ⭑ ⭑ ⭑ ⭑ ⭑ ⭑ ⭑

Sandie Pendleton

A General can be no greater than those who assist him." If these words of Dwight Eisenhower were ever appropriate, they were true of the staff of General Thomas J. Jackson of the Army of Northern Virginia. Stonewall, as he became legendarily known, surrounded himself with some of the best and brightest of his home state. For example, his chief of medicine, Hunter McGuire, would later head the American Medical Association and the American Surgical Association. But the one that Jackson came to depend upon the most, who even oversaw his mortal remains on their journey home, was Sandie Pendleton, his assistant adjuvant general.

    A hometown boy whom Jackson had met as a teen,

Sandie was very intelligent, conscientious, and courageous, but above all he was a committed Christian like Jackson himself. Indeed, he was the son of the Reverend William Nelson Pendleton, who left his pulpit to become Robert E. Lee's chief of artillery. Sandie planned to enter the priesthood himself, but first came the war.

Jackson came to depend heavily on young Pendleton to transmit orders, to communicate with his leaders, to reconnoiter, to write reports, to oversee the many details of the army's organization, and to pray with him. It was said by another staff officer that Jackson loved Sandie like the son he never had. Had he not distinguished himself in so many ways, Sandie might have been just "a son of a gunner." His best epithet from his closest coworker, Henry Kyd Douglas, identified him as "Stonewall's Man."

Alexander Swift Pendleton was born September 28, 1840, near Alexandria, Virginia, to William Nelson Pendleton and Anzolette E. (Page) Pendleton. His paternal grandfather was the grandnephew and adopted son of Edmund Pendleton, the Revolutionary patriot, and his father's mother's uncle, Thomas Nelson, had succeeded Thomas Jefferson as governor of Virginia. His mother, cousin to his father, was the granddaughter of both governors Thomas Nelson and John Page.

In 1830 W. N. Pendleton, Sandie's father, graduated from the Military Academy at West Point, where he knew among the cadets Jefferson Davis, Robert E. Lee, Joseph E. Johnston, and Leonidas Polk. Among his assignments at various military posts was a stint as assistant professor of mathematics at the academy, where he developed an interest in teaching. During this time he also struggled with the calling to resign from the military to pursue the Episcopal priesthood. Leaving the military in 1833 and being ordained in 1838, William Pendleton worked as both a minister and teacher at schools in Delaware, Alexandria, and Baltimore.

His first full-time parish, All Saints Church in Frederick, Maryland, commanded his attention from 1847 until 1853, when he moved permanently to Grace Episcopal Church in Lexington, Virginia. This rural community in the West was an excellent location to rear a family of five daughters and one son, who had been largely instructed at home by the rector. The son he nicknamed "Sandy," although everyone else in the family spelled it "Sandie."

On his first day in Lexington, Sandie entered Washington College as a freshman at the age of thirteen, passing examinations in Latin, Greek, and mathematics. The only extracurricular activities were the literary societies, where no relevant topic escaped debate. Despite a delicate build, Sandie displayed a youthful energy that provoked frequent punishments for infractions of the school decorum. In his sophomore year, to challenge the "know-nothing" anti-Catholicism mood in the country, he wrote an amazingly tolerant essay defending the contributions of the Roman Catholic Church to the world. By his senior year he was assisting in mathematics and in Latin while maintaining the top scores in his class. Honored by the faculty at the 1857 commencement with their highest academic award, he delivered the Cincinnati Oration on "Our State Character" to a prestigious assembly, while only seventeen. Following graduation, Sandie remained at home for two years and taught at his alma mater and his father's boarding school for boys. After a few trips around the state, the youthful Sandie entered the University of Virginia in the fall of 1859 to seek a master of arts, the school's highest degree, which required three years to master seven fields of study. Despite extracurricular activities with the Young Men's Christian Association, the Literary Society, and the intramural sports he helped launch at the school, he likely would have finished within two years had the war not intervened.

As the news of Sumter and secession swept across the South, many young students were torn between their studies and their state loyalties. Sandie looked to his father for guidance, but the rector, who had consistently voted with the Southern Whigs for unionist candidates, feared that extremists on both sides were likely to demagogue their constituencies into war. "At present," his father concluded, "the only certain thing for us to do is to look to God and stand by the Old Dominion."

Although Sandie wanted to complete his degree, go study at a European university, and then enter the Episcopal ministry, the gathering war clouds continued to distract him. While hoping his son could finish his degree, the elder Pendleton left his church to join the defenders of his state as a captain of artillery, reporting at Harper's Ferry. Sandie's parents quietly sought a commission for their son in the Provisional Army of Virginia, hoping to defer active service for the school term. However, upon advice of Professor Albert Taylor Bledsoe, an ardent seces-

Manassas, Va. Confederate fortifications, with Federal soldiers

sionist, Sandie left Charlottesville in June 1861 and borrowed a relative's horse to also report at Harper's Ferry.

After drilling with his father's battery, Sandie was asked by Professor T. J. Jackson, from the Virginia Military Institute in his hometown, to serve on his staff—overseeing ordinance. Jackson had been impressed with the bright young man and appreciated his Christian character. At the time Sandie reported, Jackson had been promoted to brigadier general and given command of the

First Brigade of the Army of the Shenandoah under General Joseph E. Johnston. Accompanying the army's five brigades was the Rockbridge Artillery commanded by Sandie's father and the cavalry of J. E. B. Stuart. The next few weeks saw the effective organization of the Brigade into a fighting unit as they opposed Federal advances into the Winchester area. The brigade distinguished themselves on July 21 and earned Jackson his legendary reputation as Stonewall at Bull Run Creek. There at Manassas Junction, though both Pendletons were wounded and had their horses shot from beneath them, they pressed the counter-attack that drove the Federals into Washington.

With the Union troops under McClellan on the defensive, the next few months found the "Stonewall Brigade" camping near Centreville. Sandie received a C. S. A. commission as first lieutenant and an assignment as assistant adjuvant general to now Major General Jackson. Jackson and staff were dispatched in November to oversee ten thousand troops defending the lower Shenandoah Valley. In addition to providing the merriment in Jackson's otherwise dour headquarters, Sandie was Jackson's courier of choice to communicate with his regimental leaders. When reconnoitering for Jackson at the unexpected fight at Kernstown, Sandie took over a cannon whose gunners had been wounded and began firing into the enemy himself. One staff officer, George Junkin, nephew of the unionist president of Washington College, was captured when he mistakenly wandered into the enemy lines. More vexing than the battle was Sandie's assignment by Jackson to arrest General R. B. Garrett for a court martial, charging him for withdrawing his forces prematurely. This was embarrassing because Garrett's brother-in-law, a classmate of W. N. Pendleton's at West Point, was a vestryman in the Grace parish. Jackson and Sandie were the only witnesses in the trial before its postponement by the war. Later Sandie honored General Garrett when he asked the general to serve as a pallbearer of Jackson, whom they both loved.

For most of the next year Jackson's army defeated numerous Union generals and their superior numbers in battles protecting the approaches to the Shenandoah Valley. The threat Jackson posed to Pennsylvania also kept large numbers of Federal troops in the west away from McClellan, who wanted to advance on Richmond.

From Sandie's numerous letters home we learn that the Union invaders were devastating to the countryside, burning and looting without discipline. Camp life in a tent, although humble, was not without its pleasures due to the generosity of the area families and to the supplies left by the invaders. One particular pleasure was the enjoyment of literary works thrown in the streets by looters. At the staff mess Sandie would read aloud from the essays of Charles Lamb or the works of Dickens and Shakespeare.

On November 23, 1862, came the order to bring Jackson's thirty thousand men immediately the 170 miles to Fredericksburg, where Burnside's Army of the Potomac was threatening Lee and Longstreet. Camping southwest of the town at Guiney Station, young Sandie was impressed by the contrast of the genteel Tidewater culture with his familiar western crudeness.

When Burnside began his move across the Rappahannock at Fredericksburg on December 12, Jackson's troops were rushed to protect the right of

Richmond, Va. Piles of solid shot, canister, and so on, in the Arsenal grounds; Richmond & Petersburg Railroad bridge at right

Longstreet's corps on Marye's Heights. Unfortunately, a gap was left into which the Union forces made early headway on the thirteenth before Jackson's forces drove back the invaders. In the assault Sandie was wounded but "miraculously spared." The minnie ball that hit him was stopped by a pocketknife, but still managed to cut and bruise him. Unable to transmit the counterattack order through his chief staff officer, Jackson hesitated, allowing the Union troops to flee. Meanwhile, a mile to the north, the Yankees who had ravaged the town were falling by the thousands in front of Longstreet's position on the sunken road at Marye's Heights. After withdrawing across the river, the Union troops settled into winter quarters there.

For the next three months Jackson's headquarters were set up at nearby Moss Point Plantation, one of the homes of the Corbin family, a prominent family in Virginia history. The owner of the plantation, James Parke Corbin, had lost his first wife in death in 1855. When he remarried, he established a new home nearby with his second wife. He left the use of Moss Point to three of his children. Richard Corbin had gone off to serve in the army, leaving his frivolous wife (Bertie) and their charming daughter Jane to share the manor with Catherine (Kate) and Fanny (Nettie), whose husband, Bee Dickinson, had also volunteered for the army. During the April to December 1862 occupation of Fredericksburg, most of the younger slaves had fled to the enemy lines, and Union raids had damaged the house and trashed its contents. But the manor, anchored by the three Corbin ladies and their children, still displayed its charm.

Declining the invitation to use any housing but their tents, Jackson's staff were entertained by the Corbins regularly. The highlight of those occasions was the Christmas dinner of 1862, where Lee, Stuart, and Pendleton honored Jackson.

Word also reached Jackson there of the birth of a daughter, his only child. Perhaps because of this, Jackson was smitten by the vivacious five-year-old Jane, while Sandie was only one of several officers trying to catch the eye of Kate. She invited him to tea a few days after Christmas, and he wrote his mother that he enjoyed the conversation with a well-educated woman he described as "agreeable but not pretty." Sandie, now a major, spent the winter busily completing reports and preparing for the spring campaign. During the day he rode and prayed with Jackson, but in the evening he and the young officers enjoyed visits to the manor house to sing and share with their hostesses.

In March, as the Jackson corps prepared to relocate closer to Lee, a triple tragedy befell Moss Point. The three small children each caught scarlet fever. When General Jackson visited to bid good-bye to young Jane, he ordered his surgeon to attend to the ailing child. Only moments after Dr. McGuire left the bedside, Sandie came in to take his leave and found the child dead. While trying to leave the family to grieve in private, Sandie was persuaded by Mrs. Dickinson to return to help Kate control the wild mother of the child. His holding of the grieving mother while praying and reciting appropriate words of Scripture succeeded in calming the woman—and in turning the heart of Kate. The staff stayed to tend to the funeral of Jane, delayed until her father could come from his military post. Unfortunately, within the week the two Dickinson children died as well. The only light in that dark episode was the announcement two months later of Kate's engagement to Sandie, whom she described as "a rising young man . . . a sincere, professing Christian." Jackson commented that "if he makes as good a husband as he has a soldier, Miss Corbin will do well."

Later that spring, on April 20, Jackson was visited by his wife and new daughter, referred to as "young Miss Stonewall the first." The Corbins came calling from Moss Point to see the baby, who had "eyes like her daddy's." Nine days later, their visit was interrupted by the news that the reorganized Union Army of the Potomac was crossing the Rappahannock under the new leadership of General Joseph Hooker, with 120,000 infantry, 400 cannon, and 12,100 cavalry. Against the Federals, Lee had only 60,000 men and 170 guns. Nevertheless, the Confederates were in high spirits as they fell back on Chancellorsville.

In the fight that occurred May 2, Lee observed Hooker exposing his right flank and seized the opportunity to inflict another defeat upon the superior Union numbers. Cleverly sending Jackson hastily forward along a concealed road, Lee's forces caused a near rout among the enemy late that

Amputation being performed in a hospital tent. General Jackson's arm was amputated in efforts to save his life.

afternoon. In the dull twilight Jackson and his staff rode out to watch the enemy flee. When warned by Sandie about their position, Jackson replied, "The danger is over. The enemy is routed," and sent Sandie to summon forward A. P. Hill's division to pursue. Unexpectedly, musket fire broke out and Jackson and staff galloped back toward their own skirmishers—who tragically mistook them in the dim light for attackers. Jackson was struck from fifteen paces in the shoulder, arm, and wrist, and two of his officers were killed. When Sandie learned of the wound, he raced to get Dr. McGuire, fainting from the effort after reaching him. Jackson was removed from the field and his arm amputated the next day. Sandie went to inform Hill, the next in command. Finding him also wounded, Sandie passed the command of the Second Corps to J. E. B. Stuart and then sent a courier to Lee.

Calling on his fallen chief, Sandie was greeted by Jackson, who said, "Well, Major, I am glad to see you; I thought you were killed." After briefing Jackson on the transition, Sandie asked about instructions for Stuart. Jackson, now beginning to decline, conceded, "I don't know, I can't tell; say to General Stuart he must do what he thinks best." The next day would have been difficult for the cavalry general as he commanded infantry had it not been for Sandie. After a second day of Confederate successes, the bluecoats withdrew to the north.

On May 4 the wounded Jackson was moved to the office of a doctor at Guiney Station, ten miles southwest of Fredericksburg. He was accompanied by Dr. McGuire and Chaplain B. T. Lacy. Mrs. Jackson arrived at his bedside on May 7, when pneumonia was first detected. Sandie had been prevented by his duties from visiting Jackson until Sunday, May 10. Arriving at his bedside, Jackson asked Sandie who was preaching at headquarters that day. Told that the entire army was praying for his recovery, Jackson replied, "Thank God, they are very kind." But before he began to slip away, he said to Sandie, "It is the Lord's Day; my wish is fulfilled. I have always wanted to die on a Sunday." The young aide retreated to the porch and wept. "God knows," he said to Mrs. Jackson the next day, "I would have died for him." The general's condition deteriorated and he became delirious, calling on Pendleton and others before his final words: "Let us cross over the river, and rest under the shade of the trees." Sandie dashed to the railroad station and telegraphed the news of Jackson's death to the governor and to Lee, who personally appointed Sandie to take care of the funeral arrangements and transport back to Lexington.

Mourners at the grave of Stonewall Jackson, Lexington, Virginia.

The burial of General Thomas J. Jackson was the highest state funeral the Confederacy ever observed. According to Jackson's wishes and Lee's orders, the major responsibility fell on Sandie, who was with the body almost constantly—from placing it into a casket made by the corps carpenters, through the solemn ceremonies in Richmond, to internment in Lexington. Richmond came to a halt as the train bearing the casket and family arrived on May 11 and processed to the governor's mansion, where the body remained during the evening.

The following morning the casket—wrapped in greenery and the first Confederate flag ever made, a gift from President Davis—followed a military band and escort through the downtown streets beneath pealing bells and before sobbing crowds. Following on foot behind the four white horses and hearse were the staff and pallbearers, including nine generals such as Longstreet, Ewell, and Pickett. Then came the carriages with a frail-looking President Davis and the Jackson family, trailed by officials of the state and Confederate government and an immense throng of mourners. Leading General Jackson's riderless horse, Sorrel, was his servant and cook, Jim Lewis, a freedman from Lexington. The procession circled the downtown area, returning to Capital Square and the Senate chambers where the body lay in state through the night. The next day the body was moved again to the governor's mansion for a brief service before starting for Lexington.

The funeral party proceeded to Lynchburg by a special funeral train whose passing was awaited by thousands. At Lynchburg there were more ceremonies as the funeral party processed to a packet boat on the James River and Kanawha Canal. Arriving the next afternoon, May 14, the officials of Lexington and the cadets of the military institute bore the body to the lecture hall where Jackson had taught. The following morning the entire town honored Jackson in a huge procession to the Presbyterian church, where a simple service of hymns and Scripture preceded internment in the local cemetery. The remarkable thing about the entire trek was the absence of ostentation and the sincere, spontaneous sorrow of the people. Sandie, exhausted by his duties, stayed several days with his mother before returning east.

Returning to camp after a swing by Moss Point to see Kate, Sandie found that Lee had reorganized the Army of Northern Virginia into three corps of three divisions each under Generals James Longstreet, Richard S. Ewell, and A. P. Hill. Ewell, a West Point graduate and veteran commander under Jackson, had lost a leg in battle the previous August but was recalled to active duty to head the Second Corps. Once a difficult, irreligious person before his injury, "Old Bald Head" had finally married and been confirmed by the church. Traveling to Lee's headquarters, Sandie offered his resignation, along with the rest of the staff, to allow Ewell the chance to pick his own men, but Lee refused to consider such a thing. Ewell asked Sandie to remain as assistant adjuvant general to communicate with his three commanders: R. E. Rodes, Jubal Early, and Edward Johnson. Hearing the praise from Lee, Sandie wrote Kate: "If a man is not a good soldier and ready to die doing his duty when such things are said of him by such men, I know not what stuff he is made of. I shall do my best in the sight of God and General Jackson."

★ ★ ★ ★ ★ ★ ★ ★ ★

If a man is not a good soldier and ready to die doing his duty when such things are said of him by such men, I know not what stuff he is made of. I shall do my best in the sight of God and General Jackson.

—Sandie Pendleton

★ ★ ★ ★ ★ ★ ★ ★ ★

In June 1863, Lee decided to move north and west through Winchester and Maryland into Pennsylvania. Spirits were high as the Northern papers and people led the troops to feel the war might soon be settled. Riding with Ewell, Sandie took pride in the discipline and chivalry of the Southerners, who avoided devastating the countryside, even paying for purchases from the wary townspeople. At Carlisle, Pennsylvania, Sandie and some of the staff secured passes to go into town to the Presbyterian church services and to visit Dickinson College.

Two days later Ewell's men were ordered to join Lee at Gettysburg in advance of Meade's Union forces. In the early fighting, the Confederates under Ewell and Hill drove the Federal troops back through the town to Cemetery Ridge. At this point Ewell held up his attack until Longstreet's corps could come up, a decision that allowed the Union troops to reorganize and occupy Culp's Hill. The next day the tide turned against the Confederacy as Lee was unable to dislodge the bluecoats from the high ground. The fall of Vicksburg that same day signaled the beginning of the end of the Confederacy.

For Sandie Pendleton, retreat from Pennsylvania found him promoted to lieutenant colonel. He planned to seek a furlough to be married in October, but it had to be postponed three times due to military operations and the death of Richard Corbin, Kate's brother and little Jane's father, in a skirmish. Finally, on December 29, 1863, Sandie and Kate were married at Moss Point with General Pendleton officiating and Dr. McGuire attending. After a few days in Richmond, the young couple journeyed to Lexington for their honeymoon among family and friends. Thanks to an extension of his furlough, Sandie and Kate were able to visit his oldest sister and her husband, Ned Lee (a relative of the general) before returning to Moss Point.

By mid-April the love-struck young officer was back beside an ailing General Ewell, whom Lee would replace with Jubal Early in May. With Sandie assisting him, "Ole Jube" took the newly designated Army of the Valley to chase a Union force out of Lexington, where they had desecrated Jackson's grave. Pursuing the Yankees into Maryland, Early's army routed from Monocacy Creek a defending force under General Lew Wallace (who later wrote Ben Hur). Although only a dozen miles north of Washington, Early was unable to threaten the city, so he exacted a monetary tribute from Frederick, Maryland, instead. Sandie Pendleton, who spent his early years in Frederick, received the payment and enjoyed an evening feast in a local restaurant. From this point on, it was all downhill for the Confederacy, as the new Federal commander, General Philip Sheridan, with superior numbers drove the Rebels back up the valley, defeating Early at Winchester on September 19.

By this time Kate Corbin, who was six months pregnant, had moved out of Richmond, which was threatened by General Grant, to Lexington in the valley. As Early took up a defensive position at Fisher's Hill, Sheridan aggressively struck him on September 22. As the Confederates withdrew in the evening, Sandie, while overseeing the rear guard deployment, was struck by a minnie ball that completely transited his abdomen. Accompanied by his closest friends, Henry Kyd Douglas and Hunter McGuire, the conscious but mortally wounded Sandie was carried to the home of a local doctor in Woodstock.

The enemy soon occupied the town as Sandie's friends retreated. Despite the assistance offered by Federal doctors, Sandie died on the evening of September 23, five days before his twenty-fourth birthday. "It is God's will," he said at the end, "I am satisfied." A month later, when Sheridan had withdrawn, Sandie's casket was moved from the Woodstock cemetery to Lexington, where his rector general father officiated, and Sandie was buried near General Jackson, his "soul-mate."

The Pendleton family's loss was only partly mitigated by the birth of a boy to Kate Corbin Pendleton on November 1, 1864. "Little Sandie," as he was called, soon became the joy of the family. His grandfather christened him when he returned in April from negotiating Lee's surrender in Appomattox.

Both families were impoverished by the war and struggled together in Lexington to sustain themselves. Tragically, "little Sandie" contracted diptheria in July and joined his father September 1. Kate later became a governess for a Washington College professor's family. There in Lexington in 1871 she married Professor John Mercer Brooke of Virginia Military Institute, who had converted the U.S.S. *Merrimac* into the ironclad C.S.S. *Virginia*. Upon her death in 1912, she was placed in the Stonewall Jackson Memorial Cemetery near Sandie, "Little Sandie," and Dr. Brooke.

The tragedy of families torn by needless death and devastated by the total loss of futile causes is symbolized vividly in the story of Sandie Pendleton. But in his own writings he celebrated the exuberance of living daily for the glory of God and the pride of doing your duty the best you can among men of quality.[10]

★ *Dorsey M. Deaton*

LOVE AND WAR

★★★★★★★★★

Stonewall Jackson surrounded himself with a staff of young men of character whose lives were exemplary both on and off the battlefield–James Boswell, Hunter McGuire, James Power Smith, Henry Kyd Douglas, Stapleton Crutchfield, and Sandie Pendleton. Of them all, Sandie Pendleton was the closest to Jackson. Sandie seemed the son Jackson never had; the formal Jackson even regularly called the young officer "Sandie." Both shared a strong Christian faith and were men of prayer. There was a saying among Jackson's Second Corps when speaking of a praying soldier that he "prays as much as Stonewall Jackson and Sandie Pendleton." Of all Jackson's staff, historian Douglas Southall Freeman believed Sandie was the most brilliant of Jackson's officers and the most popular with both officers and men. He had an ever-present optimism and good-naturedness about him. Even Jackson remarked that Sandie could be awakened in the middle of the night with work to be done and still have a good disposition.

After Sandie met and married Kate Corbin, they were separated often by the war. When absent, their love flourished through their letters. Many were filled with descriptions of the everyday affairs of the young newlyweds, whether on the battlefield or among Richmond's ladies, but often the letters revealed the deep humility and spiritual bond of their love. March 25, 1864, Sandie wrote his dear Kate:

There was a saying among Jackson's Second Corps when speaking of a praying soldier that he "prays as much as Stonewall Jackson and Sandie Pendleton."

It is Good Friday night. Reading your letter has made me sorrowful and ashamed. My darling, you evidently think me a great deal better man than I am. I read my Bible regularly morning & evening, & I try to do what is right because it is right, but I do fall so far short of what I know to be my duty; my prayers are so cold and feeble, my growth in grace so scarcely perceptible, & my sins so often getting the mastery of me, that I fear sometimes that I am as one having only a name to live.

Pray for me, love, for I know your prayers are heard, & I gain a blessing by them; while I recognize the fact that in this as in all other matters God helps the man who helps himself. You say that you pray more earnestly when I am away from you. With me it is just the opposite. I pray more fervently when with you. I feel so profoundly that my whole soul goes out in adoration towards Him, and as I lift up my heart in thankfulness, I feel my utter worthlessness and inefficiency and cry out for help and mercy. Thank God we can & will be a help to each other whatever be our condition & however far we may be separated. We can write & talk freely, & as husband & wife be our truest friends. I thank you very much, darling, for your letter. I believe, yes, I know, it will be of service to me. . . .[11]

As the spring blossomed, Sandie wrote Kate of the time when they could have the constant joy of each other's company and ramble among the fields and forest or tend the flowers around their own home. Until that time when they could fully be together, he felt as if he were just vegetating and only half living. Sunday, April 17, Sandie wrote Kate of the joy of worshiping together in spirit, though separated:

You ask that I will set a particular time to pray for you. I do pray regularly for you, my love, before praying for myself, morning & evening, & often in silent thought. Hereafter I will dedicate the hour at sunset, so that you may know at that time my thoughts turn to home & you.

★ ★ ★ ★ ★ ★ ★ ★ ★ ★ ★ ★ ★ ★ ★ ★ ★

How my heart yearned toward you this lovely spring morning, & longed to go with you to the House of God that we might worship together at his footstool.

—Sandie Pendleton, writing to his wife Kate

★ ★ ★ ★ ★ ★ ★ ★ ★ ★ ★ ★ ★ ★ ★ ★ ★

How my heart yearned toward you this lovely spring morning, & longed to go with you to the House of God that we might worship together at his footstool. And though in bodily presence I was unable to accompany you to St. Paul's Church [in Richmond], yet I hope & really believe I have been enabled to draw near with faith and join you in the services of the temple of the Lord. This privilege is accorded us through the instrumentality of our glorious liturgy that howsoever separated in time & space, we can unite in prayer & praise, & send up together to the throne of grace the same words of supplication, & join our voices to swell the same anthem of adoration. United church membership is an inestimable pleasure, & I trust that we may live to find it so in every vicissitude of life.

Sometimes it makes me shudder to think how far I come short of what is required of me by the profession I have made [to be a Christian]. I read my Bible regularly & try to pray, but it is hard, hard work, & I fear I don't succeed in attaining to that frame of mind which is right & proper. Pray for me that I may have grace sufficient for me in each hour of need. My sorest trial I find to be in laziness, which leads me to neglect my devotional duties, & a tendency to loose talking; I hardly know whether I should term it vivac-

ity, in consequence of which I do not keep that guard upon my tongue which I should, & am led into expressions which cause me pain & sorrow, & produce a bad effect upon others. Pray for me, my dearest one, & as I derive happiness from your love, help me to gain eternal life. I had a free & earnest conversation with [J.P.] Smith yesterday, which will, I trust, be of benefit to me. He is one of the best & purest people that I know. I shall try to emulate his example.[12]

In June, 1864, the Second Corps, now under the command of Jubal Early, with Sandie still on the General's staff, was dispatched to the Shenandoah Valley. Kate moved from Richmond to Lexington to be as near Sandie as possible. In Lexington she stayed with the Pendletons. Mrs. Pendleton loved her as a daughter, and Sandie's sisters welcomed her as another sister into the family. It was a particularly trying time for Kate with her husband away facing danger in battle and their first child on the way. On September 23, five days before his twenty-fourth birthday, Sandie was mortally wounded at the fighting around Fisher's Hill. Knowing nothing Hunter McGuire or any of the other surgeons could do would help him, Sandie sent messages of love to his dear Kate and family and requested a lock of his hair be cut off to send to his wife. He calmly faced death with Christian hope and assurance, often repeating, "It is God's will; I am satisfied."

In November, Kate, who was still living in Lexington with the Pendletons, gave birth to Sandie's son and named him after his father. Little Sandie brought joy and delight to the grieving Pendleton family; however, he contracted diphtheria and died September 1865, intensifying the grief of Kate and Sandie's family. Like the biblical Ruth, Kate took Sandie's family as her own and continued to live with his parents, helping in the school and various Christian and educational ministries they were engaged in after the war.

★ *Diana L. Severance*

FATHER AND SON

★ ★ ★ ★ ★ ★ ★ ★ ★ ★

The Civil War affected families in many ways. Sometimes brothers fought against brothers; sometimes fathers and sons joined together in the struggle. William Nelson Pendleton and his son Sandie were among the more famous father-and-son combinations fighting in the war. Brigadier General William Pendleton, a West Point graduate and Episcopal priest, was in charge of the artillery of the Army of Northern Virginia. His only son, Sandie, became adjutant general for Stonewall Jackson and continued in that capacity under Generals Ewell and Early. Sandie's Christian character and quick intelligence

were evident to all. He was graduated from Washington College at the age of seventeen and was pursuing a master of arts degree at the University of Virginia when the war broke out. He planned to become an Episcopal priest like his father.

Before hostilities began, while still at the University of Virginia, twenty-year-old Sandie wrote a letter to his father that reveals his Christian faith and the close bond between father and son:

Charlottesville, December 16, 1860

My Dear Papa,

For two letters I am now indebted to you, and have intended answering them for several days. The former I am peculiarly obliged to you for, and trust the advice you have has been of real service to me. I felt that perhaps there was some measure of apathy growing up within me in reference to my spiritual state, and that letter with its kind and affectionate warning came just in time to arouse me to redoubled diligence and prayerfulness, and now I hope that I have again drawn nearer to my Saviour. Though there is some danger, as there is and ever will be in all situations of spiritual declension, that danger is far less here than might be supposed. The weekly prayer-meetings, in which we all participate, the regular intercourse of the Christian Association, and above all, the active work in which we engage, these, in connection with the moral and religious tone pervading all here, tend to diminish in a great degree the force of the temptations lying in every young man's path, and render it comparatively easier to pursue an outwardly correct course, and be consistent, than to be otherwise. And my association with . . . the most earnest types of Christians, and all looking forward to the same ultimate work in life, is of such a character as to act as a safeguard against letting the mere intellectual development usurp first place. And I trust that, by the blessing of God, although, of course, more time must be devoted to the pursuit of secular knowledge, I am now seeking and shall ever be enabled to "seek first the kingdom of God, and His righteousness."

Thursday night the Christian Association held a meeting to pray for God's blessing and guidance for our country, and they recommended the observance of tomorrow by all the students as a day of humiliation and prayer; and surely the arm of the Almighty be not interposed in our behalf, vain is the help of man now. . . . This is Monday, December 17, 1860, the last day of the existence of the whole United States.[13]

In the early months of the war, William Pendleton remained with the artillery of the Army of Northern Virginia fighting near Richmond while Sandie accompanied General Jackson in his Shenandoah Valley Campaign. During that time, Sandie wrote in a letter to his mother that the business of the war was adversely affecting his spiritual life. His father sent him a letter of encouragement. After describing the latest military actions along the James River, William wrote:

> My main object, my son, in writing, while my time is so limited, is to say a word respecting your state of mind. You tell your mama that camp-life is destroying your religious character. Take care of this, my dear boy. "Watch and pray." If you do not make opportunities for prayer regularly you will spiritually die. Let nothing prevent this. My only sure way for getting a certain time for prayer is to compel myself to awake early, and then employ the first waking hour in steady reflection and prayer. Do this, or something

★ ★ ★ ★ ★ ★ ★ ★ ★ ★ ★

"Watch and pray."
If you do not make opportu-
nities for prayer regularly
you will spiritually die.
Let nothing prevent this.

—William Pendleton,
writing to his son Sandie

★ ★ ★ ★ ★ ★ ★ ★ ★ ★ ★

like it, and your soul will live. I find, too, that by dwelling on the several petitions of the Lord's Prayer until each word impresses on the mind its full force and stirs up feeling, I get more of the spirit of prayer than I have been able to secure in any other way. Be industrious here, and you will find spiritual health and strength the sure result.[14]

In ensuing months, the Army of Northern Virginia achieved numerous victories, and father and son each nobly performed their duties and responsibilities. Sandie, on the staff of Stonewall Jackson, was with Jackson on the day of his death and brought his body back to Lexington for burial. Jackson's death was a severe personal blow to Sandie, but he continued on and faithfully served Generals Ewell and Early when they took command of Jackson's troops.

On September 22, 1864, Sandie was mortally injured at Fisher's Hill. When Dr. Hunter McGuire, his friend and tentmate, saw that the wound was mortal, Sandie insisted that the doctor not remain with him, but go with the army where he could be of much service. Through his intense suffering, Sandie frequently repeated, "It is God's will; I am satisfied!" When William Pendleton, then stationed in Richmond, first heard of Sandie's injury, he wrote his wife:

> My beloved wife and children all,
>
> It has pleased God to permit a heavy grief to fall upon us. Our dear Sandie, so severely wounded and far away, where we not only cannot minister to his comfort, but cannot learn of his actual condition.
>
> The uncertainty and suspense render the trial perhaps

even more distressing. From the weight on my own heart I can judge somewhat what you all feel. But what precious mercy we have along with the bitter sorrow! There is a perfectly wise and kind Father watching over and ministering to our beloved in his distant suffering, a sympathizing Friend and great Physician attending unceasingly by his bed of pain, and a sustaining Comforter ever with him to soothe his spirit with sweet influences of peace. He is a child of God, a servant of Jesus, a partaker of the Holy Ghost. It cannot but be well with him. . . . Oh, how it extracts the bitterness from affliction to know that it is ordered by our Almighty Father as part of His boundless plan of righteousness and love! . . . Shall we not, therefore, submissively bow under His dealings? "Father, not my will, but thine be done."

> ### *Shall we not, therefore, submissively bow under His dealings? "Father, not my will, but thine be done."*
> —William Pendleton, writing to his wife

To the mother's heart I speak first. God may take to Himself our precious boy. Often as we have failed in our duty to that dear child, the merciful and gracious Lord has enabled us to rear him to be under grace an honor to us, a joy to his sisters, a treasure to his wife, an ornament to society, and a Christian hero in his country's service. It may be hard to give him up, should it please the Master, to take to Himself, but shall we murmur? Shall we so look upon earthly and perishable interests as to grieve intensely over disappointment there, and fail to appreciate the priceless blessing granted us in such a child, and in the heavenly

hopes we can cherish as we remember him? My darling love, I have thought of this, our dear child, as if now removed from us, with the precious little Robin we buried in his infancy, and our sainted Lucy, transplanted, as an opening flower in the sweetness of early bloom, to the garden of the Lord, with them and with our mothers and others beloved in that home, that presence, and that likeness where all are satisfied forever. . . . If it be the Lord's will to take him, never will my heart cease to feel the sorrow that on earth I shall see him no more, but not then for an instant would I wish him back. . . . Would that I could be with you all for a season now! . . . We must wait in spirit together upon the Lord.[15]

Sandie Pendleton died September 23, 1864. He was twenty-four.

✦ *Diana L. Severance*

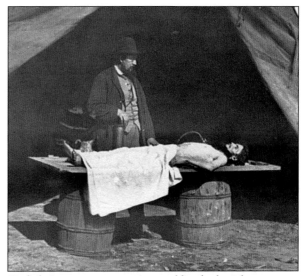

Embalming surgeon preparing a soldier for burial.

★ ★

If you're going to talk about religion and its impact on these troops, you have to start, first and foremost, with Robert E. Lee. He is the New Testament commander, and Stonewall Jackson is the Old Testament commander. Lee is a man unlike Stonewall. The difference in the way they approach their own religion is very interesting to me, especially for two men coming out of the same era, because Lee believes in a benevolent God who is responsible for everything that happens in his life, that anything in his life is a result of God's will. Jackson is a man who because of the terrible, terrible, horrible tragedies—the death of his wife in childbirth, the death of the baby, the death of his mother—actually is very much afraid of what God's going to do to him next if he doesn't do his duty. He tows the line because he has that fear of God—it's the Old Testament. Considering these two men are really very similar in so many ways, that's such a stark difference and that caught me by surprise. Again, no historian told me how to look at these characters; I had to find that out by myself.

—Jeff Shaara, *author of* Gods and Generals, *in an interview with Lili Baehr*

★ ★

Gods and Generals director Ron Maxwell, left, speaks with Senator Phil Gramm of Texas, who plays a member of the Virginia House of Delegates in Richmond during the Secession Convention.

What a cruel thing is war: to separate and destroy families and friends, and mar the purest joys and happiness God has granted us in this world; to fill our hearts with hatred instead of love for our neighbors, and to devastate the fair face of this beautiful world.

—General Robert E. Lee

A HERO'S FATHER-IN-LAW

DR. GEORGE JUNKIN

★ ★ ★ ★ ★ ★ ★ ★ ★

When Thomas Jackson came to Lexington, Virginia, to teach at the Virginia Military Institute, he became part of the intellectual elite of a college town. His friend Daniel Harvey Hill taught at Lexington's Washington College, and the faculty of both the college and VMI regularly socialized together. Often Jackson found himself in the home of Dr. George Junkin, president of Washington College. Dr. Junkin's wife, Julia, was a gracious hostess and fervent Christian; and the Junkins's two daughters, Maggie and Ellie, added a special allure to the Junkin's home.

George Junkin was born in Pennsylvania in 1790, the sixth child and fourth son of fourteen children. When he was twenty-one, he was converted through a sermon preached by Rev. James Galloway. As he described the occasion: "I found it. The way of deliverance from sin by the blood of Christ—of justification by His righteousness—of sanctification by His Spirit, all became plain. My doubts and fears passed away, and I came to enjoy a good hope. I found more comfort in secret devotion. I used to walk out in the morning for secret prayer and devotion."[1]

George studied theology, and in 1818 was ordained an evangelist at Associate Reformed Church in Gettysburg. Little could he have dreamed the Christian ministry he would have forty-five years later in that little Pennsylvania town. After pastoring churches in Pennsylvania, Rev. Junkin became president of Lafeyette College in Easton, Pennsylvania. He was zealous in his work, acting as both a father and a pastor to the young

men in his care. He had a deep affection for the students, visiting in their rooms, conversing with them about their spiritual needs, praying with them, and visiting them when they were sick. In 1848, Washington College elected him president, and Dr. Junkin moved his family to Lexington. As he had at Lafeyette College, at Washington College Dr. Junkin became a spiritual and intellectual mentor to the young men in the school. To Thomas Jackson, George Junkin became the father he had never known. Dr. Junkin accepted Thomas into his family and treated him as a son. In letters he wrote to him, he always addressed Jackson as "my dear young son."

In the Junkins's home, Jackson could relax and enjoy conversations in which everything could be discussed from a Christian perspective. Both of Junkin's daughters were lovely, devout Christians, but it was Ellie who captured Jackson's heart. The two were married in the Junkins's home by Ellie's father in August 1853. After a honeymoon in the northeast, Jackson and Ellie returned to live with the Junkins.

Sadness came, however, when Mrs. Junkin died the following February. Her sudden death was a shock to the family, but the peace with which she died was an inspiration Jackson wrote about to his sister Laura: "She, without any apparent uneasy concern, passed into that unseen world, where the weary are at rest. Her life was such as to attract around her many warm friends, and if she had an enemy in this world, it was and continues to be a secret to me. Hers was a Christian life, and hers was a Christian death . . . her death was no leaping into the dark. She died in the bright hope of an unending immortality of happiness."[2]

Mrs. Junkin's death and the family's strong Christian hope in the face of death strengthened Jackson's own religious faith. Jackson became even closer to Dr. Junkin during this time, and the two spent many hours discussing the immortality of the soul and spiritual issues.

Only eight months after Mrs. Junkin's death, Dr. Junkin suffered another severe loss. His daughter and Jackson's wife, Ellie, died in childbirth, along with her baby. The bond between Jackson and Junkin increased as both mourned the death of their wives, and Junkin his daughter as well. Their common bond and Christian hope drew the men closer together.

When the war came and secessionist sentiment swept the Washington College campus, Dr. Junkin resigned. Students had repeatedly draped George Washington's statue with a Southern flag, and Junkin vowed, "I will never have a recitation or deliver a lecture under a rebel flag." At seventy-one, Junkin left Lexington and returned to Pennsylvania. It was a mournful departure, for Lexington was where his wife, daughter, and grandson were buried and was near where other married children were living. Yet Dr. Junkin could not approve secession or compromise his principles.

On his way to Pennsylvania, Dr. Junkin stopped at Winchester, Virginia, to rest his horses. When asked why and where he was traveling, Junkin exclaimed with much emotion against the secessionists at Lexington: "I am escaping from a set of lunatics. Lexington is one vast madhouse. There is not a sane man there, nor woman either. They are bedlamites, every one. I am compelled to leave the best friends a man ever had. I leave most of my children, too, and my son-in-law, Major Jackson, who is the best and bravest man I ever knew, but he is as crazy as the rest. Yet if there is to be a war, as I fear, I tell you now, that Major Jackson, if his life be spared, will be among its most distinguished heroes."[3]

Even though they were on opposite sides of the Civil War, the Christian bond between Dr. Junkin and his fam-

ily remained strong. In the fall of 1862, after Jackson's great victory at Harper's Ferry, near the border between North and South, Rev. David X. Junkin, George Junkin's brother, asked to meet with Jackson. Though he was a Unionist, his son, also named George, was fighting for the South and was on Jackson's staff. The younger George had just been released from a Yankee prison, and his father, David, accompanied him south in the hopes of speaking with Jackson. Jackson remembered well conversations with the Revs. David and George Junkin in peaceful days. He rode off for a private meeting with David and his son George. After an affectionate embrace and recalling the happier days in Lexington, David began a long appeal to Jackson to realize the errors of his ways—that rebellion was inexcusable and that he was fighting an evil war against righteousness. Jackson listened carefully, but raised his objections and counter-arguments. The three talked for three hours, with the Maryland Heights in the background, but each maintained his convictions. Finally Jackson had to return to camp. Rev. Junkin said, "Farewell, General, may we meet under happier circumstances; if not in this troubled world, may we meet in . . . ." Tears choked back his words, and tears streamed down Jackson's cheeks as Jackson pointed upward and finished the sentence, "in heaven."[4]

In Philadelphia, Dr. George Junkin preached when called upon, gave temperance speeches, wrote theological articles, and ministered the Word of God to the army camps and war prisoners at Point Lookout and Fort Delaware. After the battle of Gettysburg, Dr. Junkin was among the first to minister to the wounded. During this time he met a young Confederate chaplain, whom he embraced with tears—the man was one of his former college students.

★ *Diana L. Severance*

IRON NERVES
DANIEL HARVEY HILL

★ ★ ★ ★ ★ ★ ★ ★ ★ ★

Daniel Hill

One of the Confederate soldiers most known for courage and iron nerves in battle was also a close friend and brother-in-law of Stonewall Jackson. Daniel Harvey Hill and Jackson had married sisters, daughters of Presbyterian minister Rev. Robert Hall Morrison. Harvey Hill first met Jackson while the two were in the Mexican War. Both had attended West Point before the war and resigned from the military after the war. Hill became a mathematics professor at Washington College in Lexington, Virginia, and was instrumental in obtaining an appointment for Jackson to teach at the Virginia Military Institute, also in Lexington. A staunch Presbyterian since childhood, Hill helped Jackson think through his spiritual questions and was one of several Lexington friends who encouraged Jackson to join the Presbyterian church there.

Jackson became a regular visitor at the home of Isabella and Harvey Hill. One time, when the Hills's daughter was ill with pneumonia and the Hills were exhausted from walking the floor with her, Jackson came to stay the night with her so the Hills could get some rest. He walked with her in his arms and prayed for her the entire night; mercifully, the child got well.

★ ★ ★ ★ ★ ★ ★ ★ ★

Oh God, give me gratitude to Thee, and may we never dishonor Thee by weak faith!

—Daniel Harvey Hill

★ ★ ★ ★ ★ ★ ★ ★ ★

Harvey Hill was an excellent teacher whose interests were not confined to mathematics. Though he did write a college algebra text before the Civil War, he also wrote two books of a theological cast: *A Consideration of the Sermon on the Mount* and *The Crucifixion of Christ*. Written in a clear style, both books revealed a familiarity with the latest biblical scholarship as well as Latin, Greek, and Hebrew.

Though Hill was often in pain and poor health, possibly due to a case of childhood polio that caused a weak spine, when the Civil War began, he promptly enlisted on the Confederate side. He had long believed war was inevitable, and in 1858 had even helped establish the North Carolina Military Institute in Charlotte, North Carolina, to prepare Southern young men for the coming conflict. When the first land battle of the war was held at Bethel, Virginia, Hill helped lead the Southerners to victory. After the battle, as the soldiers were feasting or carousing in celebration, Hill fell on his knees in thanksgiving to God, whom he believed directed the outcome of battles. The day after the battle Hill wrote his wife Isabella: "I have to thank God for a great and decided victory and that I escaped with a slight contusion on the knee. . . . It is a little singular that my first battle in this war should be at Bethel where I was baptized and worshiped till I was sixteen years old, the church of my mother. Was she not a guardian spirit in the battle, averting ball and shell? Oh God, give me gratitude to Thee, and may we never dishonor Thee by weak faith!"[5]

After the battle of Bethel, Hill was dismayed by the profanity and vulgarity among the troops. How could the Lord give victory to men who so freely defamed His name? Surrounded by unabashed godlessness, Harvey wrote Isabella: "I feel like returning to some mountain home where I would see no more mankind in large and vicious collection."[6] Excellent teacher that he was, Hill did what he could to encourage the soldiers in true godliness. A Yorktown newspaper described his address to the soldiers after one Sunday evening's sermon:

At night we had a good sermon from Mr. Yates, our chaplain, and a plenty of good singing. After Mr. Yates had finished, Col. Hill gave us a fine address, full of good advice and counsel, every word of which was exactly fitted to his hearers. He has cut off all spirits of every kind, and not a drop is to be had in camp; he is down on profanity; told us last night that he knew many regarded swearing as a sort of necessity attaching to a soldier; that it gave emphasis and eclat to the speech, but he said no greater mistake could be made; that, for his part, he would be afraid to trust to the courage of the man who had to bolster it up with whiskey and profanity. The God-fearing, moral soldier was the man to depend on. He spoke of Washington, Cromwell, and others of like caste; said they are the men to be successful; the enemy seldom saw the backs of such men. He told us that three times since we had been in this camp, the long roll had sounded, and we had promptly answered, expecting in a few hours to meet the enemy and risk our chances of success. He said he would, however, venture to say, that under these circumstances many of us had called upon God for help, who had *neglected* to do so while *they felt secure.* He appealed to them to know if, as soldiers and fair men, this was reasonable and proper. He appealed to the moral men in camp to let their influence be felt; said that a few might deride them at first, but they would be few, and if these men did their duty in all the varied scenes of camp life, these scoffers would see it, and soon hang their heads in shame.

Thus he went on for half an hour; not a man left his place, not a word was said, and save for the constant coughing of the sick, we had perfect silence. I confess this will give you but a poor idea of the best speech I ever heard, taking the time, place, and circumstances, into consideration.[7]

Hill's words and actions did have an effect on the soldiers. After his lecture, there was less profanity. Even the wicked realized that the army's success depended on the God of Battles.

As did his brother-in-law Jackson, Harvey Hill always gave God credit for victory in battle. Two days after the battle of Malvern Hill, on July 3, 1862, Hill wrote Isabella: "I am perfectly well, never better. For eight days, I have not washed my face, have slept on the ground without bed or blanket, have not taken off boots or spurs, have been struck four times without being seriously hurt once. Surely, God, even our God, ought to be adored and worshiped."[8]

Isabella was quite concerned that Harvey would be killed in battle. Since his health was poor anyway, why couldn't he resign and resume his teaching? Harvey Hill's trust in God's sovereign purposes in even the details of life made him fearless in battle, and he tried to comfort Isabella: "We are in the hands of God and as safe on the battlefield as anywhere else. We will be exposed to a heavy fire, but the arm of God is mightier than the artillery of the enemy. . . . If my work is done, I will fall. If not, all the balls on earth cannot harm me. Never distrust God."[9]

Isabella was not so easily comforted, and she wrote him a cold letter about his decision to remain in the army. Though Hill did not comply with her wishes, he wrote her back: "Poor sinner that I am, I want to hear you say that you love me. . . . God bless you darling and the dear little ones. Write often and kindly. Affectionately, Husband."

Isabella and Harvey Hill had nine children, and even when at war, Harvey's thoughts were of home. He once wrote Isabella: "God has been wonderfully kind to me. . . . Train our children to *love God*. Our gloomy Presbyterian ideas encourage *fear of God* not love for him. Let our children be taught *love, love, love*."[10]

After the war, Harvey went back to teaching and writing. He was editor of two Southern magazines before becoming president of Arkansas Industrial University (later the University of Arkansas) and then the Middle Georgia Military and Agricultural College. Though he suffered from stomach cancer the last year of his life, he continued to work until the end. He knew he was dying, and his prayers with his family more than ever before showed his close communion with his God. For Harvey Hill's funeral sermon, the preacher aptly chose as his text 2 Samuel 3:38: "Know ye not that there is a prince and a great man fallen this day in Israel?"

Diana L. Severance

AFRICAN AMERICAN HEROES

★ ★ ★ ★ ★ ★ ★ ★ ★

African American soldiers played an integral role in the Civil War, fighting for both the Union and Confederate armies. Approximately 179,000 black soldiers fought for the Union army, and an additional 20,000 served in the navy.[11] Among them was Harriet Tubman, a nurse and legendary spy for the Union army who is best known for helping more than three

Harriet Tubman

hundred slaves successfully flee through the Underground Railroad.

Close to 75,000 African Americans fought for the Confederacy, a number that doubles if the body servants, teamsters, cooks, and laborers are included. It is unlikely that most fought willingly against the Union army, which was fighting for their freedom, but there were exceptions. The Louisiana Free Blacks explained their voluntary participation in a letter written to New Orleans' *Daily Delta*: "The free colored population love their home, their property, their own slaves and recognize no other country than Louisiana, and are ready to shed their blood for her defense. They have no sympathy for Abolitionism; no love for the North, but they have plenty for Louisiana. They will fight for her in 1861 as they fought in 1814–15."[12]

Black soldiers were often given cooking duties.

Although blacks had fought in the American Revolution and the War of 1812, President Abraham Lincoln, citing a 1792 federal law forbidding blacks to bear arms, initially turned away the thousands who tried to enlist after the Confederates fired the first shot on Fort Sumter. Lincoln and various other leaders in the country were in agreement with Governor David Tod of Ohio, who said, "This is a White man's government, and they are able to defend and protect it."[13] Lincoln also believed the conflict would be short-lived, and he did not want to risk offending the border-states that favored slavery but remained loyal to the Union.

At the onset of the war, when the North suffered heavy losses and casualties, Lincoln, along with other military leaders, realized that they had far underestimated the strength of the Confederacy. Frederick Douglass, a former slave who had escaped as a young man, emerged as a powerful leader of the abolitionists and spearheaded the campaign to allow African Americans into the military, lobbying with speeches as well as articles in the newspapers he published and the books he wrote. Governor John Andrew of Massachusetts joined Douglass, stating, "It is not my opinion that our generals, when any man comes to the standard and desires to defend the flag, will find it important to light a candle and see what his complexion is, or to consult the family Bible to ascertain whether his grandfather came from the banks of the Thames or the banks of the Senegal."[14]

Finally in late August of 1862 the War Department announced, "All slaves admitted into military service, together with their wives and children, were declared forever free." Most slave owners ignored the law, but the runaway slaves who had escaped to the North joined, and as the Northern army invaded the South, thousands of slaves who were freed then joined the military. Following the Emancipation Proclamation on January 1, 1863, regiments of black enlistees commanded by white officers were established.

President Lincoln sent Frederick Douglass into the

Frederick Douglass

South to recruit African American soldiers. Douglass's own two sons joined and fought for the Union. Wearing the uniform of their country was a great victory for the African American population! Abolitionist, Methodist evangelist, and voracious orator Sojourner Truth proclaimed, "This is a great and glorious day! It is good to live in it & behold the shackles fall from the manacled limbs. Oh if I were ten years younger I would go down with these soldiers here & be the Mother of the Regiment!"[15]

African American soldiers

Life in the military, however, proved difficult for African Americans. Unwelcome by many of their Northern comrades, black soldiers' pay was less and their rations fewer. Armed with inferior weapons, the troops were sent into battle with little or no training, and sergeant major was the highest rank they were allowed to obtain. Upon President Jefferson Davis's orders, black soldiers or the white officers leading them were badly mistreated when captured. In spite of Lincoln's attempts to prevent these atrocities, tragically some captured African American soldiers were brutally executed, and others were sold into slavery.

Undaunted, Douglass continued to lobby for the rights of the African American soldiers. With his persistence, the laws were ultimately changed. Not only were their wages increased to equal that of their white comrades', but it was also made retroactive.

Sergeant William Carney was the first of sixteen African American soldiers, who fought in the Civil War, to receive the Congressional Medal of Honor. On July 18, 1863, when the color bearer was killed, Carney threw down his rifle and picked up the colors. Wounded several times, Carney literally crawled uphill on his knees urging his troops to follow as he spearheaded the 54th MA Union assault on Fort Wagner, South Carolina. Major Christian Fleetwood described the act that won Carney the medal: "Saved the regimental colors after eleven of the twelve color guards had been shot down around it."[16]

Stonewall Jackson was said to have had three thousand fully equipped unofficial African American troops scattered throughout his corps at Antietam, the war's bloodiest battle. Confederate General Nathan Bedford Forrest, notorious for terrorizing the enemy, and the only soldier feared by General William T. Sherman, had slaves and freemen serving in units under his command. After the war, Forrest said of the black men, "These boys stayed with me, and better Confederates did not live."[17]

Losing ground and in need of more troops in January 1864, General Patrick Cleburne asked President Jefferson Davis for permission to employ slaves in the army. The president adamantly refused, but by March 13, 1865, he was forced to sign General Order 14, which allowed African Americans to serve in the beleaguered Confederate army. The war ended, however, before these "official" troops could be used in battle.

More than eighty commissioned African American officers were in the Union army by the time the war ended, and black troops had played a significant role in many victories in Civil War battles, especially at Antietam, Port Hudson, Petersburg, Milliken's Bend, Fort Wagner, Fort Blakely near Mobile, and Nashville. "Milliken's Bend," said Benjamin Quarles, "was one of the hardest fought encounters in the annals of American military history."[18] "The bravery of the blacks at Milliken's Bend," observed Assistant Secretary of War Charles A. Dana, "completely revolutionized the sentiment of the army with regard to the employment of Negro troops."[19] Historians agree that the black troops at Milliken's Bend enabled Grant and Sherman to win at Vicksburg, which the president deemed significant to end the war.

Whether fighting for the North or the South, African Americans proved to be brave soldiers, and more than forty thousand lost their lives in the Civil War. Although only sixteen soldiers won the Congressional Medal of Honor, there were many unsung heroes who fought valiantly and heroically for emancipation and civil rights for future generations.
★ *Susan Huey Wales*

A UNION GENERAL
JAMES BREWERTON RICKETTS

★ ★ ★ ★ ★ ★ ★ ★ ★ ★

James Brewerton Ricketts enrolled in the U.S. Military Academy after finishing his education locally in New York City, the place of his birth. After graduating in 1839, he served on the northern frontier along the Canadian border for a time before being called to the Mexican front to fight under Zachary Taylor at the outbreak of the Mexican-American War.

James Ricketts

He returned to frontier duty after the fact, and when the Civil War broke out, he captained in the 1st Artillery. During the Union march on Manassas Junction, Ricketts commanded a battery during the battle of First Bull Run. He was left behind during the Union retreat, having been wounded a staggering four times. The Confederates captured him, and he was set for execution in anticipation of any Confederate executions in November 1861. This did not come to pass, and he became a free man in a January 1862 release. Plagued by his wounds, he did not go on active duty again until April of that same year. He received a promotion to brigadier general and took command of a brigade of Major General Edward Ord's division.

Manassas Junction, where Ricketts commanded a battery during the battle of First Bull Run

With his tenacity coming to full maturity, he led his brigade through the Rappahannock, in the counterstrike against Stonewall Jackson's move out of Richmond, Thoroughfare Gap, and at Second Bull Run. He then returned with his division to the Army of the Potomac, commanding the 2nd Division of First Corps through South Mountain and Antietam. Ricketts fell again, pinned under the second horse he rode, but refused to leave the field. In the aftermath, the injury plagued him so doggedly that he had to relinquish command before his division moved to Harper's Ferry on November 1, 1862.

Transferred to a desk job, he served on many boards, including the court-martial of Fitz John Porter. After more than a years' service, he resumed field duty on April 4, 1864, commanding a division of the Army of the Potomac in the Grant campaign against Lee. These included battles of the Wilderness, Spotsylvania, North Anna, Cold Harbor, and the beginning sieges of Petersburg. His division was diverted to Washington to counter Jubal Early's raid. In the battle of Monocacy, a staggering 50-percent-plus casualty rating earned him stout commendations from Major General Lew Wallace.

Upon Early's retreat, he joined the Shenandoah Valley Campaign with Philip Sheridan, receiving high praise for his conduct at Fisher's Creek. Misfortune knocked on Ricketts's door on October 19 when he suffered a chest wound. He never fully recovered, yet he returned to command once again two days before the Appomattox surrender. He stubbornly fought to stay on active duty, but was forced to retire at the rank of major general from his many war injuries in January 1867.

He lived the next twenty years in Washington, D.C., where he passed away on September 22, 1887. His body now rests at Arlington: "Assigned to artillery on the Canadian frontier. Served through the War with Mexico. Frontier duty in Texas. Engaged in twenty-seven battles of the rebellion. Was wounded five times. Prisoner of war in Richmond. Died September 27, 1887, from wounds received while commanding the Sixth Army Corps in the Shenandoah Valley. He gave his honors to the world again. His blessings part to heaven, and sleeps in peace."

Ted Baehr

MILITARY SERVICE
MAJOR GENERAL
WINFIELD SCOTT HANCOCK

★ ★ ★ ★ ★ ★ ★ ★

Winfield Scott Hancock became one of the top corps commanders in the Federal service after graduating West Point in 1844. He served in the infantry in the Mexican War, and at the conclusion was assigned to California, quartermaster's department. Until being called east for duty in the Civil War, he had frustrated many local secessionist movements.

Upon receiving orders, he fought at Williamsburg, leading an effective flank attack and earning himself the nickname of "Hancock the Superb." Antietam followed, and Hancock led the 2nd Corps when their commander fell, eventually taking permanent command. His division took part in the costly assaults on Marye's Height (Fredericksburg) and covered the retreat of the Union army from the Chancellorsville disaster. When General John Reynolds fell in the first day's fighting at Gettysburg, Hancock took charge on the field, recommending to Meade that the soldiers stay to fight the next day. He selected the ground where the Federal army deployed to fight on the second and third days of the battle. Hancock commanded the Union action until wounded by a nail and wood fragments that were driven into his leg by enemy fire. A long

Winfield Scott Hancock

recovery followed during which he took part in some recruiting activity.

He returned to duty in time for Grant's overland campaign. Hancock bitterly fought in the Wilderness and successfully assaulted the Confederate Mule Shoe salient at Spotsylvania. Cold Harbor found his troops slaughtered in futile frontal assaults ordered by Grant.

Because of garbled and incomplete orders, Hancock failed a brilliant maneuver ordered by Grant on the south side of the James River. Under Grant's direction he made persistent attempts to cut the rail lines leading into the south side of the city, constantly extending the network of Federal fortifications and entrenchments while fighting several battles in the process as the Confederates strove to keep them open.

With both armies going into winter quarters at the end of October 1864, he relinquished command of the 2nd Corps to General Andrew Humphreys because of his wound causing him much pain. Hancock changed gears and began recruiting the 1st Veteran Volunteer Corps, but results were disappointing at best. In early 1865, he took over command of the Washington, D.C., Maryland, West Virginia, and Shenandoah Valley areas. During this post, the military commander presided over the hangings of the Lincoln assassination conspirators in July 1865.

At the conclusion of the war, Hancock came into conflict with Grant. Hancock continued his career, holding several command positions. He also gained the nomination by the Democratic Party for the presidency in 1880,

Hancock presided over the hangings of the Lincoln assassination conspirators in July 1865.

but lost narrowly to James Garfield. He died in 1886, still listed as being on active duty.

General Grant said: "Hancock stands the most conspicuous figure of all the general officers who did not exercise a separate command. He commanded a corps longer than any other one, and his name was never mentioned as having committed in battle a blunder for which he was responsible. He was a man of very conspicuous personal appearance. Tall, well formed, and, at the time of which I now write, young and fresh looking, he presented an appearance that would attract the attention of an army as he passed. His genial disposition made him friends, and his personal courage and his presence with his command in the thickest of the fight won him the confidence of troops serving under him."[20]

⋆ *Ted Baehr*

MARSENA RUDOLPH PATRICK

★ ★ ★ ★ ★ ★ ★ ★ ★

Marsena Rudolph Patrick, born to John and Miriam White Patrick, ran away from home to make his fortune. The youth employed himself in various jobs and studies, including medicine, until securing an appointment to the United States Military Academy through General Stephen van Rensselaer, a man who paid patronage to the store where Patrick worked. He served in the Second Seminole War and the Mexican-American War after graduating in 1835. During the latter, he became commissary on General John Wool's staff.

Resigning in 1850, he took up farming outside Geneva, New York, to test out some of his scientific theories regarding agriculture. He published some of his results throughout the state, and in 1859 it earned him the presidency of the New York State Agricultural College.

Once the Civil War began, he resigned his office and joined the Union army, serving as inspector general for New York State during the first year. He accepted a brigadier general's position for the volunteers, commanding a brigade under Irvin McDowell at the Rappahannock.

His reputation as a strict but fair disciplinarian spread quickly, and his brigade became renowned for their organization.

Provost Marshal General Marsena R. Patrick and staff in Culpeper, Va.

Though stern, his kindness won over the hearts of his men. He led his brigade through Second Bull Run, South Mountain, and Antietam, earning the position of the army's provost-marshal-general during Antietam for helping reorganize the remnants of the Army of the Potomac. He operated in this capacity until being promoted by Grant to provost-marshal-general of all armies fighting against Richmond.

His new position involved dealing with intelligence officers (as part of his security duties), supervising and directing all provost marshals in their respective units, and dealing with desertion, the latter being the most intensive. To stop this problematic occurrence, Patrick set up new regulations for pursuing and punishing those who succeeded, and also coordinated the position of the marshals to ride on the outside during march to oversee troops. Maintaining camp order also fell upon his shoulders, which led to the eventual banning of alcohol in the areas held by the Army of the Potomac.

In response to his accomplishments, Patrick became major general over the volunteers on March 13, 1865. At war's end, he shifted position to being commander of the District of Henrico (which included Richmond). He held this command for only fifteen days before asking to be relieved of duty. The "stern disciplinarian" quickly came under criticism for being too kind to the poor in Richmond. He resigned three days later on June 12, 1865, and returned to New York to pursue politics in the Democratic Party.

This proved to be short lived, and he went back to farming, becoming quite prominent in the state agricultural circles. He took an office of governor over the Dayton Soldiers House in Ohio in 1880, and died eight years later in office.

★ *Ted Baehr*

A Union General
Samuel Kosciuszko Zook

Samuel Kosciuszko Zook

Samuel Kosciuszko Zook was born in Chester County, Pennsylvania, and spent most of his childhood around Valley Forge. He actively participated in the local militia until he relocated to New York City to become superintendent of the Washington and New York Telegraph Company. He sought out the militia there as well and became a lieutenant colonel in his regiment. The company came into a ninety-day service tour at the beginning of the war. Zook garrisoned Annapolis, Maryland, as one of their duties and served as the town's military governor.

Zook was a strict disciplinarian who hated cowardice, and he was known to be blunt and severe. He also excelled in cursing, and many of the primary sources comment regarding his proficient use of foul language, from his early days to his cursing exchange with Hancock prior to the battle of Chancellorsville. This trait was definitely not in keeping with his Mennonite heritage. In spite of these character traits, the men who knew him considered him to be a good-hearted man.

With regard to his cursing exchange with Hancock, T. Henry wrote to J. Ray that an incident "took place between Hancock and Zook while the 140th was on the march to U.S. Ford, destined for Chancellorsville. It was the greatest cursing match I ever listened to. Zook took advantage of

Hancock, by waiting until the latter got out of breath, and then he opened his pipe organ, and the air was very blue" (dated Jan. 29, 1902; both were members of the 140th Pa.).

Upon completion of the tour at Annapolis, Zook returned home and formed the 57th New York volunteer regiment to serve for the rest of the war. They joined the Army of the Potomac, and he was commissioned as colonel over the group. They distinguished themselves in battles such as Seven Pines and Harper's Ferry, the latter in reconnaissance missions that resulted in a skirmish with Confederate forces near Charlestown, (West) Virginia. He fought through Fredericksburg and led an assault on Marye's Heights, gallantly holding the position until nightfall, despite suffering his horse shot out from under him and 35 percent casualties. He received a high commendation from his commanding officer, Winfield Scott Hancock, about his conduct that day.

Zook briefly commanded a division of Second Corps after Fredericksburg but reassumed command of his brigade for the oncoming Chancellorsville Campaign. He received a promotion to brigadier general of volunteers on March 23, 1863, and led the Third Brigade, First Division, Second Corps (under Hancock) into battle.

Immediately after the battle of Fredericksburg, Zook wrote to his friend E. I. Wade on December 16, 1862,

> I walked over the field, close under the enemy's picket line, last night about 3 o'clock. The ground was strewn thickly with corpses of the heroes who perished there on Saturday. I never realized before what war was. I never before felt so horribly since I was born. To see men dashed to pieces by shot & torn into shreds by shells during the heat and crash of battle is bad enough God knows, but to walk alone amongst slaughtered brave in the 'still small hours' of the night would make the bravest man living 'blue.' God grant I may never have to repeat my last night's experience."

Commanding the same troops in Gettysburg, his final stand was trying to prevent a break in the Union defenses on July 2, 1863. He maintained order in the midst of pandemonium until a Confederate bullet found its way to his stomach. His men took him from the front of the company to the rear and began to tend his wound. He died before dawn on July 3, becoming one of many soldiers who fell fighting for a cause they believed to be just.

Ted Baehr

"OLD PRAYER BOOK"
OLIVER O. HOWARD

General Oliver Otis Howard was a New England abolitionist who never drank, smoked, or swore. His troops called him "Old Prayer Book."

Oliver O. Howard

Howard's brigade was routed at the First Battle of Bull Run. He blamed the Union army's horrific defeat on its decision to attack on a Sabbath.

Howard, who was widely known as "the Christian soldier," also fought at Antietam, and he was routed by Stonewall Jackson at Chancellorsville. After losing his right arm at the battle of Seven Pines, he mustered humor to say to General Kearny, who had lost his left arm, "I am sorry, General, but you must not mind it; we can buy our gloves together!"

On a Sabbath rest during Sherman's march to Atlanta, General Howard, as he occasionally did, spoke during chapel services. According to a missionary of the Christian Commission, "The General spoke of the Saviour, his love for Him and his peace in His service, as freely and simply as he could have spoken in his own family circle."

Following the war, Howard led the Freedmen's Bureau, a government effort to assist former slaves. He helped to found a university for blacks in 1867. Named in his honor, Howard University stands today, in the *New York Times*'s words, as "the largest and most prestigious black research university in America." The general also stirred controversy when he tried to integrate a church.

Howard served as chairman of the board of the American Tract Society and as superintendent of West Point. In 1869 he presented Bibles to all incoming West Point cadets, a practice that continues today.[21]

✶ Jeffery Warren Scott

YOUNG NAPOLEAN
GEORGE B. McCLELLAN

✶ ✶ ✶ ✶ ✶ ✶ ✶ ✶ ✶

George McClellan took command of the Armies of the United States in November 1861. The ambitious "Young Napoleon" was thirty-five and a newly converted Christian.

The Union had just suffered a great defeat at the First Battle of Bull Run. Some people said the Union was defeated because Federal troops attacked on Sunday morning, dishonoring the Sabbath. McClellan agreed, and he ordered that the Sabbath be observed throughout the Union army, with services held whenever military demands did not absolutely prevent worship and rest. However, devotion to God and popularity with his troops were not enough to make McClellan one of history's great commanders. He was overcautious; he continually overestimated the Confederates' strength, and he was slow to attack. Four months after becoming commander-in-chief, he was demoted by Lincoln; eight months after that, he was ordered to yield his army to General Burnside, go home, and wait for orders. They never came.

In 1864, McClellan ran against Lincoln as the Democratic candidate for president. Early on, it looked like he might win, but Union military victories boosted support for Lincoln, and McClellan carried only three states. Later, he served as governor of New Jersey.[22]

✶ *Jeffery Warren Scott*

George B. McClellan

THE PASSIONATE
CATHOLIC
WILLIAM ROSECRANS

★★★★★★★★★★

William S. Rosecrans

General William Rosecrans led his troops with the motto "God never fails those who truly trust." The *New York Times*, however, was not impressed with his dependence on divine guidance. The paper characterized him as depressive and indecisive in battle.

Following the battle at Murfreesboro, Rosecrans refused to pursue the defeated Confederate force, led by General Braxton Bragg, because he wanted his army to rest on the Sabbath.

Though known for drinking and swearing heavily, "Old Rosy" increased the number of chaplains in his company. And he often engaged his staff in religious discussions, in one period keeping them up until 4:00 a.m. for ten nights in a row. He attended Mass every day.

After maneuvering brilliantly in the 1863 Tullahoma Campaign in Tennessee, Rosecrans's forces suffered brutal losses at Chickamauga, "the River of Death." Some thirty-five thousand men fell on both sides in two days' fighting, and the heavy losses effectively ended Rosecrans's military career.[23]

⭐ Jeffery Warren Scott

Ulysses S. Grant

NO SAINT
ULYSSES S. GRANT

★★★★★★★★★★

Grant was the Union's leading general and twice president of the United States. But he was no saint.

The Grant family pew sits in the United Methodist Church of Galena, Illinois, testifying to the religious roots of Ulysses S. Grant. Finding evidence of faith in the general's adult life is harder.

At West Point, Grant (1822–85) complained that the

academy tried to mold cadets into gentlemanly Episcopalians. He resisted.

Grant's wife, Julie, was a devout Methodist. Throughout their marriage it rankled her that her husband never became a churchgoer. He claimed he didn't like the music.

Grant became known for intemperate drinking. The allegations were partially true: he drank too much when he was depressed or away from Julie.

Though passed over by the War Department at the outbreak of the Civil War, Grant eventually rose to the occasion of his life. Regarded by history as a great general, he went on to serve two terms as president.

Grant liked to say he was a verb and not a pronoun. When Lee surrendered to him at Appomattox, he let Lee's "men who claim to own a horse or mule take the animals home to work their little farms." He also sent rations to Lee's starving men.

On his deathbed, after a long battle with throat cancer, Grant was rebaptized at the insistence of his friends.[24]

⭐ *Jeffery Warren Scott*

A CONFEDERATE GENERAL
WILLIAM BOOTH TALIAFERRO

⭐ ⭐ ⭐ ⭐ ⭐ ⭐ ⭐ ⭐ ⭐

William Booth Taliaferro (pronounced "Toliver") was born in Gloucester County, Virginia, to Warner T. and Frances Booth Taliaferro. After graduating from Harvard, he started his law practice, only to be interrupted by the Mexican-American War, where he took a commission as captain, rising to the rank of major at the conclusion of the conflict.

Returning home, he picked up where he left off in his practice and also took an interest in state politics. He served in the Virginia House of Delegates (1850–53) and became a presidential elector for James Buchanan. His previous military experience led to him becoming state militia officer, and he commanded state forces during John Brown's raid of Harper's Ferry.

Taliaferro assumed command as major general of Virginia's state militia following secession and became colonel of the 23d Virginia Infantry after the state officially became part of the Confederacy. He was such a strict disciplinarian that at least one of his subordinates physically assaulted him.

After a post at Gloucester Point, his regiment moved to western Virginia (which is now West Virginia) to fight with Brigadier General Robert S. Garnett. When Garnett fell at Carrick's Ford in July 1861, Taliaferro remained there until the last month of the year and was then transferred to the Shenandoah Valley to fight under Stonewall Jackson. Taliaferro alienated Maj. Gen. Stonewall Jackson when he protested the poor conditions of the winter quarters Jackson had assigned to them.

William Booth Taliaferro

Taliaferro received a promotion to major general in the spring of 1862, despite initial friction between Jackson and himself, compounded by his becoming involved in a feud between Jackson and William Wing Loring concerning Jackson's placement of troops at Romney, Virginia. Taliaferro served with distinction during the Shenandoah Valley campaign following the promotion. In the following August at Cedar Mountain, he gained command of Jackson's old division, being given permanent command after his magnificent conduct. He led this regiment to Manassas Junction but had to step down from command temporarily because of an injury he received at Groveton (before Second Bull Run). He returned in December 1862 in time for Fredericksburg.

Taliaferro was transferred to the defenses of Savannah, Georgia, in early 1863, but transferred again to Charleston, South Carolina, to serve under P. G. T. Beauregard, preparing coastal fortifications. He received high commendation from his commanding officer for his expertly executed repelling of a numerically superior Union attack on Fort Wagner. August of the same year found him stationed to defend James Island, leaving only briefly to inspect the defenses of Florida in early 1864.

He left James Island when called to supervise the evacuation of Confederate troops from Savannah, Georgia, when William T. Sherman approached. He repeated the process for South Carolina's coastal regions and joined with Joseph Johnston's army in retreat, surrendering with him at Bentonville after a month-long fight in April 1865.

At war's end, he resumed his law practice, serving in the Virginia legislature for five years. He served as county judge for the 1890s and died in 1898 at his family home.

In spite of four volumes of diaries and letters, there appears to be no indication that William Booth Taliaferro had a strong, outspoken faith component to his life and career.

★ *Ted Baehr*

THE LORD'S BISHOP
LEONIDAS POLK

In his final year at West Point, Leonidas Polk read an evangelical tract and converted to Christ. His conversion and baptism touched off the first revival in West Point's history.

Receiving his military commission in 1827, Polk resigned it six months later in order to enter Virginia Theological Seminary. He later became the first Episcopal bishop of Louisiana.

In 1861, Polk accepted a commission as a major general in the Confederate army. Though on leave from his duties as bishop, "the bishop-general" was criticized in the North for serving jointly as churchman and warrior. Southerners saw it differently. "Like Gideon and David," the Memphis Appeal proclaimed, "he is marshaling his legions to fight the battle of the Lord."

Portrait of Leonidas Polk, officer of the Confederate army

This he did, pushing back Ulysses S. Grant at Belmont and helping lead Confederate forces at Chickamauga. During the battle of Perryville, Confederate General Cheatham advanced, shouting, "Give 'em hell, boys!" General Polk, conscious of the fact he was also an Episcopal bishop, joined in: "Give it to 'em, boys; give 'em what General Cheatham says!"

In *Battles for Atlanta*, Ronald H. Bailey reports that "on his way to battle at Resaca, General John Bell Hood confided his wish to be baptized. About midnight,

[Leonidas] Polk went to Hood's headquarters. There, while the one-legged Hood, unable to kneel, leaned on his crutches in the dim candlelight, the portly bishop dipped his hands into a horse bucket of consecrated water and performed the rite of baptism. Then he buckled on his sword and returned to Resaca."

In June 1864 a cannonball struck down Leonidas Polk, the most beloved general in the Army of Tennessee.[25]

Jeffery Warren Scott

JEB STUART
AND HIS MANY LOVES

★ ★ ★ ★ ★ ★ ★ ★ ★

J. E. B. "Jeb" Stuart is described by all as a zealous and earnest Christian. His Christianity did nothing to dampen his spirit and enthusiasm for life. Christianity made him a man of many loves. His intensity at warfare was only rivaled by his earnestness to enjoy the good things of this life when not in battle. He saw all things as manifestations of the goodness of God and saw no inconsistency at all in viewing life soberly and enjoying it to the hilt.

Stuart loved good horses and animals. He had two Irish setters he characteristically named "Nip" and "Tuck." He loved children. His staff once found him in a crowded waiting room with a baby under each arm (that he had stolen from their delighted mothers) charging all the other little children in the room with plumed hat and golden spurs, like some mad, bearded giant—roaring with laughter all the while.

Stuart loved music. Understanding the affect that music could have on morale, he sought someone who

Jeb Stuart

could provide him and his men with a good store of tunes. He found his man in Sam Sweeney. Sam Sweeney was the younger brother of Joe Sweeney, who is credited with inventing the banjo. Sam was a veritable virtuoso on the instrument, having once played for Queen Victoria. Sweeney was in the regiment of Col. T. T. Munford when Stuart met him. It didn't take long for Stuart to convince him that it would be twice the fun in the cavalry and soon sent orders for Sam to join him—to Munford's great distress.

So there was always music—even on the march. Sweeney rode behind Stuart everywhere so that Jeb could have accompaniment when he wanted to sing his favorites: "Her Bright Smile Haunts Me Still," "The Corn Top's Ripe," "Lorena," "The Dew Is on the Blossom," "Sweet Evelina," "The Girl I Left Behind Me," and, of course, "Jine the Cavalry." In the evening Stuart would gather the men who had good voices, others who could dance, Sweeney, and Bob (who played the bones), and there would be a regular variety show. People came for miles to these impromptu concerts.

There were, of course, balls and parties organized by Stuart so that life in the cavalry was never dull. Many criticized Stuart for this activity, but there was a rationale for this that few knew. Stuart revealed it in a letter to his brother early in the war. He said: "I realize that if we oppose force to force we cannot win, for their resources are greater than ours. We must make up in quality what we lack in numbers. We must substitute esprit for numbers. There, I strive to inculcate in my men the spirit of the chase."

This explains a great deal about Stuart's manner and style. He was not the vain frivolous man many thought him to be. He understood the military realities facing the South and, understanding human nature, sought to do what he could to bring about victory against such overwhelming odds. As one has stated, "His military problems were too serious to treat seriously. The weight against him, of men and horses and arms, was too great for his people to be allowed to contemplate. Therefore, he showed a happy face and led them to battle as to a fox hunt, held them joyously to hopeless odds, and fought light cavalry as nobody has fought it since Napoleon's time."

As it is with all men, the most important ingredient in Stuart's character was his faith. The foundation of all that he was and all that he did was biblical Christianity. He trusted implicitly in God and committed himself, his family, and his men to the care and keeping of the great Savior of mankind. His biographer, John Thomason, notes: "His letters, his remembered conversations, and even his official papers make it plain that his religion was an active force in everything he did, and he had a very simple earnest faith in the wisdom and the goodness of God."

Stuart was known to participate in the prayer meetings that filled the camps during the great revival among the Confederate troops in the winter of 1862–63. Even in the midst of battle he, like Stonewall, could not forget to pray. He wrote to his brother: "Pray for me in the coming struggle—with me, no moment of the battle has ever been too momentous for prayer."

He was ever careful to attribute his success to the blessing and favor of the Lord. He was active in his support of chaplains in the army, encouraging them to ride with the cavalry and giving them aid in the distribution of tracts and the holding of meetings among the men. He once angrily commented to a man who sneered at the preachers, "I regard the calling of a clergyman as the noblest in which any human being can engage."

He trusted in God implicitly. When the South was expecting intervention from Europe (France or Britain) and had hung its hopes upon this, someone asked Jeb his views on the subject. He responded, "I have strong hopes of France but depend most on our own strong arms and His aid Who can accomplish all."

In the fall of 1862, Stuart's daughter Flora fell seriously ill. Mrs. Stuart wrote him telling him of his daughter's sickness. Jeb could not go to her because of the press of circumstances, but wrote warm letters of comfort encouraging his wife to trust in God's goodness: "Let us trust in the good God, who has blessed us so much, that He will spare our child to us, but if it should please Him to take her from us, let us bear it with Christian fortitude and resignation."

On November 5, a telegram came informing Stuart of Flora's death. Von Borcke brought him the telegram. Stuart read the note and put it in his pocket, making no comment. That night after the day's work was done and out of sight of his men, he read the telegram again and gave vent to his pent-up emotions. His staff found him in his tent weeping uncontrollably. Von Borcke remarked, "I have not found a soldier who loved his family more than Jeb Stuart, or one whose sense of duty burned with a clearer flame."

On his death bed, Stuart called for his men to gather round and sing his favorite hymn, "Rock of Ages." The men were in little mood to sing, but they began the slow tune of this grand hymn, and Jeb joined in with a weak voice—weak but full of conviction.

While I draw this fleeting breath, when my eyelids close in death When I soar to worlds unknown, see thee on they judgment throne, Rock of Ages, cleft for me, let me hide myself in thee.

Later that afternoon he asked his doctor, Charles Brewer, "How long can I live, Charles? Can I last through the night?" Brewer replied, "I'm afraid the end is near." Stuart nodded and said, "I am resigned, if it be God's will. I would like to see my wife, but God's will be done." Soon afterward, Stuart turned to Dr. Brewer and gave his last

words, "I am going fast now. God's will be done." His wife, Flora, who had been rushing to get to her husband's side before he died, finally arrived at the house three hours later. Her meeting with her beloved Jeb would have to wait for another world. The greatly beloved, happy warrior was gone. He was thirty-one years old.

★ *Steve Wilkins*

AN OFFICER AND A GENTLEMAN
WILLIAM BARKSDALE

★ ★ ★ ★ ★ ★ ★ ★ ★ ★ ★

William Barksdale

William Barksdale was born on August 21, 1821, in Rutherford County, Tennessee. He was the son of William Barksdale Sr., a veteran of the War of 1812, and grandson of Nathaniel Barksdale, a veteran of the Revolutionary War. Although Barksdale was orphaned, his father left funds for his education, and he studied at the University of Nashville. At sixteen he moved with his two brothers to Mississippi, where he read for law and was admitted to the Bar at age twenty. He became coeditor and copublisher of the Columbus, Mississippi, *Democrat*, a proslavery and prosecessionist newspaper.

In 1846, Barksdale enlisted as a private in the 2nd Mississippi Rifles, commanded by Colonel Jefferson Davis, where he rose through the ranks and was eventually mustered out as captain, after being appointed commissary officer (quartermaster). He performed commendably as commissary and also kept volunteering for combat in the Mexican War.

After returning home, he married a Louisiana belle, Narcissa Smith, who brought several slaves as her dowry. His work as lawyer, journalist, and planter thrived, and his plantation grew to 639 acres, near Columbus, where he became quite active in politics. He was elected as a delegate to the 1852 Democratic National Convention in Baltimore.

In 1853, Barksdale ran for the U.S. House of Representatives against fellow Mexican War veteran Rueben Davis. Their extremely bitter campaign culminated on July 1, 1853, in a room of the Hotel Washington in Vicksburg. They had met to arrange a duel to be held across the Mississippi River in Louisiana. At this meeting, Davis backhanded Barksdale in the face, and he responded by knocking Davis down. When Davis got up, he pulled a penknife and stabbed Barksdale ten times, in his arms, chest, and side. Bloody but unbowed, Barksdale decked Davis again. Although their fight was finally broken up, and the duel cancelled, the electors were horrified that Davis had attacked an unarmed man. As a result Barksdale was elected in a landslide. He was reelected in 1855 and twice more in 1857 and 1859 without opposition.

It was customary for congressmen to go to the Capitol armed, and Barksdale, one of the most eloquent and articulate defenders of slavery and states rights, equipped himself with a Bowie knife. On one occasion, Barksdale used his knife, as well as his fighting demeanor, to escort the south-hating Representative Thaddeus Stevens of Pennsylvania from the floor. This notoriety lead to charges that he also used his knife to keep anyone from going to the rescue of Senator Charles Sumner of Massachusetts on May 22, 1856. Representative Preston

Brooks of South Carolina, offended by Sumner's reference to his father-in-law, had entered the Senate with a *gutta percha* cane and had beaten the seated Sumner into unconsciousness and permanent injury. No witnesses testified, however, that Barksdale was involved, and it is doubtful, given his experience with Davis's penknife, he would have protected even a friend and colleague, such as Brooks, in a surprise attack on another unarmed man.

When the House of U.S. Representatives was in session until 2:00 A.M. on February 1, 1858, debating the red-hot issue of slavery in Kansas, Mississippi's General John Quitman, a congressman and hero of the Mexican War, asked for special permission to explain something. Pennsylvania's Congressman Galusha Grow, who loved to bait southerners, loudly and impolitely objected, and South Carolina's Representative Laurence Keitt demanded that, in accordance with House rules, Grow make his objection from his party's side of the aisle. Following an exchange of insults, Keitt clutched Grow by the throat, and the House floor then became a free-for-all, with numerous fisticuffs and wrestling matches. Barksdale was in the thick of it when he received a fierce blow from Grow and lost his hairpiece. To cover his thinning hair, Barksdale promptly reached down for the toupee and put it on backward. His colleagues, albeit still violent, instantly noticed his mistake and began roaring with laugher. The men then all shook hands and bade good night.

While in Congress Barksdale continued to work for what he hoped could be a peaceable secession. As a born fighter, however, he told the Lowness County, Mississippi Democratic Convention in 1859, "The army that invades the south to subjugate her, their bodies will enrich southern soil. We plant ourselves upon the right of peaceable secession and there we intend to stand."

When the Mississippi legislature passed the ordnance

of secession, Barksdale resigned from Congress and returned to Mississippi to volunteer for military service. He was appointed quartermaster general for all of Mississippi's troops. But within days, he resigned to accept election as colonel of the 13th Mississippi Regiment of the Confederate States Army, organized on May 14, 1861. He was ordered to report to General Leonidas Polk, an Episcopal bishop and West Pointer, at a training center in Union City, Tennessee.

After brief training, the regiment was moved to Lynchburg and on July 20 was railroaded to Manassas Junction, arriving after dark. The following day, after reporting to General Jubal Early, Barksdale's regiment attacked the Union army's right flank with such speed and savage intensity that the Federals fled. Later that year, Barksdale's regiment distinguished itself again, at Balls Bluff, in a key maneuver against numerically stronger Union forces that crossed the Potomac near Leesburg. Barksdale's men also held off Union reinforcements at Edwards Ferry.

On December 9, 1861, the 13th was assigned to the Mississippi brigade under the command of General Richard Griffith, who Colonel Barksdale, now senior colonel, replaced after Griffith was mortally wounded in the next spring's fighting on the Peninsula. At the battles of Seven Pines, Gaines Mills, and Savage Station, the Mississippians continued to distinguish themselves with courage in combat though with heavy casualties.

Displaying the highest qualities of a leader and a soldier, Barksdale seized and carried

Pontoon bridges across the Rappahannock built by army engineers.

the colors himself at the Battle of Malvern Hill, advancing under terrific artillery and infantry fire. His command suffered 91 killed and 434 wounded. With a personal citation, the commander of the Army of Northern Virginia, General Robert F. Lee, recommended Barksdale for promotion to brigadier general on August 12, 1862.

When Stonewall Jackson took Harper's Ferry just prior to the Battle of Antietam, Barksdale's brigade and Kershaw's South Carolinians cleared Maryland Heights. The Mississippians then force-marched to Sharpsburg, where they were in some of the bloodiest fighting in that most costly one-day battle of the war. They formed their battle line under artillery fire and then advanced, driving the enemy from the woods.

Three months later at Fredericksburg, Barksdale's brigade had its most strategic effect of the war, rivaled only by their nearly breaking the Union line in Gettysburg's Peach Orchard. From 2:00 A.M. until after sundown on December 11, 1862, the Mississippians kept decimating General Burnside's army engineers as they were trying to build pontoon bridges across the Rappahannock. Finally, Burnside grew impatient with trying to dislodge the southern snipers with return musketry, and he ordered his artillery chief, General Hunt, to barrage the town with his 147 guns on Stafford Heights.

Barksdale's men took cover in cellars, but as soon as the heavy artillery let up, they came out and began shooting more Union army engineers. The artillery caused Fredericksburg homes to burn, and Barksdale sent a message to Longstreet: "Shall I have my men put out the fires?"

"You have enough to do to watch the Yankees!" Longstreet retorted.

As the barrage continued, Barksdale's aide informed him that a woman said she must see Barksdale about an urgent matter. "How can I take care of a lady's problems at a time like this?" Barksdale shouted. The aide conveyed the message to the woman but returned almost immediately with the following message: "She says you are a Southern gentleman, and that's no way to treat a lady, sir." Barksdale cursed and wrung his hands. "Bring her in."

When the lady arrived, Barksdale said, "For God's sake, madam! Go and seek someplace for safety. I'll send a member of my staff to help you find one." To which the lady replied, "My cow has just been killed by a shell. She is very fat, and I don't want the Yankees to get her. If you'll only send someone down to butcher her, you are welcome to the meat." William Barksdale, combat leader of some of the Confederacy's toughest troops, was overcome and surrendered. "I promise the cow will be salvaged and consumed to the glory of the Confederacy! Now please, ma'am, take cover."

It took two orders by Barksdale's superior, Major General Lafayette McLaws, to get Barksdale to evacuate the pulverized town, instead of remaining for some hand-to-hand. But finally, after sunset, the Mississippians evacuated and went to Marye's Heights, where their heroic delaying action under heavy bombardment gave the

"Wounded Escaping from the Burning Woods in the Wilderness" by Alfred Waud, recognized as the best of the Civil War sketch artists who drew the war for the nation's pictorial press.

75,800-man Lee, Jackson, Longstreet, & Co. time to dig in—for the December 13 Confederate shoot-out of 12,700 of Burnside's 106,000 Federals.

The Mississippi brigade remained in the area for nearly five months. During the Chancellorsville battle, they were stretched thin for three miles and given the task of halting the entire Union 4th Corps of the competent and beloved General "Uncle John" Sedgwick—more than 15,000 soldiers against part of one Confederate brigade. The Mississippians were eventually overrun, with heavy casualties, but they held long enough to keep Sedgwick from attacking Lee. For in an audacious gamble, Lee divided his army and turned loose Stonewall Jackson for his spectacular flanking of Howard's corps and another Confederate victory.

Fifty-eight days later, the Mississippi brigade arrived on the line at Gettysburg's Seminary Ridge. Here, at a great distance in front of his men, William Barksdale led his final and most spectacular charge at the sacrifice of his life. One Union army officer ordered his men to, "Aim at that big politician!" Barksdale fell with several wounds. After being kindly treated in a Union hospital, he died near dawn of July 3, still confident of Confederate victory and praying at last that God would take care of his wife and two young sons back home in Mississippi. After the general's burial, Barksdale's body servant walked from Gettysburg to Columbus, Mississippi, to make certain that Barksdale's home and family were protected and helped.

★ *Les Kinsolving*

WHO WAS JOHNNY REB?

★ ★ ★ ★ ★ ★ ★ ★

The term "Johnny Reb" usually evokes an image of a white soldier, Anglo-Saxon and Protestant and from an agrarian background. Many Southern soldiers in the Civil War, however, did not fit this mold. A number of ethnic backgrounds were represented.

For example, thousands of black Americans fought as Johnny Rebs. Dr. Lewis Steiner of the U.S. Sanitary Commission observed that while the Confederate army marched through Maryland during the 1862 Sharpsburg (Antietam) campaign, "over 3,000 Negroes had arms, rifles, muskets, sabers, bowie knives, dirks, etc. And were manifestly an integral portion of the Southern Confederate Army."

Hispanics were also Confederates. Colonel Santos Benavides, a former Texas Ranger and city attorney and mayor of Laredo, Texas, commanded the 33rd Texas Cavalry, while General Refugio Benavides protected what was known as the Confederacy of the Rio Grande. Irish Catholic immigrants also chose to fight for the South, as did a few stalwart Chinese who served nobly in Louisiana.

The largest ethnic group to serve the Confederacy, however, was made up of first-, second- and third-generation Jewish lads. Old Jewish families, initially Sephardic and later Ashkenazic, had settled in the South generations before the war. Jews had lived in Charleston, South Carolina, since 1695.

By 1800, the largest Jewish community in America lived in Charleston, where the oldest synagogue in America, K. K. Beth Elohim, was founded. By 1861, a third of all the Jews in America lived in Louisiana.

More than ten thousand Jews fought for the Confederacy.

As Rabbi Korn of Charleston related, "Nowhere else in America—certainly not in the Antebellum North—had Jews been accorded such an opportunity to be complete equals as in the old South." General Robert E. Lee allowed his Jewish soldiers to observe all holy days, while Generals Ulysses S. Grant and William T. Sherman issued anti-Jewish orders.

A number of Jewish officers were part and parcel of Southern society. They had spent their formative years in the South, defensive about slavery and hostile about what they perceived as Northern aggression and condescension toward the South. Some of the more notable among the officer corps included Abraham Myers, a West Point graduate and a classmate of Lee's in the class of 1832. Myers served as quartermaster general and, before the war, fought the Indians in Florida. The city of Fort Myers was named after him.

Another Jewish officer, Major Adolph Proskauer of Mobile, Alabama, was wounded several times. One of his subordinate officers wrote, "I can see him now as he nobly carried himself at Gettysburg, standing coolly and calmly with a cigar in his mouth at the head of the 12th Alabama amid a perfect rain of bullets, shot, and shell. He was the personification of intrepid gallantry and imperturbable courage."

In North Carolina, the six Cohen brothers fought in the 40th Infantry. The first Confederate Jew killed in the war was Albert Lurie Moses of Charlotte, North Carolina. All-Jewish companies reported to the fray from Macon and Savannah in Georgia. In Louisiana, three Jews reached the rank of colonel: S. M. Hymans, Edwin Kunsheedt, and Ira Moses.

Many Southern Jews became world-renowned during this period. Moses Jacob Ezekiel from Richmond fought at New Market with his fellow cadets from the Virginia

Military Institute and became a noted sculptor. His mother, Catherine Ezekiel, said she would not tolerate a son who declined to fight for the Confederacy.

He wrote in his memoirs, "We were not fighting for the perpetuation of slavery, but for the principle of States Rights and Free Trade, and in defense of our homes which were being ruthlessly invaded." In tribute to Ezekiel, it was written, "The eye that saw is closed, the hand that executed is still, the soldier lad who fought so well was knighted and lauded in foreign land, but dying, his last request was that he might rest among his old comrades in Arlington Cemetery."

The most famous Southern Jew of the era was Judah Benjamin. He was the first Jewish U.S. senator and declined a seat on the Supreme Court and an offer to be ambassador to Spain. Educated in law at Yale, he was at one time or another during the war the Confederacy's attorney general, secretary of war, and secretary of

Judah Benjamin

state. After the war, he settled in England, where he became a lawyer and wrote a seminal legal text.

Simon Baruch, a Prussian immigrant, settled in Camden, South Carolina. He received his degree from the Medical College of Virginia and entered the conflict as a physician in the 3rd South Carolina Battalion, where he joined the fighting before the Battle of Second Manassas. He eventually became surgeon general of the Confederacy.

While he was away during the war, his fiancée, Isabelle Wolfe, painted his portrait in the family home in South Carolina. It was at this time that Sherman began his March to the Sea. His raiders set the Wolfe house afire,

and as she rescued the portrait, a Yankee ripped it with his bayonet and slapped her. Witnessing this, a Union officer gave the attacker a beating with his sword.

From this, a romance began to blossom, but it was quickly squelched by the young woman's father, who remarked, "Marriage to a gentile is bad enough, but marriage to a Yankee, never, ever; it is out of the question." Isabelle Wolfe eventually married Baruch. After the war, they moved to New York City, where he set up what became a prominent medical practice on West 57th Street.

Mrs. Baruch became a member of the United Daughters of the Confederacy, and the couple raised their children with pro-Southern views. If a band struck up "Dixie," Dr. Baruch would jump up and give the Rebel yell, much to the chagrin of the family. A man of usual reserve and dignity, Dr. Baruch nevertheless would let loose with the piercing yell even in the Metropolitan Opera House.

Their son Bernard became the most successful financier of his time and one of the best-known American Jews of the twentieth century. Bernard Baruch was an adviser to presidents from World War I to World War II and became a confidant of President Franklin D. Roosevelt.

Simon Baruch in uniform as a Confederate assistant surgeon

Today, little remains of the Jewish Confederate South. With the mass migrations from Russia and Eastern Europe, new immigrants knew little if anything of the struggle that had ensued during the preceding half-century. Confederate Southern Jewry eventually disappeared.[26]

★ *Thomas C. Mandes*

10
FAITH, HOPE, AND LOVE
LETTERS BETWEEN STONEWALL AND ANNA JACKSON

★★★★★★★★★★★★★★★★★★★★★★★

Actors Kali Rocha as Anna Jackson and Stephen Lang as General Stonewall Jackson watch proudly as Rev. Tucker Lacy, portrayed by David Carpenter, christens the Jacksons' daughter, Julia.

My precious husband—

I will go to Hanover and wait there until I hear from you again, and I do trust I may be permitted to come back to you again in a few days. I am much disappointed at not seeing you again, but I commend you, my precious darling, to the merciful keeping of the God of battles, and do pray most earnestly for the success of our army this day. Oh! that our Heavenly Father may preserve and guide and bless you, is my most earnest prayer.

I leave the shirt and socks for you with Mrs. Neale, fearing I may not see you again, but I do hope it may be my privilege to be with you in a few days. Our little darling will miss dearest Papa. She is so good and sweet this morning.

God bless and keep you, my darling
Your devoted little wife.

—Letter from Anna Jackson to General Stonewall Jackson

THE FOUNDATION OF LOVE

★ ★ ★ ★ ★ ★ ★ ★ ★

Thomas Jackson first met Mary Anna Morrison in 1853, when she was visiting her sister, Mrs. Harvey Hill, in Lexington. After the death of his first wife, Ellie Junkin, Jackson spent a period of intense mourning, then took a three-month tour of Europe in 1856. Apparently on that trip he remembered Mary Anna and thought she would make a suitable wife for him. When he returned to Lexington, he wrote her and quickly followed up his letter with a visit to the Morrison home in North Carolina. Anna's father was happy Jackson was a "Christian gentleman," while her mother was pleased with his extreme politeness. Thomas and Anna soon became engaged. Jackson's letters to his betrothed during their engagement reveal the Christian foundation of their love:[1]

April 25th, 1857. It is a great comfort to me to know that although I am not with you, yet you are in the hands of One who will not permit any evil to come nigh you. What a consoling thought it is to know that we may, with perfect confidence, commit all our friends in Jesus to the care of our Heavenly Father, with an assurance that all will be well with them! I have been sorely disappointed at not hearing from you this morning, but these disappointments are all designed for our good.

In my daily walks I think much of you. I love to stroll abroad after the labors of the day are over, and indulge feelings of gratitude to God for all the sources of natural beauty with which He has adorned the earth. Some time since, my morning walks were rendered very delightful by the singing of the birds. The morning caroling of the birds, and their sweet notes in the evening, awaken in me devotional feelings of praise and thanksgiving, though very different in their nature. In the morning, all animated nature (man excepted) appears to join in expressions of gratitude to God; in the evening, all is hushing into silent slumber, and this disposes the mind to meditation. And as my mind dwells on you, I love to give it a devotional turn, by thinking of you as a gift from our Heavenly Father. How delightful it is thus to associate every pleasure and enjoyment with God the Giver! Thus will He bless us, and make us grow in grace, and in the knowledge of Him, whom to know aright is life eternal.

May 7th. I wish I could be with you tomorrow at your communion. Though absent in body, yet in spirit I shall be present, and my prayer will be for your growth in every Christian grace. I take special pleasure in the part of my prayers in which I beg that every temporal and spiritual blessing may be yours, and that the glory of God may be the controlling and absorbing thought of our lives in our new relation. It is to me a great satisfaction to feel that our Heavenly Father has so manifestly ordered our union. I believe, and am persuaded, that if we but walk in His commandments, acknowledging Him in all our ways, He will shower His blessings upon us. How delightful it is to feel that we have such a friend, who changes not! The Christian's recognition of God in all His works greatly enhances his enjoyment.

May 16th. There is something very pleasant in the thought of your mailing me a letter every Monday; such manifestation of regard for the Sabbath must be well-pleasing in the sight of God. Oh that all our people would manifest such a regard for His holy day! If we would all strictly observe His holy laws, what would not our country be? When in prayer for you last Sabbath, the tears came to my eyes, and I realized an unusual degree of emotional tenderness. I have not yet fully analyzed my feelings to my satisfaction, so as to arrive at the cause of such emotions; but I

★ ★ ★ ★ ★ ★

And as my mind dwells on you, I love to give it a devotional turn, by thinking of you as a gift from our Heavenly Father.

—Jackson writing to Anna

★ ★ ★ ★ ★ ★

am disposed to think that it consisted in the idea of the intimate relation existing between you, as the object of my tender affection, and God, to whom I looked up as my Heavenly Father. I felt that day as if it were a communion day for myself.

Thomas and Anna were married at the Morrison's North Carolina home on July 16, 1857. After a northern tour to Niagara and Saratoga, the newlyweds settled in Lexington.

In November 1858, they bought a house that they filled with domestic Christian love. They enjoyed working in their garden together and riding into the countryside or reading in the evenings.

In the summers, Anna and Tom would often go north to cooler weather and enjoy the mineral springs then considered so healthful. Sorrow came in May 1858 when their month-old daughter, Mary Graham, died of jaundice. Anna herself was not well the following year, and in the spring Jackson took her to New York for treatment. He had to leave her there for a time while he returned to his teaching, but his letters expressed his constant love and thoughtfulness:

May 7th. I send you a flower from your garden, and could have sent one in full bloom, but I thought this one, which is just opening, would be in a better state of preservation when my little dove receives it. Yesterday Doctor Junkin preached one of his masterly sermons on the sovereignty of God, and, although a doctrinal discourse, it was eminently consoling; and I wish that you could have heard such a presentation of the subject. You must not be discouraged at the slowness of recovery. Look up to Him who giveth liberally for faith to be resigned to His divine will, and trust Him for that measure of health which will most glorify

Him and advance to the greatest extent your own real happiness. We are sometimes suffered to be in a state of perplexity, that our faith may be tried and grow stronger. "All things work together for good" to God's children.[2] See if you cannot spend a short time after dark in looking out of your window into space, and meditating upon heaven, with all its joys unspeakable and full of glory; and think of what the Saviour relinquished in glory when He came to earth, and of His sufferings for us, and seek to realize, with the apostle, that the afflictions of the present life are not worthy to be compared with the glory which shall be revealed in us. Try to look up and be cheerful, and not desponding. Trust our kind Heavenly Father, and by the eye of faith see that all things with you are right and for your best interest. The clouds come, pass over us, and are followed by bright sunshine; so in God's moral dealings with us, He permits us to have trouble awhile. But let us, even in the most trying dispensations of His providence, be cheered by the brightness which is a little ahead. Try to live near to Jesus, and secure that peace which flows like a river. You have your husband's prayers, sympathy, and love. . . .

You are one darling of darlings, and may our kind and merciful Heavenly Father bless you with speedy restoration to health and to me, and with every needful blessing, both temporal and spiritual, is my oft-repeated prayer. Take good care of my little dove, and remember that the day of miracles is past, and that God works by means, and He punishes us for violating His physical as well as His moral laws. When you come home, I want to meet you at Goshen in a private conveyance, and bring my little one gently over the rough roads. I hope you will take my advice, and not burden yourself by carrying anything in your hands, except your umbrella and basket. You are very precious to one somebody's heart, if you are away off in New York. My heart is with my esposita all the time, and my prayers are

for her safety. How I wish you were here now to share with me the pleasures of home, our garden, and the surrounding country, which is clothed in verdure and beauty! On Wednesday your esposo hopes to meet his sunshine, and may he never see its brightness obscured, nor its brilliancy diminished by spots![3]

Portrait of General Jackson

EARTHLY WAR, HEAVENLY PEACE

★ ★ ★ ★ ★ ★ ★ ★ ★

As the war clouds gathered, Jackson foresaw the coming of war. Knowing war's horrors, he deprecated war while radicals on both sides clamored for it. Jackson earnestly spoke to his pastor about the need for Christian people to unite in a concert of prayer to avert war from their land. On April 21, 1861, Major Jackson received his orders at Lexington to immediately bring the VMI cadets to Richmond. Before he left his own home, Jackson had a special time of prayer with his beloved Anna. He read from the Bible: "For we know that if our earthly house of this tabernacle were dissolved, we have a building of God, an house not made with hands, eternal in the heavens" (2 Cor. 5:1). They knelt together, and with emotion-choked words Jackson committed them both to the care of their heavenly Father and prayed for the peace of the country. After kissing Anna fervently, Jackson left his home full of domestic happiness, never to return again.

Jackson wrote Anna almost daily concerning his military activities and the progress of the war, always interwoven with a personal, Christian perspective on events. After the Battle of First Manassas or First Bull Run, at which Jackson and his brigade received the name Stonewall, he wrote:

Manassas, July 22d

My precious Pet,-Yesterday we fought a great battle and gained a great victory, for which all the glory is due to God alone. Although under a heavy fire for several continuous hours, I received only one wound, the breaking of the longest finger of my left hand; but the doctor says the finger can be saved. It was broken about midway between the hand and knuckle, the ball passing on the side next the forefinger. Had it struck the centre, I should have lost the finger. My horse was wounded, but not killed. Your coat got an ugly wound near the hip, but my servant, who is very handy, has so far repaired it that it doesn't show very much. My preservation was entirely due, as was the glorious victory, to our God, to whom be all the honor, praise, and glory. The battle was the hardest that I have ever been in, but not near so hot in its fire. I commanded the centre more particularly, though one of my regiments extended to the right for some distance. There were other commanders on my right and left. Whilst great credit is due to other parts of our gallant army, God made my brigade more instrumental than any other in repulsing the main attack. This is for your information only—say nothing about it. Let others speak praise, not myself.

Anna thought the papers should better report on Jackson's actions and valor, but Jackson encouraged his wife not to do anything to promote his name. All promotion should come from the Lord and not be sought:

August 5th. And so you think the papers ought to say more about your husband! My brigade is not a brigade of newspaper correspondents. I know that the First Brigade was the first to meet and pass our retreating foes—to push on with no other aid than the smiles of God; to boldly take its position with the artillery that was under my command—to arrest the victorious foe in his onward progress—to hold him in check until reinforcements arrived—and finally to charge bayonets, and, thus advancing, pierce the enemy's centre. I am well satisfied with what it did, and so are my generals, Johnston and Beauregard. It is not to be expected that I should receive the credit that Generals Beauregard and Johnston would, because I was under them; but I am thankful to my ever-kind Heavenly Father that He makes me content to await His own good time and pleasure for commendation—knowing that all things work together for my good. If my brigade can always play so important and useful a part as it did in the last battle, I trust I shall ever be most grateful. As you think the papers do not notice me enough, I send a specimen, which you will see from the upper part of the paper is a leader. My darling, never distrust our God, who doeth all things well. In due time He will make manifest all His pleasure, which is all His people should desire. You must not be concerned at seeing other parts of the army lauded, and my brigade not mentioned. "Truth is mighty and will prevail."

In September 1861, Anna was able to visit Jackson for two weeks near Fairfax, Virginia. It was the first of three visits to her husband she was able to make during the war. When she left Fairfax, Anna returned to Cottage Home, her parents' home in North Carolina. She had boarded up her Lexington home and stayed with her parents while Jackson was at war. Even in the midst of intense military pressures, Jackson's letters to Anna reveal his thoughtful consideration for his wife and his primary Christian concerns:

24th September [1861]

I am going to write a letter to my darling pet esposita, who paid me such a sweet visit, and whose dear face I can still see, though she is "way down in the Old North State." If my darling were here, I know she would enjoy General Jones's band, which plays very sweetly. We are still in the encampment as when you left, and I have the promise of three more wall tents.

Monday morning. This is a beautiful and lovely morning—beautiful emblem of the morning of eternity in heaven. I greatly enjoy it after our cold, chilly weather, which has made me feel doubtful of my capacity, humanly speaking, to endure the campaign, should we remain long in tents. But God, our God, does, and will do, all things well; and if it is His pleasure that I remain in the field, He will give me the ability to endure all its fatigues. I hope my little sunshiny face is as bright as this lovely day. Yesterday I heard a good sermon from the chaplain of the Second Regiment, and at night I went over to Colonel Garland's regiment of Longstreet's Brigade, and heard an excellent sermon from the Rev. Mr. Granberry, of the Methodist church, of whom you may have heard me speak in times past.[4]

26th. I did not have room enough in my last letter, nor

★ ★ ★ ★ ★ ★ ★ ★

My darling, never distrust our God, who doeth all things well. In due time He will make manifest all His pleasure, which is all His people should desire.

—Thomas Jackson, writing to his wife Anna

★ ★ ★ ★ ★ ★ ★ ★

have I time this morning, to write as much as I desired about Dr. Dabney's sermon yesterday.[5] His text was from Acts, seventh chapter and fifth verse. He stated that the word God being in italics indicated that it was not in the original, and he thought it would have been better not to have been in the translation. It would have read: "Calling upon and saying, Lord Jesus, receive my spirit." He spoke of Stephen, the first martyr under the new dispensation, like Abel, the first under the old, dying by the hand of violence, and then drew a graphic picture of his probably broken limbs, mangled flesh and features, conspiring to heighten his agonizing sufferings. But in the midst of this intense pain, God, in His infinite wisdom and mercy, permitted him to see the heavens opened, so that he might behold the glory of God, and Jesus, of whom he was speaking, standing on the right hand of God. Was not such a heavenly vision enough to make him forgetful of his sufferings? He beautifully and forcibly described the death of the righteous, and as forcibly that of the wicked.

4th November. This morning I received orders to proceed to Winchester. I am assigned to the command of the military district of the Northern frontier, between the Blue Ridge and the Allegheny Mountains, and I hope to have my little dove with me this winter. How do you like the programme? I trust I may be able to send for you after I get settled. I don't expect much sleep tonight, as my desire is to travel all night, if necessary, for the purpose of reaching Winchester before day to-morrow. My trust is in God for the defense of that country [the Valley]. I shall have great labor to perform, but, through the blessing of our everkind Heavenly Father, I trust that He will enable me to accomplish it.

9th November. I trust that my darling little wife feels more gratitude to our kind Heavenly Father than pride or elation at my promotion. Continue to pray for me, that I may live to glorify God more and more, by serving Him and our country. If you were only here, you would have a very nice house. And if your husband stays here this winter, he hopes to send one of his aides for one little somebody. You know very well who I mean by "little somebody."

And now for an answer to your questions; and without stating your questions, I will answer them. My command is enlarged, and embraces the Valley District, and the troops of this district constitute the Army of the Valley; but my command is not altogether independent, as it is embraced in the Department of Northern Virginia, of which General Johnston has command. There are three armies in this department—one under General Beauregard, another under General Holmes, and the third under my command. My headquarters are for the present at Winchester.

During this winter, Anna came to stay with Jackson at Winchester for more than two months. The Jacksons stayed with the family of Dr. James Graham, a Presbyterian clergyman. In March, Anna returned to Cottage Home, and the two returned to letter writing:

Winchester, March 10, 1862

My darling, you made a timely retreat from here, for on Friday the Yankees came within five miles of this place. Ashby skirmished for some time with them, and after they fell back he followed then until they halted near Bunker Hill, which is twelve miles from here, where they are at present.[6] The troops are in excellent spirits . . . . How God does bless us wherever we are! [This was in reference to the kindness the Jacksons had received in Winchester over the winter.] I am very thankful for the measure of health with which He blesses me. I do not remember having been in such good health for years. My heart is just overflowing with love for my little darling wife.

April 7th. My precious pet, your sickness gives me great concern; but so live that it, and all your trials, may be sanctified to you, remembering that "our light afflictions, which are but for a moment, work out for us a far more exceeding and eternal weight of glory."[7] I trust you and all I have in the hands of a kind Providence, knowing that all things work together for the good of His people.

Yesterday was a lovely Sabbath day. Although I had not the privilege of hearing the word of life, yet it felt like a holy Sabbath day, beautiful, serene, and lovely. All it wanted was the church-bell and God's services in the sanctuary to make it complete. Our gallant little army is increasing in numbers, and my prayer is that it may be an army of the living God as well as of its country.

For three months during the spring of 1862, Jackson fought his famous "Valley Campaign" in the Shenandoah Valley of Virginia. Facing Federal forces three times as large as his, by brilliant strategy Jackson's Confederates outmaneuvered and defeated the Union troops. Jackson wrote Anna descriptions of his military operations while also writing of his love for her and his spiritual concerns:

May 12th. My precious darling, I telegraphed you on the 9th that God had blest us with victory at McDowell. I have followed the enemy to this place, which is about three miles from Franklin. The enemy has been reinforced, and apparently designs making a stand beyond Franklin. I expect to reconnoiter today, but do not know as yet whether I will attack him thus reinforced. We have divine service at ten o'clock to-day (Monday) to render thanks to Almighty God for having crowned our arms with success, and to implore His continued favor.

New Harrisonburg, May 19th

How I do desire to see our country free and at peace! It appears to me that I would appreciate home more than I have ever done before. Here I am sitting in the open air, writing on my knee for want of a table. Yesterday Dr. Dabney preached an excellent sermon from the text: "Come unto me, all ye that labor and are heavy laden, and I will give you rest."[8] It is a great privilege to have him with me.

After their success in the Shenandoah Valley, Jackson and his men joined General Robert E. Lee's Army of Northern Virginia in the defense of Richmond. After the Battle of the Seven Days, Union general McClellan withdrew from his attack on the Confederate capital:

Near White Oak Swamp Bridge, June 30th

An ever-kind Providence has greatly blessed our efforts and given us great reason for thankfulness in having defended Richmond. Today the enemy is retreating down the Chickahominy towards the James River. Many prisoners are falling into our hands. General D. H. Hill and I are together.[9] I had a wet bed last night, as the rain fell in torrents. I got up about midnight, and haven't seen much rest since. I do trust that our God will soon bless us with an honorable peace, and permit us to be together at home again in the enjoyment of domestic happiness.

You must give fifty dollars for church purposes, and more should you be disposed. Keep an account of the amount, as we must give at least one tenth of our income. I would like very much to see my darling, but hope that God will enable me to remain at the post of duty until, in His own good time, He blesses us with independence.

Gordonsville, July 28th

My darling wife, I am just overburdened with work, and I hope you will not think hard at receiving only very short letters from your loving husband. A number of officers are with me, but people keep coming to my tent—though let me say no more. A Christian should never complain. The apostle Paul said, "I glory in tribulations!"[10] What a bright example for others!

On last Saturday our God again crowned our arms with victory about six miles from Culpepper Court-House. I can hardly think of the fall of Brigadier-General C. S. Winder without tearful eyes. Let us all unite more earnestly in imploring God's aid in fighting our battles for us. The thought that there are so many of God's people praying for His blessing upon the army greatly strengthens and encourages me. The Lord has answered their prayers, and my trust is in Him, that He will continue to do so. If God be for us, who can be against us? That He will still be with us and give us victory until our independence shall be established, and that He will make our nation that people whose God is the Lord, is my earnest and oft-repeated prayer. While we attach so much importance to being free from temporal bondage, we must attach far more to being free from the bondage of sin.

September 1st. We were engaged with the enemy at and near Manassas Junction Tuesday and Wednesday, and again near the battlefield of Manassas on Thursday, Friday, and Saturday; in all of which God gave us the victory. May He ever be with us, and we ever be His devoted people, is my earnest prayer. It greatly encourages me to feel that so many of God's people are praying for that part of our force under my command. The Lord has answered their prayers; He has again placed us across Bull Run; and I pray that He will make our arms entirely successful, and that all the glory will be given to His holy name, and none of it to man. God has blessed and preserved me through His great mercy. On Saturday, Colonel Baylor and Hugh White were both killed, and Willie Preston was mortally wounded.

After the second Confederate victory at Manassas or Bull Run, the South took the offensive and entered Maryland. After the bloody battle of Antietam or Sharpsburg, they retreated again to Virginia, and Jackson's camp was again near Winchester:

Bunker Hill, October 13th

I am sitting in my tent, about twelve miles from our "war-home," where you and I spent such a happy winter. The weather is damp, and for the past two days has been rainy and chilly. Yesterday was communion at Mr. Graham's church, and he invited me to be present, but I was prevented from enjoying that privilege.[11] However, I heard an excellent sermon from the Rev. Dr. Stiles. His text was 1st Timothy, chap. ii, 5th and 6th verses. It was a powerful exposition of the Word of God; and when he came to the word "himself" he placed an emphasis upon it, and gave it a force which I had never felt before, and I realized that, truly, the sinner who does not, under the Gospel privileges, turn to God deserves the agonies of perdition. The doctor several times, in appealing to the sinner, repeated the 6th verse—"Who gave himself a ransom for all, to be testified in due time." What more could God do than to give Himself a ransom? Dr. Stiles is a great revivalist, and is laboring in a work of grace in General Ewell's division. It is a glorious thing to be a minister of the Gospel of the Prince of Peace. There is no equal position in this world.

October 20th. Don't trouble yourself about representations that are made of your husband. These things are earthly and transitory. There are real and glorious blessings, I trust, in reserve for us beyond this life. It is best for us to keep our eyes fixed upon the throne of God and the realities of a more glorious existence beyond the verge of time. It is gratifying to be beloved and to have our conduct approved by our fellowmen, but this is not worthy to be compared with the glory that is in reservation for us in the presence of our glorified Redeemer. Let us endeavor to adorn the doctrine of Christ our Saviour in all things, knowing that there awaits us "a far more exceeding and eternal weight of glory."[12] I would

Stonewall Jackson

not relinquish the slightest diminution of that glory for all this world can give. My prayer is that such may ever be the feeling of my heart. It appears to me that it would be better for you not to have anything written about me. Let us follow the teaching of inspiration—"Let another man praise thee, and not thine own mouth: a stranger, and not thine own lips."[13] I appreciate the loving interest that prompted such a desire in my precious darling. . . . You have not forgotten my little intimation that we might meet before the end of the year, but I am afraid now that your esposo will not be able to leave his command. However, all this is in the hands of the Most High, and my prayer is that He will direct all for His own glory. Should I be prevented from going to see my precious little wife, and mother should grow worse, I wish you to remain with her. In addition to the comfort it would give her, it would also gratify me to know that she was comforted by your being with her. She has my prayers that it may please our Heavenly Father to restore her again to perfect health.

November 20th. Don't you wish you were here in Winchester? Our headquarters are about one hundred yards from Mr. Graham's, in a large white house back of his, and in full view of our last winter's quarters, where my esposa used to come up and talk with me. Wouldn't it be nice for you to be here again? But I don't know how long you could remain. I hope to have the privilege of joining in prayer for peace at the time you name, and trust that all our Christian people will; but peace should not be the chief object of prayer in our country. It should aim more especially to implore God's forgiveness of our sins, and make our people a holy people. If we are but His, all things work together for the good of our country, and no good thing will He withhold from it.

VEIL OF MERCY

★ ★ ★ ★ ★ ★ ★ ★ ★ ★

On November 23, 1862, Anna gave birth to a daughter whom she named Julia, after Jackson's mother:

December 4th. Oh! how thankful I am to our kind Heavenly Father for having spared my precious wife and given us a little daughter! I cannot tell you how gratified I am, nor how much I wish I could be with you and see my two darlings. But while this pleasure is denied me, I am thankful it is accorded to you to have the little pet, and I hope it may be a great deal of company and comfort to its mother. Now don't exert yourself to write to me, for to know that you were taxing yourself to write would give me more pain than the letter would pleasure, so you must not do it. But you must love your esposo in the meantime. I expect you are just made up now with that baby. Don't you wish your husband wouldn't claim any part of it, but let you have the sole ownership? Don't you regard it as the most precious little creature in the world? Do not spoil it, and don't let anybody tease it. Don't permit it to have a bad temper. How I would love to see the darling little thing! Give her many kisses for her father.

I am so thankful to our ever-kind Heavenly Father for having so improved my eyes as to enable me to write at night. He continually showers blessings upon me; and that you should have been spared, and our darling little daughter given us, fills my heart with overflowing gratitude. If I know my unworthy self, my desire is to live

Anna Jackson with daughter Julia

entirely and unreservedly to God's glory. Pray, my darling, that I may so live.

On December 13 Jackson fought in the Battle of Fredericksburg, securing a great Confederate victory. The battle was on a Saturday, and Jackson did not write Anna the news of the battle until the following Tuesday. Though he did write of general military matters, Jackson's letters continued to express his spiritual interests, his love for Anna, and his delight in baby Julia:

December 29th. Yesterday I had the privilege of attending divine service in a church near General Hill's headquarters, and enjoyed the services very much. Dr. White says in a recent letter that our pew at home has been constantly occupied by Wheeling refugees. I am gratified to hear it. He also adds, "How we would rejoice to see you and our dear friend, Mrs. Jackson, again in that pew, and in the lecture-room at prayer meetings! We still meet every Wednesday afternoon to pray for our army, and especially for our general." May every needful blessing rest upon you and our darling child is the earnest prayer of your devoted husband.

January 17th. Yesterday I had the pleasure of receiving a letter from my esposita four days after it was written. How I would love to see the little darling [baby], whom I love so tenderly, though I have never seen her; and if the war were only over, I tell you, I would hurry down to North Carolina, to see my wife and baby. I regret to see our Winchester friends again in the hands of the enemy. I trust that, in answer to prayer, our country will soon be blessed with peace. If we were only that obedient people that we should be, I would, with increased confidence, look for a speedy termination of hostilities. Let us pray more and live more to the glory of God. I am still thinking and thinking about that baby, and do want to see her. Can't you send her to me by express? There is an express line all the way to Guiney's. I am glad to hear that she sleeps well at night, and doesn't disturb her mother. But it would be better not to call her a cherub; no earthly being is such.

Don't you accuse my baby of not being brave. I do hope she will get over her fear of strangers. If, before strangers take her, you would give them something to please her, and thus make her have pleasant associations with them, and seeing them frequently, I trust she would lose her timidity. It is gratifying that she is growing well, and I am thankful she is so bright and knowing. I do wish I could see her funny ways, and hear her "squeal out with delight" at seeing the little chickens. I am sometimes afraid that you will make such an idol of that baby that God will take her from us. Are you not afraid of it? Kiss her for her father.

February 3d. In answer to the prayers of God's people, I trust He will soon give us peace. I haven't seen my wife for nearly a year—my home in nearly two years, and have never seen our darling little daughter; but it is important that I, and those at headquarters, should set an example of remaining at the post of duty. My old Stonewall Brigade has built a log church. As yet I have not been in it. I am much interested in reading Hunter's "Life of Moses." It is a delightful book, and I feel more improved in reading it than by an ordinary sermon. I am thankful to say that my Sabbaths are passed more in meditation than formerly. Time thus spent is genuine enjoyment.

February 7th. This has been a beautiful spring day. I have been thinking lately about gardening. If I were at home, it would be time for me to begin to prepare the hot-bed. Don't you remember what interest we used to take in our hot-bed? If we should be privileged to return to our old home, I expect we would find many changes. Just to think our baby is nearly three months old. Does she notice and laugh much? You have never told me how much she looks like her mother. I tell you, I want to know how she looks. If you could hear me talking to my esposa in the mornings and evenings, it would make you laugh, I'm sure. It is funny the way I talk to her when she is hundreds of miles away. . . . I send the baby a silk handkerchief. I have thought that as it is brightly colored, it might attract her attention. Remember, it is her first present from her father, and let me know if she notices it.

April 10th. I trust that God is going to bless us with great success, and in such a manner as to show that it is all His gift; and I trust and pray that it will lead our country to acknowledge Him, and to live in accordance with His will as revealed in the Bible. There appears to be an increased religious interest among our troops here. Our chaplains have weekly meetings on Tuesdays; and the one of this week was more charming than the preceding one.

During the winter and spring of 1862–63, Jackson had time to especially encourage Christian devotion and worship among the soldiers. Not only did he hold regular devotions and prayer meeting for his own staff, but he encouraged evangelical chaplains to actively minister to the men through preaching, prayer, and personal work. A revival swept through the army, and many were converted to Christ.

On April 20, 1863, Anna and baby Julia visited Jackson at the home of William Yerby, south of Fredericksburg. It had been more than a year since Anna and Tom had been together, and Jackson was able to see his little daughter for the first time. The little family enjoyed a beautiful nine days together. During that time Julia was baptized by Rev. Lacy, chaplain of Jackson's

Second Corps. On April 29, Anna and Julia had to leave, since General Hooker had crossed the Rappahannock and a battle seemed imminent.

Before the mother and daughter reached home, while they were staying at Governor Letcher's in Richmond, news came that Jackson had been wounded—accidentally shot by his own men while returning from reconnoitering the field before the battle of Chancellorsville. Anna and Julia reached Guiney's Station May 7. Jackson's injured arm had been amputated, and pneumonia began to weaken his lungs. Anna read him Scriptures, sang hymns to him, and brought in little Julia to sit on his bed. In spite of the loving care and prayers of many, Jackson worsened.

When Jackson and the other Southern soldiers had marched off to war, Anna felt:

> It was a time of keen anguish and fearful apprehension to us whose loved ones had gone forth in such a perilous and desperate undertaking, but one feeling seemed to pervade every heart, that it was a just and righteous cause; and our hope was in God, who could "save by many or by few,"[14] and to Him the Christian people of the South looked and prayed. That so many united and fervent prayers should have been offered in vain is one of those mysteries which can never be fathomed by finite minds. The mighty Ruler of the nations saw fit to give victory to the strong arm of power, and He makes no mistakes. But for two years I was buoyed up by hope, which was strengthened by my husband's cheerfulness and courageous trust; and when he became more and more useful in the service of his country, I felt that God had a work for him to accomplish, and my trust and prayers grew more confident that his precious life would be spared throughout the war. It was well that I could not foresee the future. It was in mercy that He who knew the end from the beginning did not lift the veil.[15]

As Jackson had always wished, he died on the Sabbath. His body was taken to Lexington, where he was buried next to his first wife and daughter.

Anna remained a widow for more than half a century, beloved and revered as Stonewall Jackson's wife and as the preserver of the memory of a renowned Christian gentleman and soldier.

★ *Diana L. Severance*

★ ★ ★ ★ ★ ★ ★ ★ ★ ★ ★ ★

Jackson: O Almighty God, grant that, if it be Thy will, Thou wilt still avert the threatening danger, and grant us peace. Keep her whom I love, O Lord, in Thy protecting care, and bring us all at last to the joy of Thy eternal kingdom.

—*from the script of* Gods and Generals

★ ★ ★ ★ ★ ★ ★ ★ ★ ★ ★ ★

APPENDIX

CAST OF THE FILM *GODS AND GENERALS*

★ ★ ★ ★ ★ ★ ★ ★ ★ ★ ★ ★ ★ ★ ★ ★ ★ ★ ★

Martha / Donzaleigh Abernathy

Adjutant / Mark Aldrich

James J. White / Keith Allison

Kemper / Royce Applegate

Robb Lee Jr. / Jeremy Beck

Oliver Howard / Richard Bekins

Gnarled Vet / Wayne Bolton

James Longstreet / Bruce Boxleitner

Walter Taylor / Bo Brinkman

Gov. Oliver Hazzard Morton / Warren Burton

Joseph Hooker / Mac Butler

Beverly Tucker Lacy / David Carpenter

Old Penn / John Castle

Bernard Bee / Jim Choate

Dr. George Junkin / Martin Clark

John Wilkes Booth / Chris Conner

Kilrain / Kevin Conway

Captain Morrison / Scott Cooper

Charlie Norris / Devon Cromwell

Marsena Patrick / Ryan Cutrona

Joshua Lawrence Chamberlain / Jeff Daniels

Jane Beale / Mia Dillon

George Jenkins / Justin Dray

Robert E. Lee / Robert Duvall

Jim Lewis / Frankie Faison

John Beale / Miles Fisher

Major Gilmore / Keith Flippen

Jeb Stuart / Joseph Fuqua

John Curtis Caldwell / James Garrett

Lucy Beale / Karen Goberman

John Bell Hood / Patrick Gorman

Poague / Bo Gray

Roberta Corbin / Karen Hochstetter

Cummings / James Horan

Dooley / Con Horgan

Tom Chamberlain / C. Thomas Howell

Harrison / Cooper Huckabee

Jane Corbin / Lydia Jordan

Barksdale / Lester Kinsolving

D. H. Hill / Robert Knott

Mary Lincoln / Rosemary Knower

Thomas Jonathan "Stonewall" Jackson /
    Stephen Lang

Adelbert Ames / Matt Letscher

Heros Von Borcke / Matt Lindquist

Caesar / Marty Lodge

Sandie Pendleton / Jeremy London

Private Joe / David Lowe Jr.

Hancock / Brian Mallon

John A. Harman / Dan Manning

Ellis Spear / Jonathan Maxwell

Francis Preston Blair / Malachy McCourt

Marion Silbert / Barry McEvoy

Federal Officer / Herb Mitchell

Frederick Crouch / George Muschamp

Surgeon / Mark Nichols

Darius Couch / Carsten Norgaard

Colonel Mulholland / Tim O'Hare

General George McClellan / James Parkes

Stage Manager / Chris Potocki

Hunter McGuire / Sean Pratt

Lewis Armistead / John Prosky

Anna Jackson / Kali Rocha

McMillan / Tim Ruddy

A. P. Hill / William Sanderson

Isaac Trimble / Morgan Sheppard

Washington / Thomas Silcott

Catherine Corbin / Christie Lynn Smith

Fanny Chamberlain / Mira Sorvino

James Power Smith / Stephen Spacek

David S. Jenkins / David Stifel

Edward Porter Alexander / James Patrick Stuart

Maxcy Gregg / Buck Taylor

Glazier Estabrook / Lenny Termo

Minnis / Dechen Thurman

McClintock / Trent Walker

Ambrose Burnside / Alex Hyde White

Companion / Sarah Wiggin

Notes

★ ★

Many facts in large type placed throughout this book's pages are reprinted from *Christian History 33*, vol. 11, no. 1: "The Untold Story of Christianity & the Civil War." (www.christianhistory.net)

Preface by Susan Wales

1. *The Collected Works of Abraham Lincoln*, Roy P. Basler, ed. (Rutgers University Press, 1953).

Chapter 1

1. Alan Farley, *His Truth Keeps Marching On* (Appomattox, Va.: R.M.J.C., Inc., 1998), 14–15.

2. J. William Jones, *Christ in the Camp* (B. F. Johnson & Co., 1887), 50.

3. Ibid., 47–48.

4. Ibid., 46–47.

5. Capt. Robert E. Lee, *Recollections and Letters of General Robert E. Lee* (New York: Garden City Publishing Co., Inc., 1924), 105–106.

6. From *God Ordained This War: Sermons on the Sectional Crisis, 1830–65*, David B. Chesebrough, ed. (University of South Carolina Press, 1991).

Chapter 2

1. W. G. Bean, "Stonewall Jackson's Jolly Chaplain, Beverly Tucker Lacy," *West Virginia History* 29, no. 11 (January 1968):79.

2. Rev. Dr. Robert L. Dabney, *Life and Campaigns of Lt. Gen. Thomas J. Jackson* (New York, 1866), 647.

3. Rev. J. William Jones, *Christ in the Camp* (B. F. Johnson & Co., 1887), 519.

4. Ibid., 235–37.

5. Bean, "Stonewall Jackson's Jolly Chaplain," 87.

6. John W. Schildt, *Jackson and the Preachers* (1982), 157–58.

7. Mary Anna Jackson, *Memoirs of "Stonewall" Jackson* (Louisville, Ky.: Courier-Journal Job Printing Co., 1895), 457–58.

8. Bean, "Stonewall Jackson's Jolly Chaplain," 93.

9. Ibid., 95.

10. Jones, *Christ in the Camp*, 240. This was the conclusion of Lacy's original appeal to the Southern churches, made in March 1863.

11. Kevin A. Miller, "What PBS Didn't Tell You" *Christian History* 33 (vol. 11, no. 1) 1992, 8.

12. Mercer, 1987.

13. Albert J. Rabotean, "The Secret Religion of the Slaves," *Christian History* 33 (vol. 11, no. 1) 1992, 42–45.

14. Ibid.

15. Gardiner H. Shattuck Jr., "Revivals in the Camp," *Christian History* 33 (vol. 11, no. 1) 1992, 28–31.

Chapter 3

1. Sis Deans, *His Proper Post: A Biography of Joshua Lawrence Chamberlain* (Belle Grove Publishing Company, 1996), 24.

2. Ibid., 27.

3. Blanche Ames, *Adelbert Ames, 1835-1933: General, Senator, Governor: The Story of His Life and Times and His Integrity as a Soldier and Statesman in the Service of the United States of America throughout the Civil War and in Mississippi in the Years of Reconstruction* (published by the author, North Easton, Mass., 1964).

4. Ibid.

5. *The Cry Is War, War, War*, Michael Taylor, ed. Dayton, Ohio: Morningside House, Inc.), 102, by permission of Mrs. Jo Allman.

6. *Rev. William S. White, and His Times [1800–1873]*, M. White, ed. (Richmond, Va.: Whittet and Shepperson, 1891), 196–97.

7. Ibid., 177.

8. Mary Ann Jackson, *Memoirs of "Stonewall" Jackson* (Louisville, Ky.: Courier-Journal Job Printing Co., 1895), 79.

9. This story first appeared in *The Soldier's Journal*; the Library of Congress has no record of the date. Later the story was reprinted in *Pictorial War Record: Battles of the Late Civil War*, a four-volume work published by Stearnes & Co., New York, 1881–1884.

Chapter 4

1. John Woodbridge, *More Than Conquerors* (Chicago, Ill.: Moody Press, 1992), used with permission.

2. Used with permission of the author, Mark Noll. This article first appeared in the *Christian History* magazine issue on the Civil War (issue 33, vol. XI, no. 1, 1992).

Chapter 5

1. John Woodbridge, *More Than Conquerors* (Chicago, Ill.: Moody Press, 1992), used with permission.

2. Frank Vandiver, *Mighty Stonewall* (New York: McGraw-Hill Book Co., Inc., 1957), 88–89.

3. Mary Anna Jackson, *Memoirs of "Stonewall" Jackson* (Louisville, Ky.: Courier-Journal Job Printing Co., 1895), 72–73.

4. Vandiver, *Mighty Stonewall*, 129.

5. Rev. J. William Jones, *Christ in the Camp* (B. F. Johnson & Co., 1887), 89.

6. Jackson, *Memoirs*, 287.

7. Ibid., 503.

8. Ibid., 505–506.

9. Vandiver, *Mighty Stonewall*, 231.

10. R. L. Dabney, *The Life and Campaigns of Lt.. Gen. T. J. (Stonewall) Jackson* (Sterling and Albright, 1865), 107.

11. Jackson, *Memoirs*, 309.

12. Ibid., 78.

13. Ibid., 182.

Chapter 6

1. John Woodbridge, *More Than Conquerors* (Chicago, Ill.: Moody Press, 1992), used with permission.

Chapter 7

1. *A Diary from Dixie, as written by Mary Boykin Chestnut, wife of James Chestnut Jr., United States Senator from South Carolina, 1859–61*, Isabella D. Martin and Myrta Lockett Avary, eds. (New York: D. Appleton and Company, 1905).

2. Sources of "The Corbin Women" text: Kate Corbin Brooke Papers, in the possession of George M. Brooke, Lexington, Va.; William Nelson Pendleton Papers, Southern Historical Collection, University of North Carolina, Chapel Hill, North Carolina; Henry Kyd Douglas Papers, Southern Historical Collection, University of North Carolina, Chapel Hill, North Carolina.

3. Alice Rains Trulock, *In the Hands of Providence: Joshua L. Chamberlain and the American Civil War* (University of North Carolina Press, 1992), 5.

4. Sis Deans, *His Proper Post: A Biography of General Joshua L. Chamberlain* (Belle Grove Publishing, 1996), 92.

5. Ibid., 94.

6. Ibid., 105.

7. Ibid., 92.

8. Willard M. Wallace, *Soul of the Lion: A Biography of General Joshua L. Chamberlain* (Stan Clark Military Books, 1991), 222.

9. Ibid., 243.

Chapter 8

1. Susan P. Lee, *Memoirs of William Nelson Pendleton* (Philadelphia: Lippencott Co., 1893), 139–40.

2. Ibid., 142.

3. Ibid., 180.

4. See Genesis 14 for the account of Abraham raising an army to rescue his nephew Lot.

5. Lee, *Memoirs of W. N. Pendleton*, 235–36.

6. Ibid., 299.

7. Ibid., 344.

8. Ibid., 483–84.

9. Ibid., 45–46.

10. Author's note: The definitive biography of Sandie is William Gleason Bean, *Stonewall's Man: Sandie Pendleton* (Chapel Hill, N.C.: University of North Carolina Press, 1959). To see the faith and love of Sandie, you need to read the abundant letters preserved in the William Nelson Pendleton Papers collected at the University of North Carolina, Chapel Hill, and the Corbin and Brooke Family collections.

11. Bean, *Stonewall's Man*, 192.

12. *Stonewall's Man*, 195–96. Captain James Power Smith (1837–1923) was also on Jackson's staff. He was a divinity student before the war broke out and after the war became the Presbyterian pastor of the church in Fredericksburg, Virginia. Smith died at the age of eighty-six, the last survivor of Stonewall Jackson's staff.

13. Lee, *Memoirs of W. N. Pendleton*, 129.

14. Ibid., 202.

15. Ibid., 370–71.

Chapter 9

1. John W. Schildt, *Jackson and the Preachers* (Parsons, W. Va.: McClain Printing Co., 1982), 24.

2. Frank Vandiver, *Mighty Stonewall* (New York: McGraw-Hill Book Co., Inc., 1957), 101.

3. Mary Anna Jackson, *Memoirs of "Stonewall" Jackson* (Louisville, Ky.: Courier-Journal Job Printing Co., 1895), 487.

4. Vandiver, *Mighty Stonewall*, 388–89.

5. Hon. A. C. Avery, *Life and Character of Lieutenant General D. H. Hill* (Raleigh, N.C.: Edwards and Broughton, 1893), 13.

6. Hal Bridges, *Lee's Maverick General* (New York: McGraw-Hill Book Co., 1961), 37.

7. William W. Bennett, *The Great Revival Which Prevailed in the Southern Armies* (Bridgewater, Va.: Sprinkle Publishers, 1876): 106–107.

8. Bridges, *Maverick General*, 84.

9. Avery, *Life and Character*, 13; Bridges, *Maverick General*, 58.

10. Bridges, *Maverick General*, 37.

11. U.S. National Archives and Records Administration.

12. Thomas Wentworth Higginson, *Army Life in a Black Regiment* (Boston, Mass.: Fields, Osgood and Company, 1870), 84.

13. Bennie J. McRae Jr., *Lest We Forget* (Trotwood, Ohio: LWF Publications, 1995).

14. Ibid.

15. Sojourner Truth in a letter written for Sojourner Truth by Eumpehmia Cockrane to Mary R. Gale, February 25, 1864; Documents Division, the Library of Congress.

16. Christian A. Fleetwood, September 24, 1864, excerpt from his Civil War diary; Documents Division, the Library of Congress.

17. Higginson, *Army Life in a Black Regiment*.

18. Benjamin Quarles, *The Negro in the Civil War*, 1953.

19. Ibid.

20. Junkin and Norton, *Life of General W. S. Hancock* (New York: D. Appleton and Company, 1880).

21. Used with the permission of the author, Jeffery Warren Scott. This article first appeared in *Christian History* magazine on the Civil War (issue 33, vol. XI, no. 1, 1992).

22. Ibid.

23. Ibid.

24. Ibid.

25. Ibid.

26. Copyright © 2002 News World Communications, Inc.

Chapter 10

1. All letters are excerpted from Mary Anna Jackson, *Memoirs of "Stonewall" Jackson* (Louisville, Ky.: Courier-Journal Job printing Co., 1895).

2. Romans 8:28 was one of Jackson's favorite Bible passages, and he quoted it frequently.

3. Jackson had become familiar with Spanish while in Mexico during the war with that country. He often used Spanish terms of endearment in his letters. *Esposa* means "wife"; sometimes he used *esposita*, meaning "little wife." *Esposo* means "husband."

4. Rev. J. C. Granberry was a chaplain in the Army of Northern Virginia. He was wounded in the war and taken prisoner.

5. Robert Lewis Dabney (1820–98) was a Presbyterian theologian and professor of church history at Union Seminary, then located in Virginia. During the Civil War he served as a chaplain in the Confederate army and, in 1862, as Jackson's chief of staff.

6. Turner Ashby recruited and was Colonel of the Ashby Rangers. He was one of Jackson's most famous officers. He was killed at Harrisonburg June 6, 1862.

7. 2 Corinthians 4:17.

8. Matthew 11:28.

9. D. H. Hill and Jackson had been friends at Lexington, where Hill had been a professor of mathematics at Washington College. Hill's wife, Isabella, was Anna's older sister. Anna had been visiting the Hills when she and Jackson first met in Lexington.

10. Romans 5:3.

11. Pastor of Presbyterian church in Winchester with whom the Jacksons had stayed the previous winter.

12. 2 Corinthians 4:17.

13. Proverbs 27:2.

14. 1 Samuel 14:6.

15. *Memoirs of "Stonewall" Jackson*, 147.

CONTRIBUTORS

★ ★ ★ ★ ★ ★ ★ ★ ★ ★ ★ ★ ★ ★ ★ ★ ★ ★ ★ ★

Ted Baehr is happily married to Lili and is the father of four wonderful children. He is the author of *The Media-Wise Family*, *Getting the Word Out*, and other books, the publisher of MOVIEGUIDE®, and the chairman of the Christian Film & Television Commission. For more information, please call 800-899-6684 or go to www.movie guide.org.

- Songs in the Camp: Faith in the Midst of War
- The Great Revival
- Mary Boykin Miller Chestnut
- A Union General: Samuel Kosciuszko Zook
- Military Service: Major General Winfield Scott Hancock
- Marsena Rudolph Patrick
- A Confederate General: William Booth Taliaferro

James (Jim) Baehr is a sophomore at Dartmouth College majoring in history and government. He has written for the *Ventura County Star* and several other magazines and newspapers.

- "One of the Knightliest Soldiers"
- Quotes from an interview with Stephen Lang, who played Thomas Jonathan "Stonewall" Jackson

Gabor Boritt serves as Fluhrer Professor and directs the Civil War Institute at Gettysburg College. He has authored and edited fifteen books on Lincoln and on the Civil War. He is currently completing an illustrated book on Lincoln entitled *The Will of God Prevails*. As a set historian, Boritt was on location with director Ron Maxwell during the filming of *Gods and Generals*.

- Thanksgiving

"Miss Johnnie" Capell was born in Mount Airy, North Carolina, and attended Appalachian State Teachers College. She is married and had three sons, Jesse, Daniel Scott, and Benjamin. She is currently writing a book, *And Then There Were None*, about her faith through the death of all of her sons in separate accidents.

- Actor, Assassin, Madman: John Wilkes Booth

David B. Chesebrough holds degrees in history, theology, and sociology. Following a twenty-five-year career as an ordained minister in the American Baptist Church, he pursued a full-time career in academics, recently retiring as the Assistant Chair in the Department of History at Illinois State University. With a specialty in American religious history, emphasizing the Civil War era, Chesebrough is the author of numerous articles and seven books, including *God Ordained This War: Sermons on the Sectional Crisis, 1835–65* (University of South Carolina Press, 1991); *No Sorrow Like Our Sorrow: Northern Protestant Ministers and the Assassination of Lincoln* (Kent State University Press, 1994); and *Clergy Dissent in the Old South, 1830–65* (Southern Illinois University Press, 1996).

- God Is On Our Side: Selections from Sermons during the Civil War Era

Dorsey M. Deaton, a native of Memphis, Tennessee, earned a B.A. at Mississippi College, an M.Div. at Southern Baptist Theological Seminary, and a Ph.D. in American studies at Emory University. He taught United States history for thirty years at Emory University, Georgia State University, and Georgia Perimeter College, all in Atlanta. Deaton and his wife, Pamela Parish Deaton, serve as members of the board of MOVIEGUIDE® and manage an international family business from their home in Atlanta.

- The Faith and Values of Robert E. Lee
- The Corbin Women
- Stonewall's Man: Sandie Pendleton

John J. Dwyer is a former newspaper publisher and the author of *Stonewall,* a historical novel about the life of Stonewall Jackson; its sequel, *Robert E. Lee;* and the historical narrative *The War Between the States.* He teaches history at Coram Deo Academy, a classical Christian school near Flower Mound, Texas. (www.johnjdwyer.com)
- Standing Like a Stone Wall
- "An Epistle, Written of God"

Rebecca Hagelin is a national radio commentator for Salem Communications and a weekly columnist for WorldNetDaily.com. A political and communication specialist, she is a frequent political commentator on CNN, Fox News Network, and numerous national network radio programs. Her writings have also appeared in *USA TODAY* and other newspapers around the country. She and her husband Andy are the parents of three children.
- Contributed quotes by Ron Maxwell (director of the movie *Gods and Generals*) taken from her article, "Among Gods and Generals," part 2, *World Net Daily,* 17 December 2001; used by permission.

Tom Huntley, the great-great nephew of Confederate soldier George Job Huntley, is the manager of Dining and Event Services at LifeWay Ridgecrest Conference Center near Asheville, North Carolina. A graduate of Asheville Buncombe Community College, Huntley is an avid family history buff and genealogist. He and his wife Frieda have two sons, John and Adam.
- Portion of "Private Battles" in chapter 3

Les Kinsolving is a cousin of the Confederate General Barksdale, whom Kinsolving portrayed in the movies *Gods and Generals* and *Gettysburg.* He is a White House correspondent and talk show host for WCBM Baltimore. Formerly a nationally syndicated newspaper columnist, he was twice nominated for the Pulitzer Prize. *Talkers* magazine has selected him as one of the nation's Top 100 talk radio hosts for the past six years.
- An Officer and a Gentleman: William Barksdale

Thomas C. Mandes is a noted physician in Vienna, Virginia, with an avocation for Virginia history. He received his premed and medical degrees from Georgetown University in Virginia and did his postgraduate study at Cooke County Hospital in Chicago and Washington, D. C., General Hospital. He served as a flight surgeon in the air force. Dr. Mandes and his wife Brenda are the parents of one son, Galen.
- Who Was Johnny Reb?

Mark A. Noll was graduated from Wheaton as an English major and from Vanderbilt with his Ph.D. in the history of Christianity. On the Wheaton College faculty since 1979, he is presently the McManis Chair of Christian Thought and the cofounder and present director of the Institute for the Study of American Evangelicals at Wheaton College. Noll has been a visiting teacher at Harvard Divinity School, University of Chicago Divinity School, Westminster Theological Seminary, and Regent College of Vancouver, B.C.
- The Puzzling Faith of Abraham Lincoln

John Perry was graduated cum laude from Vanderbilt University with additional studies at Oxford, England. In 1991, he left a career as an award-winning advertising copywriter to freelance as an author and ghostwriter. John earned a Lincoln Price nomination for his book, *Lady of Arlington, The Life of Mrs. Robert E. Lee* (Multnomah Publishers) and is also the biographer of *Sgt. York: His Life, Legend, and Legacy* (Broadman and Holman). John is married to Susan Ann, and they are the parents of two children, Charles and Olivia.
- The Gentle Warrior: Mrs. General Lee in Richmond, 1863

Jeffery Warren Scott, senior pastor of Colonial Avenue Baptist Church in Roanoke, Virginia, has a Ph.D. in religion from Baylor University, a masters of divinity and masters of religious education at New Orleans Baptist Theological, and a B.S. degree from Georgetown University. The author of *Does Your Child's World Scare You?* (published by Smyth & Helwys, 1997), and also articles on church and state concerns, Scott is the adjunct assistant professor of Religious Studies at Radford University. Married to Debbie Scott, he is the father of two children, Amy and Brennan, and a member of the Fellowship of Christian Magicians.
- "Old Prayer Book": Oliver O. Howard
- Young Napolean: George B. McClellan

- The Passionate Catholic: William Rosecrans
- No Saint: Ulysses S. Grant
- The Lord's Bishop: Leonidas Polk

Diana L. Severance received her Ph.D. in history from Rice University. She is a teacher with Klein I.S.D. and chief historian of the Klein, Texas, Historical Foundation. Severance's most recent book, *Against the Gates of Hell* (University Press of America, Lanham, MD, 2003), co-authored with her husband Gordon, is based on never-before-published letters and diaries of Henry T. Perry's missionary work in Turkey from 1866–1913 and recounts the persecution of the Armenian Christians by Turkey's Ottoman rulers.

- Official Proclamations
- "Must Eternity Be Lost?": Organizing the Chaplaincy
- Comfort Ye My People
- A Man of Prayer: Stonewall Jackson
- Jackson's Mission Field
- "Old Artillery": William Nelson Pendleton
- Elevated Mules
- Love and War
- Father and Son
- A Hero's Father-in-Law: Dr. George Junkin
- Iron Nerves: Daniel Harvey Hill
- Faith, Hope, and Love: Letters between Stonewall and Mary Jackson

Susan Huey Wales is an executive producer of the MOVIEGUIDE® Awards, a noted speaker, and the author of a dozen books, including *The Art of Romantic Living* (Thomas Nelson Publishers), and coauthor with Ann Platz of the popular *Match Made in Heaven* series (Multnomah Publishers) and the *Social Graces* series (Harvest House Publishers). She is the wife of Ken Wales, film and television producer (CBS series *Christy),* the mother of a daughter Megan, and the grandmother of Hailey Elizabeth.

- Adelbert Ames: Carpetbagger or Saint?
- Private Battles
- Grandmother's Quilt
- A Dream Come True
- Abraham Lincoln quotes and letter from Lincoln to Mrs. Bixby

- The Love Affair of Fanny and Lawrence Chamberlain
- African American Heroes

Steve Wilkins holds a bachelor of science degree from the University of Alabama and a masters of divinity from the Reformed Theological Seminary of Jackson, Mississippi. Since 1989, he has served as the pastor of Auburn Avenue Presbyterian Church in Monroe, Louisiana, and is also the president of the Governing Board of Geneva Academy where he teaches Hebrew. Wilkins is the author of four books, including *Call of Duty: The Sterling Nobility of Robert E. Lee* and *All Things for Good: The Steadfast Faithfulness of Stonewall Jackson,* and coauthor with Douglas Wilson of *Slavery As It Was.* Wilkins and his wife Wendy are the parents of six children: Matt, Jeremy, Bray, Jordan, Caleb, and Charity.

- A Man of Prayer: Stonewall Jackson
- Jackson's Mission Field
- R. E. Lee and Fatherhood
- Mary Lee and Love for Others
- Jeb Stuart and His Many Loves

John D. Woodbridge is the recipient of four Medallion Awards and has written, edited, or contributed to many key works on the history of Christianity, as well as biographies including *More Than Conquerors* (Moody 1992). A research professor of church history and the history of Christian thought at Trinity Evangelical Divinity School in Illinois, he is also a visiting professor at Northwestern University and serves as senior editor of *Christianity Today.* Woodbridge earned the Doctorat de Troisième Cycle from the University of Toulouse, France, the master of divinity from Trinity Evangelical Divinity School, the master of arts in history from Michigan State University, and the bachelor of arts in history from Wheaton College. He has done postdoctoral course work at the University of Paris in France.

- Abraham Lincoln: Savior of a Nation
- Stonewall Jackson: The General Who Looked to God
- The World's Great Soldier